The Greatest

Also by Matthew Syed

Bounce: The Myth of Talent and the Power of Practice

Black Box Thinking: Marginal Gains and the
Secrets of High Performance

The Greatest

The Quest for Sporting Perfection

Matthew Syed

JOHN MURRAY

First published in Great Britain in 2017 by John Murray (Publishers)
An Hachette UK company

1

Copyright © Matthew Syed 2017
By kind permission of Times Newspapers Ltd.

A CIP catalogue record for this title is available from the British Library

ISBN 978-1-47365-365-8
Ebook ISBN 978-1-47365-367-2

Typeset in Celeste by Hewer Text UK Ltd, Edinburgh
Printed and bound by Clays Ltd, St Ives plc

John Murray policy is to use papers that are natural, renewable and
recyclable products and made from wood grown in sustainable forests.
The logging and manufacturing processes are expected to conform
to the environmental regulations of the country of origin.

John Murray (Publishers)
Carmelite House
50 Victoria Embankment
London EC4Y 0DZ

www.johnmurray.co.uk

For Evie and Teddy

Contents

Introduction

When I was in my teens, a careers adviser asked what I wanted to do for a living. When I said that was I interested in writing about sport, she smiled a little, as if to emphasise the naivety of such a hope. 'Sport isn't a career choice,' she said emphatically. 'It probably won't be very big in twenty years' time, anyway.'

It is remarkable how common this view was three decades ago. Sport, it was thought, would be superseded by computer games, consoles and the futuristic vision of virtual reality. A new leisure age, driven by technological sophistication, was going to usher in recreational pursuits of which Nintendo's Game Boy was considered a precursor.

Why would anyone wish to kick a football around a field when you could be transported into a scintillating alternative reality by immersing yourself in a computer program in your own living room? Children, in particular, were never going to bother with anything as passé as games using balls made from cork, leather or plastic.

And yet sport has demonstrated curious staying power. It has grown over recent decades, not diminished. There are many ways to calibrate this growth, such as the burgeoning space in national newspapers, the way that stories have become front-page news (rarely the case thirty years ago), and how television content, particularly football, has soared in value.

The question, however, is why? Why has sport, as a cultural institution, confounded the expectations of those who so confidently wrote it off? What has driven its growth in the teeth of myriad scandals, institutionalised cheating, and maladministration of a quite epic kind, not least within the Fédération Internationale de Football Association (FIFA) and the International Olympic Committee (IOC)? What are the internal qualities of sport that make it so durable and cross-culturally intoxicating?

This book of collected columns attempts to uncover some of the answers. It examines the way in which sport, while superficially frivolous, is underpinned by themes which are basic to the human condition: heroism, drama, competition, hierarchy, psychology, morality and, perhaps most important of all, the quest for greatness. How do we become the best that we can be, as individuals, teams, and organisations?

Back in 2012, Tim Hallissey, the sports editor of *The Times*, telephoned to suggest that I travel out to Ancient Olympia, the sanctuary in the Western Peloponnese where the original Olympics took place. It was a long trip, including getting lost on gravel roads with no signal to gain help from Google Maps, but it was, for me at least, a seminal experience.

Standing above the sanctuary on the slopes of Mount Kronos, one could glimpse sport from a fresh vantage point. This festival was a central aspect of Greek culture and unified the warring city states. Every four years, peace emerged so that athletes and spectators could travel to the Games. For almost 1,200 years, it took place without a single interruption. Virtually no other cultural festival can match this kind of staying power.

To put it a slightly different way, sport gripped the imagination of the ancient world, just as it grips the modern. Sport isn't, in that sense, a post-Romantic institution, one that started with the encoding of rules of play by Victorian schoolmasters and moralists, as is sometimes suggested. It didn't begin with the inauguration of FIFA, or the International Tennis Federation, or any of the other governing bodies which effectively operate as monopoly providers of the games that dominate today's landscape. No, sport is far more ancient and quintessential.

Introduction

I was struck by a quote from Lucian , the great historian, who wrote about his infatuation for the Ancient Games: 'Oh, I can't describe the scene in mere words,' he said. 'You really should experience first-hand the incredible pleasure of standing in that cheering crowd, admiring the athletes' courage and good looks, their amazing physical conditioning, their unbeatable determination, and their unstoppable passion for victory.'

Couldn't this have been written about a great sporting event today? Could it not have been written about the Wimbledon final, a long-awaited Champions League showdown or a fiercely contested Test match? Doesn't it capture why we go through the turnstiles and tune in on television? And, on the wider point, isn't it precisely because sport is simple and, in a certain sense, trivial that we can so clearly perceive its dramatic qualities? It seems to transport us to what is essential about competition and, yes, the nature of greatness, too.

There were many pioneering athletes in the ancient world through whom these themes were personified. Milo of Croton, an associate of Pythagoras, won five men's wrestling titles between 536 and 520 BC. Coroebus of Elis, a cook by profession, was the first Olympic champion by winning the stadion (200 metres). Leonidas of Rhodes was an all-rounder, winning the stadion, the diaulos (400 metres) and the hoplitodromos (400 metres while carrying heavy armour) at four straight games from 164 BC. That's almost as many golds as Michael Phelps.

Today, sport continues to produce cultural icons. Few who have watched tennis can have failed to be moved by the beauty of Roger Federer, the gutsiness of Raphael Nadal or the indomitability of Novak Djokovic. In many ways, the rivalry between these three, joined more recently by Andy Murray, has provided peerless insights into how competition spurs innovation, a never-ending upward spiral as competitors dare each other to greater heights, a theme discussed in Part I.

Introduction

Success is also about great teams. We have had powerful examples in sport, including the All Blacks, Manchester United under Sir Alex Ferguson, FC Barcelona, Leicester City and, rather improbably, the British women's hockey team, which won gold in Rio 2016. But how do teams become great? How do they combine seamlessly? As we will see, many of the insights of how humans combine are emerging from improvisational jazz. There are also powerful lessons to learn from aviation and the military.

We also look at the dynamics of intrinsic motivation, the fight, flight, freeze response, risk-taking, the ironies of self-belief, and the importance of resilience. We look at the techniques adopted by top athletes, coaches and scientists to build mental strength. Success, in sport as in life, often hinges on these elusive psychological factors.

My own sporting career provided a number of profound lessons about how success happens. When I became the England number one, around half of the top players in the country at that time didn't just come from the same town as me, or the same suburb, but the same street. It was a perfectly anonymous road, snaking a mile or so through the suburbs of Reading, but it was a ping-pong Mecca.

It was clear to me, even as a teenager, that this wasn't because we were all born with extraordinary talent. We didn't share the same genes. No, we had benefited from a series of covert advantages that, over time, proved crucial. The top coach in the country taught at the school adjacent to the road. He gave us access to superb training and mentoring. We also had the advantage of each other, this small group of players, vying for supremacy.

Perhaps the crucial advantage, however, was that we all had access to the only purpose-built table-tennis club in the south of England. Instead of going to a local sports centre and having to wait for the badminton or yoga to finish, we could go to a wooden building explicitly built for table tennis. You would walk through the door, turn on the lights, put on the little heater in the corner, and then play for as long as you liked. Almost everyone on the street had a set of keys, so we trained before school, after school, weekends.

The secret of our success, then, was about subtle cultural and social advantages. It was about long-term practice, easy-to-access facilities, great coaching, committed parents, and mentoring. In Part I, Building a Champion, we look at these themes in greater depth, exploring the world-class support teams that stand behind the greatest sportspeople, the power of volunteers and motivators, and the many other subtle factors that drive success, but are so often ignored in our individualistic culture.

Perhaps the most chastening lesson I learned as a sportsman was the time I choked. It happened at the Olympic Games in Sydney, an experience etched on my consciousness, the only time that I suffered a total meltdown in what was, unquestionably, the most important contest of my career. There seemed to be a breakdown in communication between mind and body, a catastrophic loss of feeling and touch, and a defeat so one-sided that my Olympic dream (four years of build-up) was over in thirty minutes flat.

The experience, while tortuous, did provide the impetus to study the mental qualities that are implicated in success. These were central to my two books, *Bounce* and *Black Box Thinking*. So in Part II, The Mental Game, we examine both those who have had the uncanny mastery to hold their nerve under great pressure, such as Michael Jordan and Nick Faldo, and those who melted in the metaphorical heat, such as Greg Norman and Jimmy White. By looking at both sides of this mental divide, we will learn new things about the psychology and neurophysiology of success.

Greatness, in sport and beyond, is an elusive concept. It is about being the best, but are there not other factors that impinge upon how we relate to champions? We are interested in the

Introduction

hardships they have faced, the lessons they have learned, the way they play the game, the values they express. We are fascinated by the way they impact upon wider society. All of these themes require a slightly different lens, moving beyond the field of play and looking at history, culture, aesthetics and the complex relationship between sports and politics. This we do in Parts III and IV, On Beauty and The Political Game.

In the final section, we look at more than a dozen sporting icons. Most have revealed greatness in one form or another, providing lessons about commitment and nerve, but also about the many temptations that can subvert the path to greatness. Lance Armstrong attempted to cheat the system. Jake LaMotta took a bung to throw a fight. Other champions have, conversely, demonstrated great integrity and moral courage. Billie Jean King was a seminal figure in the modern history of feminism, Muhammad Ali in the fight for racial equality.

Bringing these columns together (edited highlights from more than two million words) reminds me of what a privilege it is to write about sport, and the breadth of the canvas it permits. I have been influenced by many books, including *Fooled by Randomness* by Nassim Nicholas Taleb, *The Golden Bough* by Sir James George Frazer, *The Mighty Walzer* by Howard Jacobson, *The Meaning of Sport* by Simon Barnes, and, more recently, *The Secret of Our Success* by the evolutionary geneticist Joseph Henrich.

Sport, in one sense, is trivial, but it is also profound. My hunch is that it is here to say, not just for decades, but perhaps even for centuries (if we do not destroy ourselves in the meantime). It is thrilling to watch, and captivating to play, an activity as old as our species itself. But sport has another wonderful use, too: as a metaphor, it helps us to delve deeper into the nature and construction of greatness.

Matthew Syed
October 2016

I
Building a Champion

What does it take to reach the top? We typically think about this question in terms of the individual. He or she needs talent, will-power, mental toughness and other ingredients that are routinely discussed in the context of high achievement. When we analyse performance, we therefore wish to focus, closely and intimately, on the specific person. What are they like? What do they do? How do they live?

The truth is, however, that it's often by looking beyond the individual that the true picture of greatness snaps into focus. Understanding the culture and circumstances into which the champion was born, the commitment of parents, the fortune to have a fine coach, perhaps even to be born in the right city or state, or at the right time of year (a factor known as the relative age effect), all contribute – subtly but indisputably – to the flour-ishing of genius.

In this section, we look at this wider story. We meet visionary coaches, mentors who gave a crucial nudge at the right time, volunteers working behind the scenes whose selfless actions propelled the aspiring champion forward. We meet parents who made untold sacrifices, world-class support staff who found astonishing innovations, and explore the powerful rivalries and animosities that help to drive performance ever higher.

Ultimately, we will glimpse one of sport's most vital lessons: greatness is about remarkable individuals, to be sure, but it is about getting a remarkable amount of help along the way.

The Trainer

3 February 2012

There was something both beautiful and revelatory about Angelo Dundee's relationship with Muhammad Ali. The trainer, who died yesterday at the age of ninety, was with Ali throughout his tumultuous career, from the early days when a naive professional dreamt of a shot at the title, to the glory years of the mid-Sixties, through the tribulations of Vietnam and all the way to the tragic denouement when an ageing Ali was humiliated by younger, fitter opponents.

It is not merely that Dundee experienced the most thrilling ride in the history of sport, clinging to the coat-tails of Ali as he danced his way into the hearts of the world; in many ways, Dundee helped to guide the journey, to shape it. He was an essential component of the legend that Ali became. Indeed, it can plausibly be argued that, given his influence upon the most important sportsman of the twentieth century, Dundee changed the world.

It was a soft influence, but no less profound for that. Dundee recognised, as early as that fateful conversation in 1961, when Ali probed the knowledge and tactical awareness of a potential new cornerman, that he could not play the role of dictator, benign or otherwise. His young charge was too headstrong, too opinionated and altogether too sure of his direction of travel for a trainer to impose an alternative world view.

He also knew that, given the growing influence of Ali's handlers in the Nation of Islam, who preached that white men are devils and looked darkly upon any relationship, business or personal, with the 'enemy', that he would have to act with great cunning if he were to survive.

That he remained with Ali for more than two decades, despite the drip-drip of poison fed into the ears of the champion by his religious advisers, is an astonishing testament to his savvy.

And that is the real story of Dundee. He cared about his boxers, to be sure. He knew how to inspire them, to train them, to give them the trademark left jab and overhand right, to imbue them with a sense of belief even as their reserves of energy were depleting during the championship rounds.

But more than anything – and the secret of his long and extraordinary success – was his ability to navigate the myriad relationships, the egos and the endlessly fragile sociology of a boxer's entourage.

His quick wit was evident in more prosaic ways, too, and many of the fond obituaries that have been penned in the past twenty-four hours have focused on his ringside Machiavellianism. He illegally assisted Ali to the corner after the famous left hook of Henry Cooper in 1963, administered smelling salts and allegedly splitting Ali's glove, giving him a few extra seconds of recovery time.

He is also alleged to have loosened the ropes of the ring in Zaire, enabling Ali to lean back and 'rope-a-dope' the fearsome George Foreman in the Rumble in the Jungle in October 1974.

Dundee often gave conflicting accounts of his role in these and many other controversies. At one point, he said that he had actually attempted to stiffen the ropes in Zaire, rather than loosen them, and had nothing to do with the rip in Ali's glove in the bout against Cooper. At other times, he confessed to his antics with a glint in his eye and a smile on his face.

Perhaps he merely wanted to add to the mystique; the sense that, when it came to Dundee, nobody could really be sure how he sprinkled his magic.

What is certain is that he was among the most accessible sporting icons in the world. He volunteered his phone number to reporters and would graciously and often thrillingly share hours of his time reliving the Ali years, offering sage opinions about the new pretenders.

'I put an arm around his shoulder in the dressing room before he went out to face Foreman,' he once told me. 'Ali was an enigma. He was utterly convinced of his own destiny, but he also needed reassurance.'

It was not just Ali, of course. Dundee also guided the career of Sugar Ray Leonard, arguably the greatest and certainly the most poetic boxer to have emerged in the years since Ali's prime. Perhaps the most rousing intervention, as well as the most storied, occurred during Leonard's epic welterweight unification bout with Thomas Hearns in 1981. With Leonard trailing on all three scorecards at the end of the twelfth round, Dundee uttered the immortal words: 'You're blowing it now son, you're blowing it!' Leonard rallied to stop Hearns midway through the fourteenth, and would later credit Dundee for helping to unlock the inspiration.

In all, Dundee trained thirteen world champions, but it was the relationship with Ali that defined his career and ultimately secured his place in history.

It is fitting that one of his last public appearances before being hospitalised with a blood clot was to attend the seventieth birthday of Ali last month. 'It was the way he wanted to go,' Jimmy, Dundee's son, said yesterday. 'He did everything he wanted to do.'

The last of the great trainers, and one of the few remaining links to the most seminal era in the history of sport, has left us.

The Parents
3 March 2010

What is the more remarkable tale: that of Tiger Woods winning fourteen major titles in golf, or that of his late father making untold sacrifices to bulldoze his son's path to greatness? What is the more inspirational: the virtuosity of the Williams sisters in tennis, or the stoicism of their redoubtable father, a man who endured mockery, insults and threats as he coached his anonymous daughters on bullet-riddled courts in the ganglands of Los Angeles?

What is certain is that if you deconstruct the success of almost any great sportsperson, you will glimpse the heroism of a much maligned demographic – parents. You will see love, devotion, compassion, fidelity and passion; you will see a willingness to share in the joy of victory and to alleviate the pain of defeat; most of all, you will see untold quantities of self-sacrifice. Sure, there is something Darwinian about all this parental dedication, but does that make it any less stirring?

Yesterday Lewis Hamilton split professionally from his father, Anthony, the man who has managed his career since he arrived in go-karting as an eight-year-old. 'Over the past few years we looked around to see if we could bring someone else into the picture to help with the situation – whether to help with guidance, or sponsors or whatever it was,' Hamilton said. 'I think now we're at the point where we are looking to take that step – and I think it is a positive step.'

Many will find sympathy with Hamilton's assessment, given that his father lacked the experience to conduct negotiations with leading sponsors and to handle an often voracious media, but it cannot have been easy for Hamilton Senior to stand down. For seventeen years he has willingly lived his life by proxy, marginalising his own ambitions for those of his son, agonising not about his own problems but those of his boy, and now he is being shunted to one side, albeit for eminently sensible reasons.

Letting go – that is the essential paradox of parenthood. You care, you nurture, you sacrifice, and then you watch as the little ones fly into the great unknown, often shouting recriminations as they depart. You experience the stomach-clenching pain of separation, but you do so with a smile and a hug, aware that the desire to protect and love must never morph into the tyranny of mollycoddling.

Who would be a parent? Who would seek what Freud described as the toughest of human assignments? The questions that must be answered by a parent every day of the week are as urgent as they are unanswerable: when does devotion morph into oppression? When does discipline shade into authoritarianism? When does one cross the line between offering encouragement and exerting undue pressure?

We read often about the excesses of pushy parents, and there is much to learn from those who have got it wrong. Growing up in competitive table tennis, I saw some dark episodes: the bespectacled boy from the Isle of Wight who was humiliated to the point of tears by his father after an unexpected defeat; the twelve-year-old girl from Derby whose father left her to make her own way home because she executed the wrong tactics; the boy from Wolverhampton who was thrown into an outdoor swimming pool after a crushing defeat.

But for every appalling act of excess, for every parent who has got it wrong, there are hundreds who have got it right. Men and women who would never dream of thrusting themselves forward as parental role models, who would not think to preach about how it should be done, but who – through countless acts of sacrifice, love and devotion – have done their best by their children. They do not expect thanks or praise, they do not demand recognition; they merely crave the joy of witnessing the happiness of those they nurtured.

So, even as Hamilton Senior steels himself for a new beginning, leaving his son's career in the hands of cold-eyed professionals, he can take great credit for what he has achieved as a father. He not only forged the opportunity for his son to thrive in Formula One, not only coaxed him along the often treacherous path to world championship glory, he also sustained the respect and admiration of the boy whose career would have got nowhere but for the intrepidness of his dad.

'He has really been the most incredible father and supporter throughout my life,' Hamilton said. 'He's been there through the toughest of times. He's always had my best interests at heart, he's always been there to guide me in the right way. The amount of work and effort and commitment he's put in throughout my whole career has taken all of him to be able to do that.'

As a homage to his father, the words were both heartfelt and moving. But Hamilton also spoke for countless others whose gratitude to their parents, whose recognition of their sacrifice and quiet heroism, is no less earnest and no less profound.

Practice Makes Perfect
4 September 2013

One of the great things about science is that it has taught us to be sceptical about surface appearances. The world seems flat, but it is, in fact, round. Tiger Woods looks as though he was born to play golf – but was he really?

The idea that Woods was genetically predisposed to hit balls seems, on the surface, self-evident. You only have to look at the way he swings a club to realise that genius was encoded in his DNA. A similar analysis might be applied to the free-kick taking of David Beckham, or the tennis playing of Roger Federer.

In *Bounce*, my 2010 book, I challenged this view, following in the steps of authors such as Malcolm Gladwell. Much of the intellectual ballast for the book was provided by the work of Herbert Simon, a cognitive scientist who won the Nobel Prize in 1978, and Anders Ericsson, of Florida State University. According to this approach, what looks like talent is, in fact, the consequence of years of practice. Hence, the idea that 10,000 hours is what it takes to attain expertise.

Woods, for example, started playing golf at the age of one, played his first pitch-and-putt round at two, and had practised many thousands of hours by the age of ten. When he became the youngest winner of the Masters in 1997 and was acclaimed by pundits as having been born with a 'gift', Woods laughed. 'It looks like a gift, but that is because you haven't seen the years of dedication that went into the performance,' a colleague said. This is the danger of surface appearance.

Recently, the debate on nature versus nurture has ignited again. *The Sports Gene*, a book by David Epstein, has sought to elevate the role of genetics in the analysis of success. It is well written, and many of the examples about running, jumping and other 'simple' sports are uncontroversial. There is little doubt that it helps to have fast-twitch muscle fibres if you want to be a sprinter. Similarly, a long Achilles tendon is helpful if you aspire to be a high jumper. The anatomical advantages enjoyed by many top athletes in simple sports are often caused by genetic differences.

But the 10,000-hour notion was supposed to apply only to complex areas of sport, and life. Take the case of reaction speed in sport. For a long time, it was thought that those, such as Federer, who could react to a serve delivered at more than 150 m.p.h., were blessed with superior genes. The idea was that

Federer was born with instincts that gave him the capacity to react to a fast-moving ball, where most people would see a blur.

Federer's speed is, according to this analysis, a bit like Usain Bolt's fast-twitch fibres: encoded in DNA.

This turned out to be quite wrong. On standard tests of reaction, top tennis players are no faster on average than the rest of us. What they possess is not superior reactions but superior anticipation. They are able to 'read' the movement of their opponent (the torso, the lower part of the arm, the orientation of the shoulders) and thus move into position earlier than non-elite players. In fact, they are able to infer where the ball is going a full tenth of a second before it has been hit. This is a complex skill encoded in the brain through years of practice; not an inherited trait.

One of the reasons why practice is so important is because it transforms the neural architecture of the brain. To take one simple example, the area of the brain involved in spatial navigation – the posterior hippocampus – is much bigger in London black cab drivers than the rest of us. But, crucially, they were not born with this; it grew in direct proportion to years on the job.

Proponents of talent tend to respond by saying: 'Are you seriously saying that talent counts for nothing?' Well, that depends on what is meant by talent. The problem is that different notions are used interchangeably. What does it mean to say that Jonny is more talented than Jamie at, say, tennis? Does it mean that Jonny is better at the moment? Or that Jonny is improving faster? What if Jamie starts to improve faster than Jonny? Is Jamie now more talented than Jonny? In many fields, it has been found that those who start off below average (who might be said to lack talent) improve, over time, faster than average. In others, those who start out learning faster continue to accelerate. In one study of American pianists, those who would go on to achieve greatness were not standing out from their peers even when they had been studying intensively for six years.

Practice Makes Perfect

At what point do we decide who is talented? After a week, a month, ten years? The answer may be different depending on the time-span chosen, not to mention the level of motivation and the quality of coaching brought to each hour of practice. In the studies cited by Epstein, these variables are rarely taken into account. What this shows, I think, is that a simple notion of talent (which still rules much of the world) is misleading. Complex skills are not hardwired like height, and neither is the disposition to learn.

Many of the differences in the world today when it comes to sporting prowess are determined not by genetic differences, but by differences in the quality of practice. Brazil once had the top team in football because of highly efficient training techniques. Instead of learning from them, English coaches, obsessed with talent, said: 'Brazilians are born with superlative skill; our players could never do that.'

The consequence was that we didn't teach technical competence to our youngsters. Our eleven-year-olds continued to play on full-size pitches, hoofing the ball up to the front man, and touching the ball infrequently. No wonder we went backwards. Spain superseded Brazil because they found a way of accelerating skill-acquisition beyond their competitors.

I would have no problem with the notion of talent if it was amended to incorporate the complexity in human performance. The problem with the simplistic notion prevalent today is that it can destroy resilience, as many studies have shown. After all, if you are struggling with an activity, doesn't that mean you lack talent? Shouldn't you give up and try something else?

It is worth remembering that SF, a famous volunteer from memory literature, went from below average to world-class level in memory skill with two years of training. Was he talented? Ultimately, it depends on how you conceive of talent. What is clear is that the present notion is deeply misleading. The power of practice, on the other hand, remains vastly underrated.

Delegation
31 August 2016

In his seminal account of how the tide turned in the battle against Al-Qaeda in Iraq (AQI) between 2005 and 2008, General Stanley A. McChrystal talks about the power of delegation. The commander of Joint Special Operations ripped up the rigid hierarchical structure of the forces combatting the insurgency and took what seemed like a high-risk decision: he pushed authority down the chain of command.

'[I realised that] the role of a senior leader is no longer that of controlling puppet master, but that of a crafter of culture,' McChrystal would later say. 'When you give people responsibility, more often than not, they step up.'

The turnaround had many components. The US forces on the ground had real-time information that the leaders back at base couldn't possibly keep pace with. Allowing people to take decisions without going up and down the command enhanced agility and speed. AQI, small in number but fleet of foot, suddenly found a previously sluggish opponent right on its heels.

Something else happened, too. As the level of responsibility increased, so the troops became more responsible. Instead of requesting or, worse, hogging crucial assets (like unmanned aerial vehicles), they started to share. They realised, as McChrystal put it in his book, *Team of Teams*, that 'it would be used in a context even more critical than their current situation'. They were already working gruelling hours, but found renewed energy, too. Slowly, the tide began to turn.

I was thinking of all this in the context of a fascinating hour on Monday spent in the company of Helen and Kate Richardson-Walsh. They are not just outstanding athletes who helped Team GB hockey to gold in Rio, but deep thinkers, too. Kate, the captain, is almost certainly a future head coach. Helen, who is doing a psychology degree, reads copiously on strategy and leadership.

Delegation

Perhaps their most startling insight was the extent to which Danny Kerry, the outstanding coach, delegated authority 'down the chain of command'. The players decide when they do their daily training. They determine the written rules and behaviours against which they are held to account. They choose the captain via a vote. For some, this must sound like anarchy. In fact, the chain of command became stronger.

'If you give people responsibility, if you bring them into the decision-making, they take ownership. They become more committed. The entire dynamic changes,' Kate said. 'Even the younger players step up. Why would you wish to break a code you helped to create? There have to be well-defined limits, of course. We all understand that many key decisions are taken by the coach. But it isn't weakness to delegate; it is a sign of strength.'

Richardson-Walsh's insights tally with rigorous research into corporations. The psychologists, Jay Conger and Rabindra Kanungo, found that empowerment improved employee satisfaction. Kenneth Thomas and Betty Velthouse, two management academics, found that 'the decentralisation of authority created intrinsic motivation'. As McChrystal put it: 'People who make the decision are more invested in it.'

Football, however, typically adopts the opposite model. Authority, both de jure and de facto, is centralised in the manager. He takes all the decisions. The players are (all too often) conceptualised as lazy, unintelligent and mutinous. They receive instructions like labourers and are expected to mutely carry them out. Motivation is of the crudest carrot-and-stick variety.

When they play badly, players are shouted at. I have seen pre-match team talks that have consisted of little more than ranting. Managers are so wary of allowing players to think for themselves that they wave wildly from the touchline. Treated like infants, players become infantilised. They start to misbehave. Incipient leadership qualities are crushed. Initiative is obliterated. Players opt out of decisions even when it comes to their own personal lives, delegating to often duplicitous agents. After all, how is an infant to make a judgement call for himself?

You can trace this, as surely as night follows day, to the way England play in major competitions. As the pressure intensifies, the more they look around. When they are required to step up, as against Iceland, the more they retreat into institutionalised insecurity. The more the coach gesticulates, the more they quiver at the very prospect of taking responsibility on the pitch.

This hints, too, at the competitive advantage of Germany. Football, there, is positioned as an intelligent game. Players are brought into decision-making on training, development and rehabilitation. They are encouraged to take further education. The class divide (gaffer-manager against player-labourer) is seen for the sordid anachronism it is. This why their national teams are so imbued with leadership qualities on the field of play when it matters most.

Sir Dave Brailsford, the architect behind the success of Team GB cycling and Team Sky, deploys a model very similar to British hockey. He calls it CORE, an acronym for Commitment, Ownership, Responsibility, Excellence. 'When you give cyclists responsibility, you empower them,' he said. 'Bringing riders into decision-making, while retaining ultimate authority, has been one of the most important cultural changes we have made.'

That doesn't mean that coaches never speak sharply. Shane Sutton resigned as technical director for British Cycling after allegations of bullying, which he denies. But it is vital to realise that there is, psychologically speaking, all the difference in the world between being chastised for breaking rules that you yourself created, as opposed to rules dictated from above. Many of the most successful riders in Rio thanked Sutton for reminding them, sometimes forcefully, when they flouted the code they had personally authored.

Some readers will doubtless say that footballers should be treated like idiots for that is how they behave. This is to get things the wrong way around. They behave like idiots for that is how they are treated. There are limits to rational delegation, to be sure, and it takes true leadership to define and enforce them. But without meaningful delegation, you lose an irreplaceable resource: the initiative and resolve of the most important people of all – those on the front line.

When American forces left Iraq, AQI started to grow again, but the turnaround between 2005 and 2008 was nothing less than spectacular. When McChrystal tried to improve performance without delegation, the number of raids increased from ten to eighteen. When he judiciously delegated, this figure 'sky-rocketed' to 600. 'These raids were more successful, too,' he has said. 'They were eliminating a higher percentage of their targets.'

The McChrystal gambit remains one of the most influential events in recent military history, but it has implications that extend way beyond modern warfare. Football, please, take note.

The Volunteer

4 February 2015

Brian Halliday will only be familiar to a handful of readers. He was a quiet but determined man, but he rarely featured in newspapers, not even in his home town of Reading. But Halliday, and others like him, are, to my mind, the most important people in British sport, indeed in British society. Halliday was a volunteer.

Lots of words are aspirational in sport. Champion, victor, icon, legend, hero, to name a few. But volunteer, although a word with less effusive connotations, should command similar prestige. Halliday was the chairman of the Kingfisher Table Tennis Club for more than twenty years. He worked for the English Table Tennis Association for a decade. He wrote the newsletter for the seniors (over-40s, -50s and -60s) for so long that he became an institution.

Marx was wrong about many things, but on one issue he wrote with haunting clarity. He recognised that, while money has lots of uses, it can undermine many important things. Love is corrupted by money. Friendship is, too. These things are precious precisely because they are not about money. The moment you pay someone to be a friend is the moment that the friendship ends.

Halliday was never paid for his tireless work. I remember seeing him at our local club (I have been a member of Kingfisher for most of my life), sitting at a table in a corner patiently going through sheaves of paperwork. We caught each other's eye and he smiled, before carrying on. He wasn't working for money; indeed, to have been paid would have compromised the very act he was undertaking. He did it, like so many volunteers in sport and beyond, out of love.

He loved table tennis. He loved the fellow members of his club, just as we loved him. He loved to be a part of an institution that helped people to grow, to share, to be together. These relationships were anchored not by money, but something with a deeper power. It is the power that David Cameron sought to harness in his idea of a Big Society. But Cameron didn't realise that the beauty and the mystique of this power is precisely why it is not amenable to political manipulation.

Halliday gave up weekend after weekend to build the club that we shared together. All of us did. In the cold winter of 1986, when the idea of a new table-tennis club in a small plot of land in suburban Reading was first proposed, about thirty of us undertook the spadework. We didn't have the money to pay a professional builder, so we built it ourselves.

The Volunteer

First we dismantled a prefab in north Reading. Then we transported it over to a place called Woodley, where we had been granted the land. Then, under the auspices of Jim Hodder, a builder and table-tennis player for whom the construction of the club became a personal act of devotion, we started to reassemble it.

The weekends were long. They were cold. Gloves were vital. But the collective endeavour, the sense of camaraderie and mutual support, will never leave me. Over the past thirty years, pride in the club has never wavered.

Halliday became one of the longest-serving volunteers, but he was not alone. Colin Dyke, a bearded defensive player with an impressive forehand slice, has acted as an officer for more than two decades; Hodder is still an honorary vice president. Today (the club has moved a hundred yards to a new location because the initial plot was required by a local school) a new generation of volunteers are assisting in the work.

Dozens of local young people are members. They do not see the behind-the-scenes work that makes it all tick, but they do see the welcoming faces, the willing coaches, the sense of inclusion.

This is what great volunteers create. It is not about the majesty of the venue (Kingfisher is functional and rather small); rather, it is about the sense of purpose, fun and adventure. This is the real meaning of sport.

I sat down while writing this column and wrote the names of all the people who had shaped my life for the better. To my surprise, almost all were unpaid.

My parents, my siblings, my friends, my wife: they go without saying. But I also noted a group who gave up their time out of what I can only describe as a sense of duty and humanity. I suspect that Peter Charters, my coach, spent more than 5,000 hours nurturing me and other aspiring players at the Kingfisher club and its precursor. He is still the coaching officer today.

Building a Champion

The notion of volunteering often sounds twee. The Unsung Hero award at the BBC Sports Personality of the Year can (entirely unintentionally) feel a bit worthy, and more than a little sentimental. But volunteerism has a moral force that endures. And it evokes a vital imperative: for if those of us who have benefited from the actions of others do not offer that kindness to the next generation, these beautiful ecosystems of mutual support and friendship will wither and die.

Kingfisher is just one club that anchors this urgent truth. Ormesby in Cleveland, Cippenham in Slough, and a hundred more clubs up and down the country – in cricket, swimming, dance and everything in between – also capture the magic that emerges when people come together in a shared cause.

Table tennis may be the proximate reason for the association at Kingfisher, but it is, at bottom, about the human instinct for sharing and mutual support.

According to a think-tank, 971 million people volunteer in a typical year across the globe, either through organisations or directly to persons outside their household. The monetary value of their time is estimated at $1.5 trillion (about £1 trillion). But this is the least important dimension of volunteering. What these people contribute to a nation is not measured in money, but in soul. It is in these acts of solidarity and love, both making and receiving them, that life finds meaning.

Halliday, who was seventy-nine, passed away last week. His funeral will take place tomorrow morning. I noted on Twitter that Maria Tsaptsinos, whom he nurtured to the top of the junior rankings (I had almost forgotten that Halliday found time, even after the onset of cancer, to coach one of the nation's most promising youngsters), wrote: 'Rest in Peace Mr Brian Halliday #number1coach.'

But I leave the final word to Tom Maynard, another top player, who not only captured Halliday, but hundreds of thousands like him: the men and women who, quietly but emphatically, make this country great.

'Very sad to hear of the passing away of Brian Halliday, such a kind and gentle man. He will be remembered fondly by so many. RIP.'

Small Margins
3 November 2010

Sport is pedantic. It is defined by the quest for very small things. You could call it a lifelong exercise in hair-splitting.

Adrian Moorhouse, the swimmer, is fond of telling people that the difference between first place and last place in the final of the 100 metres breaststroke at the 1988 Olympic Games was a tenth of 1 per cent.

That was the wafer-thin margin that separated the Englishman, who won gold and many plaudits, including the MBE, from Christian Poswiat, of East Germany, who finished eighth and won very little.

Linford Christie has often talked about letting fly on the 'B of Bang'. It was his way of saying that, when launching off the blocks, it is imperative for the leg muscles to be twitching even as the crack of the pistol is registering in the inner ear. Christie defeated his nearest rival in the 100 metres final at the Barcelona Olympics by a margin roughly equal to the time it takes to blink an eye.

Paul Gascoigne frequently laments the *Sliding Doors* moment when he came within a toenail of putting England through to the final of the 1996 European Championship. It was 1-1 against Germany, the nation was on tenterhooks, and a ball was sent across from the right flank by Alan Shearer. Gascoigne lunged, but failed to make contact. England were eliminated on penalties and a nation mourned.

Sport is pedantic. It is defined by the quest for very small things. Professional athletes get up at 6 a.m., work flat out until their lungs feel as if they are going to go on strike, and then wake up the next morning and go through the same purgatory all over again. All for the sake of a fraction of a second here or a couple of millimetres there. All in pursuit of the wafer-thin advantage that means nothing and everything.

For many years, athletes thought that they could find an edge by working harder than any of their rivals. Daley Thompson always ran on Christmas Day because it was the one time of the year when he could steal a march on competitors. Christophe Legout, the French table-tennis ace, would steal back into the training hall on the outskirts of Paris after lights out to practise his serve.

Hard work remains central to the quest for athletic advantage, of course, but sport has moved on. Today, the edge is as likely to be found via engineering and technology as via sweat and toil. Football clubs and Olympic academies are populated not merely by athletes, but by scientists seeking to squeeze an advantage in everything from equipment to medicine and from engineering to psychology.

Sportsmen are no longer, like Alan Sillitoe's long-distance runner, lonely individualists. They are the point men in larger and more complex dynamics. The mythology of sport continues to demand the eulogising of the individual who breasts the tape or lands the knockout blow, but the more complex and revelatory story is often to be told about the men and women in the background whose proxy battle is more clandestine but no less ferocious.

Sometimes, teams get so caught up in the pursuit of small things that they lose sight of the bigger things. Bloodgate, Crashgate, Liegate, and the other 'gates' that have rocked the sporting world in recent years, appalled because of the institutionalised cheating that defined them. On each occasion, it was all about finding an edge even when that meant an entire organisation colluding to break the rules. The edge was the rather prosaic one of willing deceit.

The terminology 'sports science' has lost some of its sparkle recently. It is the term given to humdrum university courses about physiology and newspaper articles about oxygen testing on exercise bikes. The modern reality is infinitely more exciting. It is not just a story about sport, but about the world beyond sport. It is the story of how the imperative of gaining an edge on the field of play is changing, in various small ways, the way we live.

Innovations in Formula One designed to gain a fraction of a second around the rollercoaster of modern circuits are transforming the functionality of the mass-production car.

Orthopaedic techniques developed to drastically speed up recovery time for injured footballers are being co-opted into everyday medical procedures. NASA technology is changing the fabric of the running shoe. The spin-offs are often unintended, but they are no less real.

Where sport was once a metaphor for life, it is now becoming a paradigm. In the same way that coaches such as Sir Clive Woodward examine every conceivable angle for an edge, entrepreneurs are seeking to do the same. Soon, the workplace could be transformed by performance-enhancing clothing, ergonomics and nutrition. Prozone, the ultimate time-and-motion study in football, may soon morph into a real-time methodology to evaluate and monitor performance in the office.

The morality of progress is always complex. The most explosive branch of sporting innovation is the embedding of advantage not in training methods or equipment but in the very DNA of athletes. How do you feel about gene doping? Is it wrong to engineer genetically extra speed or bulk? Would your answer alter if it became possible to engineer longer life or immunity to cancer? It is an ethical debate that could shape the future course of humanity – and sport is at its forefront.

Social commentators have long debated the place that sport has carved for itself in the modern age. A couple of hundred years ago, sport was barely existent in organised form, and fifty years ago it rarely featured on the evening news unless England happened to be in the final of the World Cup. Today, it eclipses other forms of entertainment, driving traffic on the internet and subscriptions to pay television channels. It is part of the national psyche and the national conversation.

But we are seeing the curious new beginnings of sport as something more than a cultural phenomenon. We are seeing sport on the cutting edge of engineering, of medicine, of technology. We are seeing sport driving innovation in business and commerce, and vice versa. We are seeing the first signs of a powerful interplay between sport and science.

In short, sport, and its quest for 'small things', is slowly redefining our perception of the possible.

Competition
12 November 2014

Watching Roger Federer at something close to his imperious best yesterday, beating Kei Nishikori at the Barclays ATP World Tour Finals, reminded me of just how lucky we have been over the past decade or so.

It is not just Federer, of course, but also Rafael Nadal, who is sadly absent from London with a back injury, and Novak Djokovic, who was virtually error-free in his 6-1, 6-1 demolition of Marin Čilić on Monday.

This three-way rivalry has been among the most revelatory in sport. It is not just the epic encounters that they have served up in Melbourne, London, New York and Paris, but the deeper sense that in their quest for supremacy, they have spurred the most rapid evolution seen in the game. They have been rivals, but they have also been collaborators in an exploration of the limits of tennis.

Competition

Federer, I suppose, will always be considered the grandmaster. It is not just his results, but also the grace that he brings to the court. Sue Mott, the sports writer, once described his conquest of tennis as 'a beautiful tyranny', and the phrase strikes just the right note.

He is a poetic player, but also possesses a ruthless will. I once thought that his eyes were soft and sensitive, like those of a novelist. But I have come to realise that they are piercing and wholly unsentimental, more like those of an assassin.

There is a deep irony in that Federer, while widely acknowledged as the finest player to have flicked a racket, has a losing record to Nadal. The Spaniard leads 9-2 in grand-slam events and 23-10 overall.

Nadal is generally credited for his strength and power, but his fierce tactical brain should never be underestimated. He has the ability to adapt mid-match, sometimes even mid-point, if he feels that the narrative is slipping away from him.

The Wimbledon final of 2008 will probably always be considered the greatest of their matches. People have hailed it for the quality of the tennis but, for me, it was like watching two sharks circling each other, seeking out a fatal weakness.

First Nadal tried to expose the Federer backhand with that high, spinning forehand; Federer responded by taking the ball on the up; Nadal started to switch the play, using the court and testing his opponent's legs; Federer responded by flattening his forehand, giving Nadal less time, as the match reached the denouement.

By the end, of course, tactics and technique had become almost irrelevant, which is often the way in a career-defining contest. As the day faded to twilight, both men were naked, left only with their respective wills.

There was something elemental about the climax. Both men were spent. Each was exhausted. But they knew that in the quest to destroy each other, they had discovered new dimensions of greatness within themselves.

So to Djokovic, who, to my mind – and many will disagree – has, in his day, produced the finest tennis of all. Exhibit A for this argument is the 2011 US Open, where the Serb played with an authority that took the breath away. This was a new kind of tennis, in which he had found the zone within the zone. Watching the final against Nadal, I remember thinking that this must have been what it was like to watch Muhammad Ali in the mid-Sixties, or the Brazil football team in 1970.

It wasn't just the scoreline, it was the manner. Everyone knows – it is probably in a textbook somewhere – that you never engage Nadal on reverse diagonal (a right-hander's backhand to the Spaniard's forehand). Nadal's forehand is so heavy, so laden with topspin, that it is liable to bounce over your head. The trick with Nadal is to pin him down on the backhand, playing only to the wide forehand to keep him guessing and to stop him stepping around.

Djokovic had other ideas. It was obvious from the outset that he wanted to beat Nadal at his own game. He willingly traded backhand to forehand, stepping close to the baseline, leaning into his double-hander, flattening the stroke.

Many insiders started rubbing their eyes, but he kept at it, hitting the ball so true that Nadal struggled to recover in time to play his next shot, stumbling ever farther behind the baseline. It was like going toe to toe with Mike Tyson and muscling him into submission. It was shocking, almost transgressive. And it was utterly compelling.

The Darwinian paradox at the heart of sport and life is that beauty and truth emerge not from good intentions, but from competition. Michael White, the author, has shown that innovations from the Internet to encryption were spurred by military rivalry. He has also shown how Alexander Graham Bell invented the telephone in fierce competition with Elisha Gray, and how Crick and Watson cracked the secret of DNA, not because they were motivated by the good of mankind, but in a demented race to beat rival teams who were closing in on the discovery.

In sport, this evolutionary truth is writ large. Nadal without Federer would have been bereft. And Djokovic would have suffered mightily if he had not had Nadal in his sights, raising the bar, forcing him to jump higher than he knew possible.

The on-court rivalry is only the half of it. It is the stuff not seen: the training regimens, the nutrition, the quest for small margins in everything from flexibility to stamina.

The grand slams, in effect, are culminations of rival strategies; the battle is ultimately between rival teams, rival philosophies, each evolving in the light of the most recent encounter.

It is to the eternal credit of Andy Murray that, for a while, he broke into this closed shop of genius. The boy from Dunblane did not intrude momentarily, either. For a season and a half, he raised the bar. He triumphed at the London Olympics, was too strong at the 2012 US Open, then, most memorably of all, outplayed Djokovic to capture Wimbledon in 2013.

He combined athleticism with tactical wit. If Murray does nothing else (and I suspect he could win more grand-slam championships), this achievement alone will guarantee him a place in the pantheon of great British sportsmen.

The victory of Čilić at the US Open this year caused many to talk about a changing of the guard, but this was surely a little premature. My sense is that Djokovic and (injury permitting) Nadal will be dominant forces in the grand slams for the coming season, and probably beyond.

Federer will pose a threat, too, as he tries to take his grand-slam total to the seemingly impossible number of eighteen. But, one day, this three-way rivalry will begin to fragment and disappear. Other players will emerge. Federer, heaven forbid, will retire, and Nadal and Djokovic will call it a day, too.

It is then that people will look back on this era with longing and wonder. They will recall the Australian Open clash between

Djokovic and Nadal in 2012, which lasted five hours and 53 minutes, a record for a final in the open era.

They will remember Federer's tears after his pulsating match against Nadal down under in 2009. They will recall Nadal's multiple victories in Paris, those of Federer in London and Djokovic's in Melbourne. And they will shake their heads and acknowledge that these were the best days of their lives.

The Numbers Game
8 October 2011

To say that Billy Beane has changed sport is a bit of an understatement. He has, in many ways, changed the world. He has become an icon not merely for baseball aficionados the world over, but for an entire subculture devoted to peeling away layers of reality to reveal the hidden truths beneath.

He is as likely to be quoted by hedge-fund managers as sports journalists and is probably more beloved by maths graduates than baseball fans. He is in demand as a speaker and consultant and sits on the boards of a number of companies. He is also played by Brad Pitt in a film that was released last month.

'My approach is to understand the world through numbers,' he says when we meet in Central London. 'It is about looking ever more deeply into the connections between different phenomena and figuring out whether conventional wisdom has it wrong. If it has, there is an opportunity to step in and make a killing.'

That is precisely what Beane did with Oakland Athletics (the A's), a relatively impoverished baseball franchise. Beane was able consistently to exceed expectations by wielding (and helping to shape) the new science of sabermetrics (baseball stats). Data revealed that the assumptions of the gum-chewing baseball aristocracy (scouts, managers, owners) were seriously flawed. They were too focused on established numbers such as batting averages, and were overlooking things such as slugging percentage. To put it another way, the market was overvaluing certain attributes and undervaluing others.

'Bill James [an amateur baseball statistician] and others had been carefully putting together all sorts of incredible data,' Beane says. 'Nobody paid attention to them, but Sandy Alderson, my predecessor as general manager of the A's, realised that this information could be incredibly useful to our decision-making.

'I just took it up from them. I am not a scientist or mathematician, but I have confidence in the power of statistics to provide answers. And I am prepared to back the numbers with action.'

Beane's story has powerful appeal because it synthesises two different narratives. First, there is the story of the outsider, the bold iconoclast, stealing a march upon the settled order. This has particular resonance in baseball, a sport that inhabits American consciousness like no other and which, until Beane's arrival, had its own set of seemingly immutable truths.

Then there is the second and, in some ways, even more beguiling part of the story: the idea that beneath observable reality is a world of hidden correlations that can only be uncovered by patient code-breaking. This has captivated anyone – and not just sports coaches – interested in finding the patterns in complexity.

'For a long time, science was thought to be austere and dispiriting,' Beane says. 'The great thing about *Moneyball* [the best-selling book about Beane, written by Michael Lewis] is that it helped to glamorise statistics. After all, stats can be applied to any situation, not just baseball.'

This raises the question of whether the insights of *Moneyball* can be applied to football. It is a question with particular appeal for fans of lower-division clubs, yearning for some statistical magic that might enable them to move up the divisions. But the idea has been scoffed at by many within football, who argue that a fluid and open-ended game is far less amenable to analysis than an episodic activity such as baseball.

Beane, for his part, is in no doubt. 'Of course statistical analysis can boost performance in football. There are critical metrics that apply to every sport and to every business,' he says. 'Just because a game is dynamic and fast-flowing doesn't mean you can't measure it. You may not have as strong a correlation, but there are inevitably going to be some events that make more of a contribution to the outcome than others. The skill is in identifying the right metrics and then placing the right value on them.'

Beane's views have not been lost on at least some of the top clubs, many of whom wield statistics, and not just Prozone. Damien Comolli, director of football at Liverpool and avid admirer of Beane's, is also taking part in the discussion.

'There are clubs that are already using advanced statistics,' Comolli says. 'I have been working on it for six years and we have made fantastic progress.

'One of the first players we properly analysed was Gareth Bale when I was at Spurs. We knew as soon as we got the numbers that we had a very special player, even though he was only seventeen years of age. It was just a question of keeping him fit and making sure he stayed mentally strong. Since then, the use of statistics has grown and grown. We employ three people at Liverpool who analyse statistics.'

This is two more statisticians than are employed by the Oakland A's. 'We only have one guy who is a graduate student,' Beane says. 'He is a very highly regarded mathematician, but he is also great fun and highly inventive. We would love to have more, and we outsource a lot of the statistical work to outside experts, but it is a question of money. We just don't have a lot of cash. The New York Yankees [the richest baseball franchise] have twenty-one stats people.'

Of course, finding a statistical correlation is only useful to a team or manager if it is not already well understood by the opposition. When a particular insight is already established, it is priced into the market. To put it another way, information has to be proprietary for it to provide a competitive edge. That is why Beane's arrival in baseball was so propitious: it was not just a time when sabermetrics was taking off, but also a time when the baseball establishment was hostile to the data.

One of Beane's biggest problems since the publication of *Moneyball* (the performance of the A's has been less stellar since 2003) is that other teams have incorporated his analysis into their hiring and firing decisions. His competitive advantage has been diluted just as surely as if a patent had expired. Or, to use the vernacular of the financial markets, the information has been arbitraged away.

'We have been looking at other correlations to try to regain an advantage,' Beane says. 'Things like defensive skills, which may be undervalued, and other things that I won't discuss publicly. I am also interested in finding ways to improve the medical situation, because if you can get players back from injury faster, or hire players who are less likely to get injured, you are going to significantly improve performance. That is a key field of analysis right there.'

I ask Comolli if any counterintuitive results have been thrown up by the data in football. 'I don't want to go into too much detail,' he says with a nod towards arbitrage, 'but there are a couple of things we have found. Firstly, there is less of a correlation between possession and success than we supposed. We lost 1-0 to Stoke this season, for example, even though we had more than 70 per cent possession. That does not mean possession is irrelevant – you only have to look at Barcelona – just that it tends to be overrated by most clubs.

'We have also found that winning challenges, the battles around the pitch, are less important than we had previously thought. We have found a few other things, too, which are directly relevant to what we have been saying, but I can't really talk about them.

'We will keep looking, keep searching, because the information has to be useful. It may take a while for it to affect results, because the correlations may be relatively small, but over the long term it will make a difference.'

Beane is nodding vigorously. The man who revolutionised baseball remains in thrall to the magic of numbers.

All in the Details
28 July 2015

Tension and exhaustion. These were the dominant feelings inside the Team Sky bus when it pulled into Modane for the defining, penultimate stage of the 102nd Tour de France on Saturday. The riders, who had raced through more than 3,000 kilometres and climbed the equivalent of Mount Everest during the previous twenty-one days, were slumped in their seats, half-naked, legs bruised and battered, their lithe upper bodies pale against the gloom.

The shutters had been closed and the lights dimmed for the final, crucial team briefing. At the front, Nicolas Portal, the respected sports director, slowly but assuredly went through the race plan. 'It has been a long race, but this is the final day of the war,' he said. 'It is 110 kilometres between the start and finish line. It is not far, but much could happen.'

On a screen at the front, the route was flashed up, together with key parts of the stage. An almost imperceptible murmur swept through the bus as the bare numbers were outlined. A downhill start would be followed by a 31-kilometre climb, culminating at the Col de la Croix de Fer, then a descent to the valley. Finally, after turning left and crossing the river, they would confront perhaps the most fabled climb in all cycling: the fearsome Alpe d'Huez.

The faces of the riders were steady but the emotion was obvious. Three weeks of pain, their bodies crying out for some rest, some sleep, some recuperation, and now they were going to make new and unreasonable demands on their legs and lungs. Richie Porte, at the front, looked around at his team-mates and nodded his head grimly. 'The body is no longer willing,' Portal had said. 'It is only the mind that keeps you going now.

A year of preparation hinged on the next three hours. Chris Froome, sitting at the back, eyes scanning the map, led the General Classification (GC) by two and a half minutes. That was a significant but not insurmountable margin for Nairo Quintana, of Colombia, his main rival, to overcome. The day before, Team Sky, for the first time, revealed vulnerability. Geraint Thomas cracked and slipped from fourth to fifteenth in the GC. Even Froome, who had seemed bulletproof, rode in obvious torment.

'This isn't over,' Sir Dave Brailsford, the team principal, said minutes before the meeting. 'The riders have been magnificent, they have given it everything, but they are on the absolute limit. The tanks are nearly empty. It is crucial that Froomey has team-mates with him. If he gets isolated, we might lose the race right here. I am nervous . . . very nervous.'

Froome then asked the question that had been hanging in the air since the first slide had gone up on the screen. 'It is almost sure that Quintana is going from the bottom of Alpe d'Huez. Do I let him go and ride at my pace, or do I get straight on the wheel? If I am alone, I mean; just me, him and the other GC contenders. Do I go or do I wait?'

There was silence for a moment, then a short debate. Some said that he should respond immediately, while others argued that going flat out might kill his legs or, as Portal put it, 'put yourself in the red'. 'You should ride at your own pace,' Porte said. Froome listened and thanked the team for their input. Then he closed his eyes in contemplation. 'I will judge it at the time,' he said. 'There are too many variables to make a decision now.'

Now, it was Brailsford's turn. The team leader invariably has the last word before the riders hit the start line. He is a man of scrupulous rationality who likes to examine numbers and data, but he has a deeply competitive instinct. He calls it the 'animal within'. Like the whole team, he had been bruised by unsubstantiated allegations about the integrity of Team Sky: the newspaper reports, the booing, the spitting, the cup of urine thrown into the face of Froome. It is one thing to compete in the Tour, but it is quite another to do so while having one's moral character systematically impugned.

'You have done a fantastic job, guys, and you are sixty miles away from winning this race. That's it,' he said. 'G [Geraint Thomas]: manage yourself. Wout [Poels] you did a brilliant job yesterday, manage yourself. Leo [Leopold Konig]: I know you had a crash, we understand that, but it's the same for you – and for Nico [Nicolas Roche]. Richie: you have to be there. You are one of the best climbers in the world. You can be at the top of the mountain for sure. Manage yourself up there. That is the massive, massive part of the day. Get Froomey to the bottom of Huez and he can do his thing.'

Heads were nodding. One or two of the riders reached across the aisle to pat one another on the shoulder or thigh. The last remnants of Team Sky's collective energy were beginning to stir. And then the peroration. Brailsford's voice, usually so matter of fact, cracked as he urged his team to a final, do-or-die push. 'Pull together like a team like you have never f****** pulled together before. You can f****** do it. Get to the top of that f****** climb and this race is won . . . Let's do it.'

The crucial first step towards victory in the 2015 Tour de France did not occur on 4 July, when the riders set out from

Utrecht on the Grand Départ. It happened on the penultimate day of the 2014 Tour on 25 July. It was a six-hour drive from Périgueux to Paris. In the Team Sky car alongside Brailsford were Tim Kerrison, Rod Ellingworth and Carsten Jeppesen, senior members of the management team.

The 2014 Tour had been chastening. Froome had crashed out in the early stages and plan B had been found wanting. Porte had developed a virus and was out of contention. The muttering had started. Team Sky were said to have blown themselves out. Brailsford, it was whispered, had made serious miscalculations.

'It was ground zero,' Brailsford said. 'I said to the guys: "Right, we have been successful for a long time but if we are going to get to the next level, we have to question ourselves. We have to look at every assumption, every procedure, everything we have taken for granted. We have to rip it up and start again."

'We had worked together, the four of us, for a long time. We had become aligned in our thinking. When we were faced with problems, we tended to respond in the same way. That can be a strength, but in the long term, it can also be a weakness. Your perspective is not challenged.'

Team Sky brought in Simon Jones, a new performance scientist, with a specific brief to speak up, to ask searching questions, to force the leadership out of its comfort zone. They also hired a new dietician, James Morton. 'It was threatening in some ways, but I loved the challenge. New ideas began to flow,' Brailsford said. 'I started to write down a new plan in the black book that chronicles what it takes to win.'

Brailsford points to three key changes, two designed to improve the culture and one to improve the technical aspect, as crucial. 'I am convinced that successful teams emerge from emotionally robust cultures,' he said. 'Cycling is often described solely in terms of wattage and power outputs. But the human side is vital and often underestimated by performance scientists.

'We created a "winning behaviours" app. It sounds cheesy as hell, but it was fundamental. An example of a winning behaviour is, "I don't moan". A losing behaviour is, "I moan". If you get pissed off with somebody and start moaning about it, and then he tells his mate, who tells someone else, that is cancerous within a team. It sounds small, but it can destroy you.'

He took out his iPhone and showed me the app. The behaviours were listed down the left-hand side and then there was a sliding scale of emoticons: a happy face, a less happy face, all the way down to a sad face. With each behaviour, Team Sky members are required to provide weekly self-reports, which are sent through to Brailsford, who conducts regular one-on-one meetings.

Brailsford started inputting his data from the previous stage. Question one is: 'I am in control of my emotions.' 'I wasn't in control of my emotions today,' he said. 'I need to improve that.' Another question was 'I don't allow personal problems to affect my work.' Brailsford gave himself a happy face. 'I never allow my personal issues to affect my job,' he added.

Other behaviours included: 'I don't criticise the team; I seek out marginal gains; I seek and give constructive feedback; I continuously look to learn; I actively listen; I proactively solve problems for my team-mates.' Brailsford said: 'I can't tell you how important that last one is. People say: "You could have helped me." The response is invariably: "If you'd asked, I would have." That isn't enough. They shouldn't need to ask. Proactivity is the difference between a good and a great team.

'I have a profile of everyone, where they are at all times. That is how you change a culture. It is no good writing your values down on paper. You have to alter the way people actually behave. The app has brought the change to life. Everyone knows that when the heat is on, like in the team meeting today, they have to get their behaviour right. It is like a filter, preventing damaging actions before they even happen.'

The second change was a systematic effort to improve motivation. Brailsford calls it 'the Hunger Index'. 'We drilled down into everything that could possibly influence motivation,' he said. 'We had found that some riders in the last year of their contract tend to work like crazy to earn a new contract. They tended to fight hard in the first year, too, particularly if they had come from outside, to impress the new team. But, for a few riders, we had detected a slump in motivation in the second year. We decided to address that directly by tweaking contractual arrangements. We also looked at how they were in their personal lives and the training data. We developed a Hunger Index for every rider and tracked it. If there were any warning signs, we addressed them instantly. A dip in motivation is a clear negative. But if you are proactive, you can prevent a dip before it happens.'

The third change was technical. The algorithms used by Team Sky are among the most sophisticated in the sport. Guided by Kerrison, they delved into their assumptions and, in particular, the dynamic relationship between diet and power. 'It is not just about training but the way you fuel the training,' Kerrison said. 'Every training is fuelled differently in order to obtain the adaptation you are looking for. We do some sessions with low carbs to train the body to work more efficiently using fat. We do some with more carbs to optimise performance. But we started to explore different variations. Over time, we learnt crucial things about how different nutrition, with different levels of cadence, dynamically interact to effect the power outcome.'

Sky made other changes, too, altering the bike design for the cobbles and hiring a Spanish coach to improve communication with Spanish riders. This came on top of marginal gains such as vacuuming the riders' rooms to cut down on infection, transporting individual mattresses and using dehumidifiers, air-conditioning units and filters in the rooms.

They also expanded the training base in the south of France.

'Many teams are dispersed around the world,' Kerisson said. 'Bringing seven of the riders together to train week in, week out, had many benefits. It forced them to raise their game, to keep up with each other. It also helped them to bond. Most importantly, it gave them a chance to develop an intuitive understanding. They could tell how each other were feeling on a climb, say, so they would know when to help and when to push.'

The improvements were obvious to team members as the Tour approached, but outsiders gave them a more sinister interpretation once the race had started, particularly after Froome's blistering ascent up La Pierre Saint-Martin. Brailsford responded to an onslaught of doping allegations by releasing technical data and pointed out that the team had gone farther than any other in terms of transparency. Froome was the first rider to agree to 24-hour in-competition testing if the authorities deem it necessary.

'It is impossible to prove a negative,' Brailsford said. 'That is the great frustration. We would be happy to release more performance data along with the other teams. But I suspect that whatever we do, there will remain doubts.' Overall on the mountain stages, Froome actually lost out to Quintana, somewhat mitigating the idea that the British rider had superhuman power on the climbs. The overall margin of victory for Froome in the GC was a mere 72 seconds after 85 hours of racing.

'We are clean.' Brailsford said. 'I can't urge that strongly enough. In 20 years, nobody within the set-up has questioned the integrity of the set-up either in the GB team or with Team Sky. We are all about honest, systematic improvement. That is what the last 12 months were all about. We were building, finding slight improvements. None of them were decisive. But when you added them all up, it gave us confidence that we could regain the yellow jersey.'

The radio crackled as Portal offered guidance to the riders as they hit the slopes of Col de la Croix de Fer. In the reconnaissance car,

Ellingworth kept murmuring. 'Just a bit more Froomey, just a bit more.' But he knew that the words were meaningless now. As the riders climbed ever higher, they were beyond encouragement, beyond support, alone with their ambitions and neuroses, running on little more than fumes.

As they neared the summit, Vincenzo Nibali, the Italian, attacked to close the gap to Quintana, who had raced ahead. Froome responded and for a few haunting moments the Team Sky leader was isolated. 'This could be disastrous,' Ellingworth said. 'Stay calm, Froomey, just stay calm.' But even as the staff were recoiling in fear, the attack petered out. As the pace slowed, the other Team Sky riders made it back and rode, once again, in front of Froome, punching a hole in the air for their leader, sacrificing every last ounce of energy to shepherd him towards the final agonies of Alpe d'Huez.

As they rode up that final ascent, snaking one way and another, the astonishing beauty of the Alps revealed as if from a dream, the emotions began to tell. Brailsford, who had driven ahead to the finishing line, could no longer contain himself, unable to watch, unable to look away, beseeching Porte to stay with his leader. On the radio, Portal, whose job as sports director is perhaps the most gruelling of all the staff, was running on pure adrenaline. 'Just four kilometres,' he said. 'Just four.'

All eyes were on the clock. Quintana had built a lead of more than a minute and Froome, suffering with a slight chest infection, was nearly spent. At times, he urged Porte, the only teammate left with him, to slow down. The Australian, with whom he had trained for months, was acutely sensitive to his friend's needs, calibrating his input, head down, legs turning the wheels, sweat cascading down his brow. This was no longer a race, but a metaphor: in that final, ultimately victorious climb, teamwork, sacrifice, discipline, heroism and many other aspects of humanity were illuminated.

As Froome crossed the line to take the GC by a little more than a minute, and tears started to flow among the Team Sky staff, Brailsford closed his eyes. There was no sense of euphoria or internal fireworks; just the measured quota of grim satisfaction that accompanies all of his triumphs. 'I just don't seem to experience the elation that most people seem to,' he said, those pale eyes blinking in the sunshine, as if wondering what it would be like to experience conventional human feelings. 'I don't even feel relief. I just feel, well, satisfied,' he said.

Even as Froome was bathing in the flashbulb light of the world's photographers up at the finishing line, the other Team Sky riders were arriving on their bikes at the hotel, 500 metres away. One of the cruel ironies of the Tour is that it is a team event, perhaps the ultimate team event, and yet the garlands are reserved for one man. 'It's fine with me, it's the way we have always done it in this sport,' Thomas said, shivering in the breeze. 'He is a great athlete. He deserves everything he gets.'

As the sun lowered over the distant peaks, the riders of Team Sky shared dinner in the hotel restaurant. They allowed themselves a beer, the one nod to their triumph, and were now reloading. They still had the ceremonial ride into Paris to come, as well as a long drive to get to the starting line for the final stage. Porte was so tired, he could scarcely lift his fork. 'How are you feeling?' I asked. 'Nothing left,' he said, smiling wanly. 'But we did it.'

Across the table, Froome, whose most conspicuous quality in the team meeting, in the bar, and in his post-race interviews, was his courtesy, fixed his team-mate with a long look. 'Thank you,' he said. It was a small, inconsequential moment, but it freeze-framed the chemistry of a remarkable group. 'You have been amazing,' he continued. 'I owe it to you guys.'

A couple of hours later, the restaurant was deserted except for Richard Usher, the Team Sky doctor, and Portal. The cleaners were vacuuming and it seemed like an extraordinary day was coming to an end. But suddenly, there was the patter of foot-steps on the stairs and Brailsford darted into the room, clutching a sheaf of papers. His eyes were glinting. 'I have just agreed to sign one of the world's most brilliant young riders,' he said.

Since the end of the race, Brailsford had not paused. He had conducted a dozen interviews, overseen a debrief, accompanied Froome to meet journalists, but had then arranged to meet agents in the bar to sign new riders. 'You have to keep looking forward,' he said. 'As soon as you acknowledge the applause, you are finished. We will go through the same process of question-ing every assumption, challenging every procedure. That is the only recipe for sustained success.'

'Have you phoned Lisa [his long-term partner]?' I asked. Brailsford sighed and his face contorted. 'Damn, I haven't,' he said, and then smiled. As he began to write a text message to her, he said: 'It's a long time away from home, but next week we are going to America with Millie [his ten-year-old daughter] and some other close family,' he said. 'It should be good.'

Is it a break? 'Yes and no,' he said. 'We are going to relax, but I am going to visit the [San Francisco] 49ers and the Oracle sail-ing team. That's one thing about this job. There is always room to learn. If you think you have all the answers, you may as well give up.' He paused, and his face softened. 'We all have different views about life, and I respect people who like to take it easy. That is one way to live. But I want to keep going, keep pushing.

'Keep pushing until there is nothing left.'

II
The Mental Game

The psychological factors underpinning greatness are perhaps the least understood. Why do some people perform seamlessly under pressure while others choke? Why do some sustain their motivation over many thousands of hours of practice while others fizzle out?

Why do some athletes learn from failures and setbacks (David Beckham had his most dazzling season after his sending off at the 1998 World Cup) while others are overwhelmed by them? And why do some teams combine as if governed by a unifying intelligence, while others flail around, unable to gel?

The exciting thing about psychology is that the subject remains in its infancy. New experiments are being conducted daily around the world. Cognitive neuroscientists are learning more about what is happening in the brain when we perform and make decisions, while anthropologists are discovering fresh insights about the evolutionary development of the mind.

Sport is a powerful vehicle for exploring these themes because it is psychological factors that are often the difference between victory and defeat at the highest level. Whether it is Sampras v. Agassi, Ali v. Frazier or Ferguson's Manchester United against Wenger's Arsenal, these contests illuminate the mental qualities that define greatness.

Matter over Mind

11 March 2014

Pete Sampras always seemed like a man hidden in open view. He dominated tennis for almost a decade and was a regular presence in the media, but he sustained an enigmatic quality that never dissipated, even as he took the long walk into retirement. The emotional contrast with Andre Agassi, who wore his heart on his sleeve, added to a scintillating rivalry.

Only two things we knew for sure about Sampras. The first was that he served and volleyed like an angel. The second was that he was surrounded by an almost mystical calmness. His most memorable press-conference answer came after his three-set demolition of Agassi in the 1999 Wimbledon final. He won on a second-serve ace. What was going through your mind before that serve, he was asked. 'There was absolutely nothing going through my mind,' he replied.

When I meet Sampras in central London, I am keen to explore how he was able to attain what Simon Barnes, my colleague, has compared to a state of Zen. How was he able to find such unusual serenity amid the maelstrom of a grand-slam final? Sampras raises his eyebrows and leans forward. 'I could talk about that for hours,' he says. 'The mind is the area of sport that fascinates me the most.

'The strange thing is that I was always incredibly nervous on the morning of a grand-slam final. At Wimbledon, I would often wake up at five thirty a.m., my body pumping with adrenalin.

47

My mind would be racing. I had a terrible fear of failure. I lost a few times in grand-slam finals and it sucked. The hard truth is that nobody cares about the loser. It was the fear of failure that drove me.

'But something would happen when I walked on to play at two p.m. Suddenly I felt in control. In control of myself, in control of my emotions, in control of the crowd. I was comfortable. My head would clear out all the other stuff and focus on something incredibly simple. I would lose/myself out there. The best way to describe it was like the body taking over the mind.'

It is a revelatory phrase. I ask how easy it was for the mind to cede control to the body. 'You need confidence to be able to do it,' he says. 'Don't get me wrong. Before that second-serve ace, I was nervous as hell. During matches, I would get feelings of anxiety. But the act of playing would free my mind: when I toss the ball up, my arm swings and my body takes over. It just clicks. It's about repetition as a kid; it's about good technique; it's about having everything in place. It's about confidence and muscle memory. It's the 10,000 hours.'

Sampras is very reserved. The interview takes a while to warm up. But he undergoes a transformation as he talks about performing under pressure. His face works. His eyes gleam. Every now and again, he throws his hands forward.

'The day of a grand-slam final has a particular feel,' he says. 'At Wimbledon, I stayed in a house with my coach and girlfriend of the time. I would load up on carbs at eight a.m., always waffles. I would go for a walk, or jog. I would hit at noon for forty minutes and then have a little snack at one p.m. Then the walk on to Centre Court at two p.m.' Deep in his eyes, he is almost back there in SW19.

Perhaps it is little surprise that Sampras, who won fourteen grand-slam tournaments, has struggled to find his way since hanging up his racket. 'The first four years were tough,' he says.

Redefining failure

'I had fun, put on weight, ended up at over 200 pounds. I played golf every day, played poker and basketball, but I needed something more. I was bored. I began to think: what next? Playing tennis in exhibitions helped me get back into shape and gave me some focus. I had structure in my day again, and started working out in the gym. I have enjoyed it.'

Last week, Sampras took part in World Tennis Day, an initiative launched by the ITF to increase the number of young players in the sport. Although he lost to Agassi by two sets to love, he intends to continue playing the occasional competitive match. 'I think the tennis gives me balance,' he says. 'I also play a little golf and spend time with my wife and two kids [11 and 8]. I have my slow days: days when you don't have much to do. But life after tennis was never going to have the intensity of a grand-slam final. You have to accept that.'

As the interview draws to a close, I find myself warming to Sampras. It is not his love for tennis that shines through so much as a thirst, so powerful it feels almost existential, for the chase. For the intensity of battle. 'There is nothing like it,' he says. 'You work so hard for it, grind out those hours in the gym and on the practice court, push yourself to your limits. And then it is all about delivering on the big stage. The great players find a way to do that.'

Redefining failure
6 July 2016

In his mesmerising account of his time on the Galápagos Islands, Charles Darwin writes of the astonishing tameness of the indigenous birds. 'All of them are often approached sufficiently near to be killed with a switch, and sometimes, as I myself tried, with a cap or hat,' he says in *The Voyage of the Beagle*. 'A gun is here almost superfluous; for with the muzzle I pushed a hawk off the branch of a tree.'

Darwin, initially, couldn't make sense of this. An avid bird-watcher as a boy, he was aware of the reticence of British birds, which flew away if he came within twenty feet of them.

But then he realised what was going on: the birds here didn't have predators. Humans were conspicuous by their absence. Their willingness to expose themselves to danger was because they hadn't evolved the instinct of fear in quite the same way.

What does this have to do with football? Well, in the aftermath of England's defeat by Iceland, much of the post mortem has become bound up with this primal emotion. Steven Gerrard talked about a 'culture of fear', and Martin Glenn, the FA chief executive, about a team 'held back by fear'. These comments will resonate with fans who witnessed the collective meltdown last week. At times, the players looked terrified.

On the other hand, Wales (and what a marvellous tale this has been) have played without inhibition. In an inspiring post-match interview, Chris Coleman, the manager, said: 'Don't be afraid ... if you work hard enough and you're not afraid to dream, then you're not afraid to fail.' As pundits have noted, fear, in the Wales team, is conspicuous by its absence.

So, let us return to Darwin for a moment, to explore the biology of fear to see what it might mean for football. Darwin realised that, like all mammalian instincts, fear plays a crucial role in survival. Birds in the UK flee from humans because ancestors who possessed this facility escaped predators. A Galápagos bird transported over here would have been eaten for breakfast.

This is also true of humans. SM (her name is anonymised), a woman who couldn't experience fear due to a lesion to the amygdala, an ancient part of the brain, kept placing herself in harm's way. She was held up at both knifepoint and gunpoint, was almost killed in a domestic violence incident, and received explicit death threats on multiple occasions. And yet she did not exhibit any signs of desperation, urgency, or other behavioural responses normally associated with such incidences.

Fear, then, is useful: we want ourselves and our children to possess it. And yet it is also damaging: we want the England football team to be freed from its grip. How to resolve this paradox?

Fear, as Darwin noted, evolved to help us to avoid predators and other existential threats. That is why the primal response (shared by all mammals) is so exquisitely calibrated to assist in these situations. We freeze to evade detection. The inhibition of stomach function means that even digestion ceases. If detection is established, however, we run. The acceleration of heart and lung function primes the muscles for activity. In extremis, if cornered, we fight. The Fight-Flight-Freeze response needs to be fast, so it bypasses rational control.

But now suppose that instead of facing a predator, you are standing on a football pitch. The threat, here, is not to life and limb, but to ego and reputation. You don't want to fail. You don't want to become the scapegoat. Gerrard talked of the mind drifting to 'what the coverage is going to be like back home and the level of criticism you are going to get. You cannot stop yourself.' The stakes are high, and the consequences real, so fear is a natural response (which is why most of us experience the FFF response in similar, 'judged' situations, like giving a speech or doing a job interview).

And yet the evolved response, here, couldn't be less appropriate. Freezing means you cannot kick the ball. In cricket, you are stuck to the crease. In darts, you struggle to let go of the arrow. In speeches and job interviews, your brain can't access the information ('I've gone blank!').

Running away, the second possibility, isn't much good, either. We have all experienced, when facing a pressurised situation, that visceral desire to get the hell out of there. This can sometimes be so extreme that people won't walk on to the field of play, inventing excuses ('I'm injured', 'I am not feeling well') to legitimise their reluctance. Even if they do get on to the pitch, they stay away from the action. Here, we sometimes say: 'They have gone missing.'

Fighting isn't going to assist, either, even if you sometimes see sportsmen when put under extreme pressure, like Zinedine Zidane in the 2006 World Cup final, lashing out.

What this tells us is that familiar species of meltdown in sport and life – choking, the yips, aggression, 'going missing' – represent an instinct that is trying to be useful but is triggered by a situation for which it is singularly unsuitable. And the tragedy is that while we recognise that freezing isn't terribly helpful when taking a penalty, it is damn difficult to switch off the primitive system responsible for it.

And this brings us back to football. Much of modern performance psychology is about mitigating the FFF response. It is about 'managing the chimp', controlling 'inner demons' and the like. These techniques can be useful, but rewind for a moment to the words of Coleman, for they hint at an alternative methodology. Coleman is not talking about mitigating FFF response through conventional psychological techniques, but through the redefinition of a word: failure.

Failure is generally considered a pejorative. It has profoundly negative connotations. But, to Coleman, it has a very different meaning. 'I'm not afraid to fail,' he said. 'Everybody fails. I have had more failures than I've had success.' His point was simple and powerful. Failure is central to life and learning. It is how you grow, develop, and ultimately flourish. As Michael Jordan, the basketball ace, once put it: 'I fail. But that is why I succeed.'

If failure is stripped of its negative associations, if it is no longer an indictment of who you are, but an opportunity to learn, what reason is there to be fearful? If football is a game of expression, and you accept the mess-ups that are inherent to any creative enterprise, why freeze at the point of executing a pass?

And if you are with a group of like-minded people, cohesive and strong, united in resolve and ambition, why worry what the media might say if things go wrong?

What Coleman has done is a feature of all great leadership. By redefining failure, he has turned an environment of high consequences into one of joy and collective expression rather than worry and trepidation. Football, despite Bill Shankly's famous dictum, is not more important than life and death. The Darwinian FFF response is therefore not just unhelpful but often devastating. Take the sting out of the concept of failure and you surgically remove fear from the primitive midbrain.

And you end up playing the game of your life.

Risk-Taking

14 April 2010

Jack Nicklaus once said that the art of winning tournament golf is to understand when to defend as well as when to attack. It is a strategic insight with which most of us would agree, particularly in the context of Augusta National, a course where mistakes tend to extract penal consequences.

But in the pine needles at the side of the thirteenth fairway on Sunday, Phil Mickelson, a mild-mannered, gentle, some might almost say anaemic character, offered us a rather different philosophical proposition.

Faced with an aperture only a few feet in width between two encroaching trees, and with the potential for catastrophe staring him squarely in the face, the American went for broke.

It was a 200-yard carry over Rae's Creek, with the pin just a few paces on to the green – the kind of shot that would require scrupulous accuracy even with an obstacle-free trajectory and a perfect lie. In the circumstances, the shot seemed not merely brash but insane. Even when he took his six-iron from his bag, many of us assumed that he was laying up with a low scuttler rather than risking his chance of winning a third Masters by tilting for the green.

It was a shot selection that invited not merely dissent but ridicule. The headlines would have written themselves. Mickelson led by a shot, he had time on his side, the coming holes suited his game, he might still have made his birdie by laying up and Rae's Creek was snaking its way across the trajectory of his ambitions. Everything spoke against the decision he made.

But it is for moments such as this that golf, and sport, have meaning. In the instant he struck the ball, the 2010 Masters, which had already provided thrills and spills aplenty, was elevated into one of the great sporting events of recent times.

It was not just the sweetness of the shot, the soft landing of the ball just inches from the edge of the water and its gentle passage to within a few feet of the hole; it was, even more so, the thrilling audacity of its contemplation.

In the days when Nick Faldo and Seve Ballesteros were at the top of their games, commentators often speculated as to why the Spaniard had such a powerful emotional hold over the watching public when Faldo did not. Why was Ballesteros revered, even loved, where Faldo was only ever admired and respected? Some offered the view that the Englishman was altogether too sullen compared with the emotionally exuberant Spaniard, but this does not begin to tell the story.

We glimpse a deeper truth by looking at the way they approached the game. Faldo was the arch strategist, weighing each shot in the scales of his own ambition, methodically charting his way around the course as if golf was, at some fundamental level, a problem of algebra or geometry.

Ballesteros was quite different, playing shots from the gut, flying by the seat of his pants, selecting strokes for the sheer delight of their audacity. In short, Ballesteros was a risk-taker – and we loved him for it.

Risk is a strange and intoxicating thing. We are drawn towards it, as fans and spectators, not just because it holds out the tantalising prospect of improbable riches for the risk-taker, but also because it offers the flip side of calamity. As the roulette wheel spins and the white ball dances, we are held in a netherworld of uncertainty, riches juxtaposed with impoverishment, triumph with despair, the fabled green jacket with the stony depths of Rae's Creek.

Most of us are, to use a term from economics, risk-averse. We avoid risk, we try to live our lives by minimising its influence, we hedge our bets. That is why there is rather a large sector of the economy known as the insurance industry and why we hike millions of pounds into its claws. But it is also why we are mesmerised, at some profound level, by those among us who embrace uncertainty, who take the daring course, who risk the world to gain the world.

Alex Higgins is not the nicest chap on the planet, but his place in our hearts was consummated with his impulsive, almost suicidal shot selections en route to capturing the snooker world championship in 1982. Ayrton Senna is not the most successful Formula One driver of all time, but he is among the most revered; the maverick gambler to Alain Prost's professor. Jan-Ove Waldner did not win untold adulation in the world of table tennis just because he won so often, but because he so brazenly flirted with defeat.

And Mickelson is adored by the American public not simply because he is a decent chap with a nice demeanour, but because he has an affinity with boldness and adventure no less profound than that of Ballesteros, Arnold Palmer and the other swashbuckling legends who illuminated the history of golf.

It is because, when playing shots such as those from the pine needles on the thirteenth hole at Augusta, he provides a glimpse of the way life could be if we dared to live it beyond the cocoon of safety and certainty.

In *Being and Nothingness*, Jean-Paul Sartre wrote that the vast majority of us are inclined to misgauge the calculus of risk. We fear to step outside the comfort zone because of a morbid trepidation of what might lie beyond, when the unspoken reality is that, whatever we do, however much we insure and barricade ourselves in, the existential endgame is always the same.

'Fear?' he wrote. 'If I have gained anything by damning myself, it is that I no longer have anything to fear.'

Responding to Adversity
25 May 2016

Most of us think we are better than we are. In fact, the tendency is so powerful that psychologists have given it a name: illusory superiority. When a group of drivers were surveyed to see how they rated themselves in terms of their driving skills and safety, for example, 93 per cent thought that they were better than average.

This phenomenon also affects the super-intelligent. In a survey of professors at the University of Nebraska, '68 per cent rated themselves in the top 25 per cent for teaching ability, and more than 90 per cent rated themselves as above average.'

I was thinking of all this in the context of the exclusive story in *The Times* yesterday that Chris Ashton – after not being selected for the England rugby union tour to Australia – had refused the invitation, possibly in a fit of pique, to go with the Saxons (effectively the B team) on their tour to South Africa, potentially burning his bridges with Eddie Jones, the England head coach.

Selection processes, you see, inevitably lead to resentment and rancour. This would be so even if we were objective about our worth to the team, and merely upset that we hadn't made the cut.

But this is magnified many times over by the phenomenon of illusory superiority. After all, if we all suppose that we are significantly better than we really are, it is almost impossible to accept that the person who dropped us from the team acted in good faith.

You see this in corporations where even the lowest-performing employees are horrified (in an entirely sincere way) that they haven't been promoted. 'Doesn't the boss realise how brilliant I am?'

You see it in politics, too, where almost every person who fails to get into the cabinet within eighteen months of entering Parliament wonders about the sanity of the prime minister. You also see it in newspapers, where editors seem to be unpopular with at least 90 per cent of their writers. Why? Because every journalist thinks he is pretty much the finest writer on the paper, and should therefore be given privileged access to the limited space. 'Surely my piece should have walked into the section? It was much better than the rubbish they put on page ninety-eight!'

But perhaps the phenomenon of illusory superiority is taken to its apotheosis in sport. When I was sixteen, I was selected for the table-tennis world championships in New Delhi. It was a close call for the selectors, because there were two older players, called Jimmy Stokes and John Souter, around the same ability level, whom they could have plumped for instead. In the end, they went for youth.

Many disagreed with the decision, and yet accepted that the selectors had acted in good faith.

But for Souter and Stokes, it was a betrayal they couldn't get their heads around. They pretty much quit table tennis on the spot. Stokes became a plumber in his dad's firm and Souter a courier. 'If they aren't going to select me now, when I am clearly the best player around, there is little point in continuing' was their thinking, or something to that effect.

I still feel saddened by their decision, all these years later, because they loved the game, were marvellous team-mates, and would have made it to the top had they continued. And yet they effectively burned their bridges.

Don't we see these kinds of outbursts again and again when people are dropped, in sport and life?

For a contemporary example, take cycling. We don't yet know the outcome of the independent inquiry into – among other things – whether Shane Sutton used unacceptable language to his riders, but I seriously doubt that he dropped Jess Varnish on anything other than performance grounds. This is a man who may have acted in a way that was unacceptably offensive, but most sane people would agree that he was single-mindedly focused on winning medals. Varnish seems to believe that he acted in bad faith. I suspect that this is her illusory superiority rather than Sutton's supposed prejudice.

I remember talking to David Beckham about when he was out of favour at Real Madrid under Fabio Capello. Many felt that the Italian had made a mistake by dropping the midfielder, and it would have been easy for Beckham to have regarded the decision as prejudicial. He was wealthy, famous, popular, and could have coasted through his remaining months at the Spanish club before joining Los Angeles Galaxy. In extremis, he might have had a slanging match with his coach.

Instead, he forced himself to accept that Capello was doing what he thought was best for the team, which was the first step in trying to convince the coach to change his mind. 'I knew that Fabio wanted the club to do well, and that the best way to get back into the team was working harder, showing my stuff on the training pitch, giving it everything,' Beckham said.

A few weeks later, Capello, an arch rationalist, performed an about-turn. 'I started to see that he was working hard and this week he has trained perfectly,' the coach said. 'He was better than good. He has behaved like a great professional . . . the only thing that has influenced my decision is the work that Beckham has put in. This is not about the players saying they want him back in the squad and nor do I think that my decision to recall him undermines my authority.'

When it comes to Ashton, doesn't the same analysis apply? If I had been in Jones's position, I would probably have given Ashton the nod for the tour to Australia, but I certainly don't think that the head coach acted unreasonably. And that is why Ashton should have seized his moment with the Saxons. Jones is clearly an admirer, given that he gave Ashton a place in his RBS Six Nations championship squad. By accepting his place on the Saxons tour, the twenty-nine-year-old would have demonstrated commitment and could have mentored the younger players. He might even have enjoyed it.

The phenomenon of illusory superiority is not, by any means, all bad. When we rate ourselves highly, we tend to become more positive, optimistic and resilient, as Martin Seligman, the psychologist, has noted. But when we are overlooked, it can lead to a sense of injustice that can be destructive. Every now and again, isn't it worth accepting that we failed to make the cut, not because the boss or selector is a raving lunatic, but because we were not good enough? This means that, instead of stewing or, worse, quitting, we find new ways to improve.

The Shoot-Out
26 February 2014

A couple of years ago, Ap Dijksterhuis, a brilliant Dutch psychologist, designed a now famous experiment. It was about the capacity of experts to predict the outcome of football matches, but it also has much to say about how to take penalties.

The Mental Game

The experiment was pretty simple. Dijksterhuis took some football experts and asked them to predict the outcome of a set of matches. One group was given the opportunity to think the matches through for two minutes. They could sit and ponder, consider head-to-head results, whether the star player was having a good season and anything else they considered pertinent.

The second group had an additional complication, however. They had the same set of matches to predict, but instead of thinking it through for two minutes, they were distracted with a demanding memory task. Indeed, they were so focused on the memory task that they had virtually no bandwidth remaining in which to ponder the football matches.

The findings were both emphatic and paradoxical. Those who had time to think were poor at picking the outcome of matches. They would have done just as well picking the results randomly. Those who had to juggle the memory task, on the other hand, did far better. The distraction actually improved their performance.

The findings go to the heart of delivering under pressure. The problem for the first group was that their conscious deliberations got in the way. Thinking too much was a curse. For the second group, however, the conscious mind was distracted. It was forced to focus on the memory task. This freed the subconscious – which is far more powerful – to come up with the answers.

What does this have to do with taking penalties? Well, Roy Hodgson has mooted the possibility of hiring a psychologist to work with the England team in the build-up to the World Cup finals. The England manager has recognised that successful penalty-taking is largely about the mind. 'It will be about their character, their confidence and their ability to block out the next morning's headlines,' Hodgson said. 'If a psychologist can find a way to block that out, then we'd be very, very happy.'

But what would a psychologist actually do? The Dutch experiment provides a hint. Taking penalties is (in one sense) like predicting the results of football matches. The conscious mind can get in the way. If you think about it too much, you are likely to mess up. Glenn Hoddle, who took part in the discussion with Hodgson on Monday, made precisely this point when he talked about the moments leading up to a spot-kick. 'It's the worst walk in football – the walk from the halfway line to the spot,' he said. 'Taking a penalty technically isn't the problem.'

Why is the walk so perilous? Well, in large part, because it provides an opportunity to think. It provides half a minute to ponder the ramifications of failure; about the millions of people watching on TV; about the humiliating Pizza Hut commercials. No wonder the walk seems like an eternity. And, in this situation, it is all too easy for the conscious mind to become even more engaged, making a bad situation worse.

Thinking is often held up as a panacea, in sport and life. If you are struggling with a business decision, you are told to think it through a little more. If you are struggling with penalty-taking, you are told to analyse the way you are striking the ball. Of course, these things can help in the right context. The problem is that, in a performance environment, thinking can be nothing less than fatal. Sometimes, we need to think less, not more.

The same goes for effort. Often when England lose, whether on penalties or in open play, the players are admonished for not trying hard enough. The idea seems to be that better performance is fundamentally about greater application. But this is also misguided. Imagine a guy with impotence being told by his doctor that, to get an erection, he needs to try harder. Wouldn't it make the problem worse? When we try too hard, we often destroy the very thing we wish to achieve. Many things can only happen when we try less hard, when we relax, when we switch off the conscious mind.

The power of the subconscious has much to do with the basic architecture of the brain (according to neuroscientists, the subconscious can process up to 11 million bits of information per second while the conscious mind can only process 40), but it can also be gleaned from the testimony of top performers. When a sportsman (or, for that matter, musician) is at peak performance, the conscious mind is often very still. Very serene. Rather, it is the subconscious competence, built up over many years of practice, that is given full rein. There is a gargantuan amount of processing going on, and a huge amount of effort, but it is all taking place beneath the radar of conscious awareness. The zone in sport, rather like the state of Zen, can be compared to a duck gliding effortlessly across the water while its legs are going like the clappers.

The job of any psychologist working with the England team will be to help the players to resist the temptations of over-thinking. There are many well-established techniques, such as distraction (of the kind used in the prediction experiment) and artifice (taking the pressure off by pretending that the outcome doesn't really matter). But none is a panacea. Much will depend on the relationship between player and mind coach, which is why Hodgson is right to want any psychologist to be a part of the camp rather than someone who pitches up and delivers a lecture.

What seems certain is that if England are to improve their disappointing track record in penalty shoot-outs (one victory from seven), they will have to alter their methods. As with so many areas of life, success and failure will be less about technique and more about conquering the paradoxes of the mind.

Staying Power
9 September 2015

Longevity is a fascinating phenomenon because it is so deeply implicated in greatness. We have all seen temporary excellence: sports stars who have burnt brightly for a month, perhaps a year, before fizzling out. We see prodigies, such as Jennifer

Capriati in tennis, or the footballer Freddy Adu, not failing to reach the elite level, but failing to sustain it.

Then there are those who remain at the top, pushing the boundaries year after year, even when they are into the twilight of their careers. Just two months ago, Federer played one of the matches of the year when he defeated Andy Murray in the semi-finals at Wimbledon. His shots oozed artistry and precision, and his first-serve percentage was stellar. He may not have won a grand-slam title for three years, but at the age of thirty-four, he is still competitive. He still has a title in him.

The secrets of longevity are evoked not just by Federer, of course, but by many other celebrated athletes. Jack Nicklaus won his eighteenth major at the age of forty-six. Ryan Giggs was still playing majestic football at forty after more than 650 games for Manchester United. Sir Steve Redgrave pushed his body to five consecutive Olympic golds. You will be able to think of others, too.

But how does longevity happen? In a world of diminishing attention spans, the so-called 'five-second generation', how do these remarkable figures sustain their motivation and intensity not just for years, but for decades?

Perhaps a good place to start is at Aorangi Park, the practice courts at the All England Tennis Club. I love spending time there during Wimbledon fortnight because it provides so many insights into the various champions. On a morning about midway through the event this summer, I watched Federer going through his paces with a young hitting partner.

It was a revelation. The session lasted about fifty minutes and had a number of components (Federer hit a hundred or so serves, then they exchanged groundstrokes, and finally played six games of competitive tennis), but there was one constant throughout: Federer's smile. He took absurd delight in a drop shot that left his opponent motionless at the back of the court, lifted his hands above his head and applauded when he was a victim of a crosscourt lob.

The Mental Game

In the third decade after first starting to play tennis as a schoolboy, and almost twenty years after beginning his life as a jobbing professional, it seemed as though Federer was still revelling in the inherent fascination of the game. He was like a kid at the local courts.

A similar story emerges from the lives of other storied champions. A few years ago, I interviewed Nicklaus at St Andrews and asked him what had kept him going into his forties and beyond. His answer was simple and, in its way, reminiscent of Federer. 'I love the game,' he said. 'Without that, I couldn't have done it.' Billie Jean King said something similar. Asked about whether she ever got bored of tennis, she countered: 'How could I? I've never seen a ball cross the net in the same way twice.'

We live in a world where motivation is often conceptualised through the prism of money. If you want someone to persevere and be productive, give him the lure of a bonus. This is what you might call an external motivator. But the likes of Federer and Nicklaus hint at the idea that there is another form of motivation that underpins the most thrilling kind of longevity. It is not about external factors, but about the internal qualities of the game. The activity is a reward in itself.

The problem, of course, is that the joy of so many sports is often coached out of youngsters, just as the fascination inherent in science, or art, or music is driven from young minds by the instrumentalist view of education so prevalent today.

Instead of allowing young people to develop a love for these things, they are positioned as routes to a high income, or a decent CV, or some other 'objective'. But this serves to obscure why we do these things in the first place.

There are doubtless counter-examples: people who have achieved great things purely through the lure of external motivators, in sport and beyond. Andre Agassi springs to mind, although I never quite believed him when he said that he 'hated' tennis. If so, why did he keep playing after he had made his fortune and escaped the orbit of his pushy father? In an interview last year, he admitted, almost apologetically, that he had often thrilled to playing the game.

None of this is to decry money. We all want to be paid a fair amount for a day's work. I am merely arguing that you cannot purchase ever more motivation with larger pay cheques. Indeed, bigger bonuses are likely to crowd out these deeper instincts, driving short-termism, which is the very opposite of longevity.

But this is not a danger with Federer. When he plays, when he dances around the court, he evokes the notion that passion is not some ethereal add-on, but the psychological stuff of creativity and drive. His abilities may be remarkable, but without his love of the game, they could not have been realised. Tomorrow, he will attempt to reach an astonishing thirty-eighth grand-slam semi-final.

That is the kind of staying power that money cannot buy.

Speed of Thought
31 March 2014

This is a piece about chess, radiology and what high-velocity aircraft pilots call situational awareness. Mainly, however, it is about the neck of David Silva, the Manchester City player who, among his many accolades, has won two European Championships and a World Cup.

Silva has had a fine week. He was virtually unplayable in the Manchester derby last week, finding space between the lines, channelling attacks and, in general, creating mayhem disproportionate to his diminutive size. In the first half against Arsenal, too, he was, at times, close to sublime.

There is certainly much to admire about the Spaniard: a silky first touch, the ability to manipulate the ball in limited space and, particularly in recent weeks, a willingness to take risks in forward positions. But I would argue that none of these things would mean very much without his most important attribute: a flexible neck.

How it must ache after a match. His head spins one way, then the other. The most wonderful thing is the way he shoots a glance over his shoulder even as the ball is travelling towards him, often at pace. There is something revelatory in that: Silva is willing to take risks with his first touch to maximise his spatial awareness.

When Clive Woodward became head coach of the England rugby team, he hired a vision specialist. He wanted to figure out, among other things, if his players were efficiently using the available space. He found that the characteristic tendency of the players was to track the ball, following its progress around the pitch, and figuring out their movements in relation to its path. Woodward realised (partly through the use of Prozone) that key opportunities were being missed. Huge chunks of space were underutilised.

So he created a new strategy. He christened it 'Crossbar, Touchline, Communicate'. The idea was for the players to look at the crossbar, then at each touchline, to build a more global perspective on what was happening around them. 'They were suddenly able to pick up on all the visual cues for where the next passage of play could develop,' Woodward said. It was arguably the key innovation of his time as head coach, and was central to the team's World Cup success.

In football, coaches often encourage players to create a picture in the head. The phrase, to my mind, is unfortunate. It suggests that awareness on a football pitch is static. A picture may tell you a great deal about where players are now, but it tells you nothing about where they will be in a couple of seconds' time.

Constant scanning is infinitely more powerful. It tells you where players were, where they are and, by implication, where they are likely to be after you have executed a pass.

Andrés Iniesta, one of the standout playmakers of the modern era, was once asked about the secret of his success. His answer focused on the importance of situational awareness. 'Before I receive the ball, I quickly look to see which players I can give it to,' he said. 'Always be aware of who is around you . . . Try and put yourself in space to get the pass: the more space you have, the more time you have to think.

'The best players are the quickest thinkers. Where is my team-mate going to run to? Will he stay onside? Which one has space? Which one is looking for the ball? How do they like the ball – to their feet or in front? You can be the best passer in the world, but without your team-mates being in the right position, it's no good.'

Xavi Hernández, his team-mate, has made the same point. 'Think quickly, look for spaces. That's what I do, look for spaces,' he said in a newspaper interview. 'All day. I'm always looking. All day, all day. [Xavi started gesturing as if he was looking around, swinging his head.] Here? No. There? No. People who haven't played don't always realise how hard that is. Space, space, space. It's like being on the PlayStation. I think, the defender's here, play it there. I see the space and pass. That's what I do.'

In his pioneering experiments into chess, Herbert Simon (the great psychologist and Nobel Prize winner) discovered that grandmasters are able to extract more information from a single glance at a chessboard than amateurs taking twenty times as long. This is now a familiar finding in expert performance. Top radiologists, for example, are able to elicit rich diagnostic information from radiograms that amateurs cannot see.

The best footballers, too, think with their eyes. The difference is that they have to work in four dimensions rather than two, which is why the neck is so vital. A player who has spent his whole life swivelling his head, building perceptual judgement; a player for whom constant scanning has become second nature, has an advantage that cannot be exaggerated. Football, like art, is about the appreciation of space and time. The great players do not have it by accident, but by design.

Spanish players do not have a monopoly on head-swivelling. Many footballers from other nations, including England, have supreme situational awareness. My point, really, is that this message needs to be constantly emphasised in youth football. Coaches should talk less about the importance of a good right peg, or ability to head the ball. They should talk less about dribbling and shooting. Instead, they should talk about the neck. They should make it a condition of every training session that players swivel their heads before taking possession of any pass.

There was a wonderful moment against United when Silva nudged the ball sideways and slightly behind him, into the path of Yaya Touré. The commentator, if I remember rightly, described it as a blind pass. It was an understandable phrase, but it was the opposite of the truth. Silva had glanced backwards twice in the build-up. It was not a blind pass, but one of supreme vision. A flexible neck gives you eyes in the back of your head.

Collapse
10 July 2014

The Art of War by Sun Tzu, which was written around 500 BC during the Warring States period in China, remains the most widely read book in military history. There is a simple and compelling reason: it is not really about warfare. Look closely at its dense pages and enigmatic aphorisms and you will see that it is ultimately about human psychology and the art of intimidating opponents. And that is why its applications reach into politics, business and sport.

On Tuesday, we were treated to one of the most graphic capitulations in football history. It wasn't just a collapse of a team who were rated by most bookmakers as pre-competition favourites; it was something more profound. For a period in the first half, between Germany's second goal and their fifth, Brazil underwent a curious metamorphosis. They abdicated any sense of tactics, technique or endeavour. They seemed to experience a collective loss of willpower. They lost 7-1.

In chapter two of *The Art of War*, we are given a clue as to what was going on. Tzu introduces the concept of 'rapid dominance', the way in which morale can be destroyed by a small number of selective strikes. These strikes are designed not for military reasons, but for psychological ones. They are chosen to sow panic in the opposition, to cause them to believe that the task is hopeless. And (as during the Warring States period) they can be devastating.

Tzu's theory has become a dominant theme in military doctrine: if a critical mass of one's opponents lose the will to fight, this hopelessness is likely to spread. It has been picked up in the German concept of the Blitzkrieg: 'The application of precise, surgical amounts of tightly focused force to achieve maximum leverage,' and the American doctrine of Shock and Awe: 'To affect the will, perception, and understanding of the adversary to fight or respond.'

The psychological applications extend way beyond the battlefield. In his bestselling book, *The Tipping Point*, Malcolm Gladwell explores the idea of the social epidemic. He showed that ideas, products and messages (such as the fall in the New York crime rate after 1990 and the sales of Hush Puppies in the mid-1990s) can spread like a virus. The same kind of analysis applies to societal breakdowns, bank runs and the contagious effects of fear.

An echo of these ideas can be seen in sport, too. Batting collapses can sometimes be random sequences of poor decisions or bad luck. But every now and again, they are much more than that. Five or six beautifully delivered balls that remove the opening few batsmen can sow panic in the middle order. The psychological impact is, in many ways, far greater than the statistical one.

The incoming batsmen lose the will to fight. The opposition seem too powerful. Demoralisation goes viral. As Mark Ramprakash once told me: 'There are times during a collapse when you are walking out to the crease and, in your own mind, you are already walking back to the pavilion. It can be almost overpowering.'

It is worth pointing out, here, that I am not in any way comparing sport to war. They are very different things with radically different importance. I am merely pointing out that human psychology has distinctive features that transcend particular situations. And that is why the science of the mind has grown so rapidly over the past three decades: it is of significance everywhere from the war room to the boardroom to the dressing room.

Germany had scored two goals by the twenty-third minute. This was not an insurmountable deficit for Brazil. But the manner of the goals seemed to have a particular impact. They were slick, neatly constructed and carried the accusation that the Brazilians, deprived of Neymar and Thiago Silva, were outmatched. In psychological terms, they were like surgical strikes. The stadium was shocked. The Brazil players, as they walked back to the halfway line, looked discombobulated.

It has been pointed out, rightly, that there was a gulf in ability between the teams. But think about what happened over the course of the next seven minutes (as Brazil conceded three more goals), and beyond: the gulf became a chasm.

Alan Hansen, the BBC pundit, said: 'That is a woeful, woeful performance that could not get any lower. Nobody could have summed this up.' Gary Lineker said: 'On nigh on half a century of watching football, that's the most extraordinary, staggering, bewildering game I've ever witnessed.'

The capitulation was dramatic because it was, at bottom, sociological. This was a batting collapse taking place on a football pitch, an epidemic of panic spreading in real time during a World Cup semi-final. In many ways, this is the most compelling sports story of the year because it has revealed, once again, how games such as football, cricket and the like allow us to peer deep into the human psyche to witness its beauty and precision (Germany were mesmerising), but also its many ironies.

In the aftermath, David Luiz, who had captained his country for the first time, faced the cameras. 'We couldn't do it,' he said. 'I'm sorry, everyone. Sorry to all Brazilians. I wanted to see my people smiling.' But his words were less revealing than his manner. He was shocked, confused, as if he couldn't quite bring himself to comprehend what had happened. Tears were streaming down his face.

A group of professional sportsmen, desperate to win, had been drained of every last shred of willpower and hope. It was left to Júlio César, with the unique perspective of a goalkeeper, to offer the quote of the night: 'We got lost,' he said. And then he cried, too.

Belief

11 December 2013

Just like the England cricket fans watching their team being dismantled in the Ashes winter tour of 2013–14, Liverpool supporters were close to despair as their team trudged off at the end of the first half. Rafael Benítez's team had been handed a lesson by Kaká, Hernán Crespo and Andriy Shevchenko of AC

Milan. About forty fans had walked out when the third goal went in, unable to cope with the humiliation. The only question was by how many goals they would lose the 2005 European Cup final.

Up in the stands, a contingent of Liverpool fans began to sing. 'It started hesitantly, with an undertone of anger,' Tony Evans, who was there for *The Times*, wrote. 'But suddenly it turned into the ultimate assertion of culture and belief. When it finished, the tension had lifted and the 40,000 Liverpool fans were no longer broken and defeated, even if the team were.'

But the team weren't broken, either. Down in the dressing room, in the bowels of the stadium, Benítez was making a crucial tactical change. Off went Steve Finnan and in came Dietmar Hamann, given the task of neutering the creativity of Kaká. Benítez then began to speak. He argued that Milan might be tiring, that they could be psychologically vulnerable having lost the Serie A title late in the season to Juventus. The players, initially slumped on the benches, began to listen.

When they came back on to the pitch, they heard the tumult from their fans in the stands. Nobody, at that point, could have predicted the scoring of three goals in six minutes, the heroics of extra time, the penalty shoot-out at the climax of one of the most compelling sporting contests of the age. Liverpool had no right to turn things around. The fans had no right to believe that a miracle might be in the offing. But that is the essential paradox of the comeback: miracles happen only if you believe.

Shelley Taylor, an American professor of psychology, has studied this phenomenon. Even on the most mundane tasks, those who have unrealistically high expectations of their own efficacy (who believe, in effect, they can create miracles) perform significantly faster and with more efficiency. Self-belief bolsters performance. Those who are more realistic about the difficulties of the task, on the other hand, tend to be slower and more easily distracted. Sometimes they give up. Put simply, optimism often contains the seeds of its own fulfilment.

We saw this in the European Cup final six years before the 'Miracle of Istanbul'. Manchester United trailed Bayern Munich 1-0 as the clock ticked late on, but that United squad knew all about miracles. They had come back (in astonishing fashion) against Juventus in the semi-final second leg; they had held out against Arsenal in FA Cup semi-final replay with ten men (the most pulsating match I have seen): self-belief and an unwillingness to accept defeat had become part of their DNA. As Sir Alex Ferguson put it: 'The time to give up is when you are dead.'

In his autobiography, Gary Neville reflected on those final few moments, as he sprinted, despite his exhaustion, to take a throw-in high up the pitch on the opposite flank. 'Why did I do that?' he wrote. 'What was I doing running all that way? And it's simple really: it's what I'd been taught to do since I was a kid at United. You keep playing, you keep driving, you keep sprinting until the death.' United scored from an ensuing corner and, in the closing moments, scored again.

The England cricket team, at present in Australia, need a miracle or something close. Logic says that, with a 2-0 deficit and a Test at the dreaded venue of Perth on the immediate horizon, they are pretty much doomed. Logic says that all their efforts will likely end in vain.

But this is a moment to ignore logic. When the odds are dwindling to an invisible speck on the horizon, rationality is, perhaps, the greatest enemy of all. What the England team need is the lunacy of optimism.

Forgive me for telling a brief table-tennis story. In the European Top 12 in the early 1980s, a prestigious round-robin event, Mikael Appelgren, of Sweden, lost his opening two matches. In the third match, he trailed by two games to love and 15-5. It seemed all over. With a third defeat, any chance of winning the title was gone. But as he came to retrieve the ball,

Stellan Bengtsson, his coach and a former world champion, whispered the words that would become legendary within the game. 'You have to believe in the small chance.'

What a beautiful and contradictory piece of advice. As a species, we are used to apportioning our beliefs to the evidence. This is the hallmark of civilisation and of science. But Bengtsson recognised that it was no good, from a practical perspective, for Appelgren to believe that his chances had been vanquished. This would have been rational, but deadly. Far better to believe that he could still do it, to fill his mind with the (slim) possibility of success. Appelgren went on to win the competition.

Comebacks in sport are wonderful because they represent a deep truth about the human condition. Doggedness and optimism often fail. Most teams trailing by three goals to nil at half-time end up losing, and most table-tennis players who lose their opening two matches do not go on to win the European Top 12. In much the same way, the majority of scientists involved in the battle to find a cure for cancer fail to make a breakthrough and the majority of charity workers fail to make inroads into the scourge of global poverty.

But it is also in the crucible of optimism that the alchemy of greatness is created. It is in the blind refusal to accept the evidence of one's own senses and the doggedness to ignore surface rationality that miracles become reality. This is true of technology, of democracy, of the conquest of the New World, of civilisation itself. All of these miracles required an essential lunacy, a willingness to keep striving towards a goal while the sane majority snigger down their sleeves.

Sport is beautiful because it articulates this truth more powerfully than any other arena. That is why epic comebacks amaze and confound us. They show us what is possible when people to refuse to give up, when they hope beyond hope. From Istanbul to the Nou Camp, pioneers of the miraculous believed in the small chance.

Risk Averse

6 January 2016

It is natural to want to protect things that are precious. We protect our children, our homes, our lives. In fact, the more precious the thing, the more we are inclined to adopt a protective mode. Biologists call it the 'shield tendency'.

This happens in sport, too. One thing that golfers don't want to do is drop a shot. They want to protect their scorecards from the dreaded red ink. The language is revealing. If you hole out in regulation, you have made a par. That is pretty admirable, is it not? But if you hit one shot too many, you have made a 'bogey'. It sounds almost shameful.

The language in cricket is revealing, too. One of the most precious commodities in the game is a wicket. You have to preserve your wicket, nurture it, protect it, particularly in Test cricket. If you play a loose shot, you are said to have 'thrown away your wicket'. Coaches rail against 'flashing' outside the off stump, playing 'loose shots'. If a wicket really matters, are you not honour bound to protect it, not just for yourself, but for your team, too?

But here, I wish to focus on the risks associated with being overprotective, whether with one's wicket, one's kids, or whatever else. In the context of children, this is a familiar lament. Parents were once so worried about their little ones getting hurt playing sport, or going on adventures, or climbing trees, that politicians imposed strict liability on teachers and carers to prevent this happening.

The health and safety industry was predicated on the concept of removing children from risk. A teacher who took kids on a field trip, for example, would get hauled over the coals if a child so much as scratched her knee. Risk aversion was not only a legal requirement, it became a mindset. It wasn't until recently that people woke up to the risks associated with caution: kids stuck in classrooms, losing their sense of adventure, their spirit, their resilience, their joy.

But the dangers of risk aversion can be seen in sport, too. To return to golf, players are so worried about making a bogey and protecting their scorecards from red ink that they often run birdie putts up to the hole so that they can be sure to tap in for par. They feel good about this because they have avoided the golfing equivalent of a faux pas. But they rarely stop to consider that cautious putts have consequences – namely, that they don't make as many birdies.

A scientific study showed that this tendency (sometimes called 'loss aversion') costs the average professional about one stroke per 72-hole tournament, and the top twenty golfers about $1.2 million (around £820,000) in prize money a year. Just as with the health and safety lobby, undue caution is causing golfers to undermine the very objectives that matter most.

I was considering this while watching Ben Stokes hitting a double century at Newlands. I am guessing that I was not alone in being transported back to the halcyon days of Headingley in 1981. As with Ian Botham, that other all-action hero, Stokes seemed to play that innings, particularly on the second day, with a devil-may-care attitude. It was as if his wicket meant nothing at all.

But this was, of course, an illusion. The idea of Stokes (or Botham) as a maverick who cares less about his wicket than his team-mates may seem seductive, but it is quite wrong. Stokes is among the most diligent players in the England team. As Alastair Cook, the captain, put it: 'If anyone goes to the nets, they will see that the first guy hitting the ball, half an hour before anyone else, is Stokesy.'

Stokes, then, cares deeply about cricket, just as he cares deeply about his wicket. But he also recognises that the value of his wicket relies on the extent to which he can use it to further

England's cause. And, given his strengths as an attacking batsman, that means scoring fast, cowing opposition bowlers and
igniting the crowd. If he were to protect his wicket or approach
the crease with that mindset, he would be far less effective. To
put it simply, Stokes's aggression is not about derring-do; it is
about a rational calculation of risk and reward.

I have long suspected that the tendency in Test cricket is for
batsmen to be too risk averse, rather like professional golfers.
Mike Brearley, the former England captain, made this very point
in a newspaper column last summer. The moralistic condemna-
tion of people who get out 'cheaply', allied to the instinctive
tendency to focus on the risks of action rather than those of
inaction, has historically conspired to create batsmen who are
overprotective of their wickets.

That is not to say that everyone should play like Stokes;
rather, it is to say coaches should be more balanced in the way
that they articulate the risk–reward spectrum. When they rail
against Stokes for getting out 'cheaply', they should consider
that his superb 258 in the second Test against South Africa
couldn't have happened without risky shots.

And when they praise a batsman for leaving a ball outside off
stump, they should remember that this could have been a scoring stroke (and that he might get out soon, anyway). As Wayne
Gretzky, the ice hockey great, put it, 'You miss 100 per cent of the
shots you don't take.'

It is noteworthy that Ed Smith, the former England player, no
longer accepts the terminology of the 'bad dismissal'. Why?
Because he has never seen a 'good' dismissal. 'David Gower
scored thousands of Test runs playing majestic cover drives,'
Smith wrote. 'He also got out numerous times doing it. To argue
the dismissals were "soft" while believing the runs were "invaluable" is a simple contradiction. He could not have scored the
runs without risking the dismissals. It's a question – all taken
together – of whether Gower playing cover drives was a better

bet than a potential replacement doing something else. And, of course, Gower was the right choice.'

This is not just about cricket, it is about life. We cannot discover value unless we can encompass the risks that good things entail. When we are overprotective, we take ourselves away from the very outcomes we crave. Above all, we need to strike a more enlightened balance between risk and reward, and develop a new vocabulary for the rational risks that occasionally lead to bad outcomes. That way, we may indeed make a few more bogeys, but we will make far more life-enhancing birdies, too.

The Hand of God

21 January 2009

Kaká belongs to Jesus even if he will not, after all, belong to Manchester City. This may upset priests here more than City fans, however, given that his evangelism is even more potent than his goalscoring.

The appearance of the AC Milan forward in a Christian advertising campaign in his native Brazil reportedly led to thousands turning to Christ, hundreds more being freed from demonic possession and dozens of drug addicts being cured. It is even said that a former voodoo princess has seen the light, although there are, as yet, no reports of water being turned into wine in downtown Rio.

Kaká became a Christian at twelve, but it was not until he was eighteen that he fully committed to the Lord after slipping on a swimming pool slide and hitting his head on the bottom of the pool. The injury to his neck could have spelt the end of his career but it healed within two months. 'That was when I knew that God was looking after me and that He was on my side,' Kaká said.

The Hand of God

I am often struck by the selectivity with which Christians perceive the Hand of God (if you will forgive the expression). Kaká, presumably, did not discern the influence of the divine in allowing his foot to make contact with the slide, in permitting the slide to be slippery, or even in allowing gravity to propel his head towards the concrete floor. But God, bless Him, did miraculously pop up to heal the vertebra in his neck, enabling him to recover quicker than expected. It all smacks of hindsight bias, if you ask me.

But even if some of us doubt the rationality of Kaká's beliefs, none of us can doubt their potency. The idea that the Creator is on your side, guiding your footsteps, taking a personal interest in your recovery, deriving pleasure from your victories, providing solace in your defeats, orchestrating the world such that, in the words of St Paul's Epistle to the Romans, 'all things work together for good to those who love God' – all this must have a powerful impact on the efficacy of a sportsman, or, indeed, anyone else. As Muhammad Ali put it: 'How can I lose when I have Allah on my side?'

Ali was talking in the build-up to his showdown with George Foreman in 1974, a bout that few, even in his own camp, believed he could win. Norman Mailer, Ali's most eloquent chronicler, feared that the boxer might lose his confidence and vitality in the build-up to the contest, such was the apparent gulf in ability between the ageing former champion and his fearsome young opponent. But Mailer failed to factor in the divine: how could Ali fall victim to self-doubt when his strength flowed, not from within, but from the Almighty?

Ali's God was, of course, different from Kaká's. The Black Muslims believed in the teachings of W. D. Fard, a door-to-door salesman turned messiah, who preached that God – a divine being created from a single, spinning atom 76 trillion years ago – will save black people from the apocalypse in a wheel-shaped spaceship. Kaká, on the other hand, believes in Jehovah, the God of the Bible. My point is that these two belief systems say very different things, so only one (at most) can be true. Or, to put it another way, either Ali or Kaká (or both) has benefited powerfully from false beliefs.

Jonathan Edwards, the triple jump world record-holder, made precisely this point in an interview last year in which he opened up about his apostasy. 'Looking back now, I can see that my faith was not only pivotal to my decision to take up sport but also my success,' he said. 'Believing in something beyond the self can have a hugely beneficial psychological impact, even if the belief is fallacious. It provided a profound sense of reassurance for me because I took the view that the result was in God's hands.'

If a born-again atheist can testify to the power of religious belief, who are the rest of us to doubt him?

Last week I met Nicky Gumbel, a leading Anglican vicar and founder of the Alpha Course. At the end of an amiable discussion, he handed me his book, *Is God a Delusion?* – a riposte to a work by Richard Dawkins, the atheist – in which he contends that religious faith need not be irrational. While Gumbel makes some powerful points, his argument is surely doomed from the outset.

How can faith be rational when it asks us to believe in something – the existence of God, the divinity of Fard, the holiness of Shiva – for which there is insufficient evidence? Faith, by definition, is about believing in that which cannot be proven – which is precisely, I would suggest, why it has such power over the human mind.

But there is an altogether different sense in which faith is rational. If we aim not at truth but at success – in sport or otherwise – faith is not merely helpful but essential. Even those who do not believe in God hold beliefs that stray beyond the boundaries of reason. Kevin Pietersen believes in fate; something that, he says, provides him with the confidence to bat without inhibition. 'What will be will be,' he told me when I asked him whether he gets nervous before a big innings. 'Things happen for a reason.'

Others partake in what might be described as secular irrationality. Andy Murray tells us that he believes he will win whoever he is playing, which is nothing less than crazy. If Murray is up against Rafael Nadal on clay, he should (on mathematical grounds) believe he is going to lose. But Murray knows that doubt is a dangerous thing on a tennis court.

To win, one must proportion one's belief, not to the evidence (as in science), but to whatever the mind can usefully get away with. As Jesus rather metaphorically put it: 'If you have faith the size of a mustard seed, you will say to this mountain, "Move from here to there", and it will move.'

Sports psychology was invented to help non-faith sportsmen to garner some of the psychic power of religion, and its potency – like that of religion – derives from the placebo effect. The psychologist is not a scientist, but more akin to a homoeopathist – he seeks to instil beliefs that are not true but that create results (which are a different kind of truth). That is why sports psychologists are not technicians, but articulate and often charismatic advocates for their methods. I guess I am not the only one to have noticed their similarity to Christian evangelists.

It is not just sportsmen: none of us can get by without carefully constructed myths. We accentuate the positives, suppress the negatives, block out the traumas, create mini-narratives about our lives and loves that, on honest reflection, have little basis in reality; we do this not merely to win, but to survive.

Reason without inhibition is a perilous thing, as anyone who has studied the lives of the philosophers will testify.

In that sense the religious apologists are right: we all make assumptions that cannot be justified, even mathematicians. The problem is that, for me at least, religion fails the test of minimalism – it attempts to explain the lesser (the world) in terms of the greater (God) and thereby provides no explanation at all.

Yet even as I dispute the beliefs of Christians, Buddhists, Sikhs and other believers, I cannot help but acknowledge the unreason of my atheism. We each of us reach for beliefs beyond explanation.

Gádel, Aquinas, Kaká, Ali, Edwards: all, in their different ways, found an irrational way to triumph in the strange game we call life.

Problem Solving
30 May 2016

Football, at its best, is a game of intelligence. I am thinking of the turn and take of Andrés Iniesta against Paris Saint-Germain last year, how the Spaniard not only had the dexterity to control a ball, but caressed it into his stride, head up, already scanning the field ahead, computing the possibilities, the ball now moving forward at his feet, his body encroaching on the halfway line.

Only when Neymar, his Barcelona team-mate, had moved into space, and Iniesta had drawn the other defenders, did he release the pass, yards from the area, allowing the Brazilian to execute the shot into the back of the net. In a matter of seconds, Iniesta had demonstrated perception, judgement, versatility, and not an insignificant amount of guile.

It is not just attacking players, of course. Think, too, of the skill revealed by the world's greatest defenders and holding midfielders; how they patrol the space, constantly making probabilistic decisions about danger: how close they need to be to team-mates, how aware of the offside potential, while making interceptions and collisions, and, when the need arises, moving up field.

Anybody who supposes that footballers are not intelligent has not, to my mind, grasped the meaning of the word. Footballers may not be theoreticians. They do not solve, say, differential equations in any formal way. But they are practical problem-solvers. They make sophisticated calculations every minute of every game. And they do so with crowds baying at them and opponents kicking at their ankles.

Nassim Nicholas Taleb, the philosopher and mathematician, has discussed the power of this kind of intelligence. He notes how the industrial revolution was inspired not by theoreticians but by often semi-literate ministers, trying to solve practical problems, patiently tweaking their machines through trial and error. Indeed, these machines were so marvellous that it was only afterwards that pure scientists were forced to come up with theories to explain how they worked. The laws of thermo-dynamics were inspired by the industrial revolution, not the other way round.

Or think of James Dyson, working his way through 5,126 prototypes for his cyclone vacuum cleaner, hand-writing the results into a notebook in his workshop. He was a practical prob-lem-solver: testing, learning, adapting. By the end, his device could separate microscopic particles of dust from air at orders of magnitude way below those predicted by the theories of the day. The same pattern is found in cybernetics, derivatives, medicine and the development of the jet engine.

Footballers are problem-solvers in precisely this sense. They build skill and understanding via trial and error (also known as practice), developing implicit understanding of the laws of grav-ity, momentum, friction and inertia, while developing sophisti-cated pattern recognition and motor skills of the kind that, in the case of Tottenham's Dele Alli against Crystal Palace on 23 January, permitted him to control a moving projectile with a dab of his foot, before turning and firing into a net from twenty-odd yards against Crystal Palace – *Match of the Day*'s goal of the season.

If you want to know how far artificial intelligence is from doing such things, google 'robot football' (really do: it's quite funny). You will see that machines currently play at about the level of three-year-olds. AI will do amazing things in the coming decades, not least through 'temporal difference learning': effectively, setting up machines to practise day and night, and constantly learn from mistakes (machines develop expertise through iteration, too). But robots will not, any time soon, play football like Messi.

And this brings me to my point. Once we accept that football is a game of intelligence, the question becomes: how do we inculcate it? The hallmark of the finest players is not that they have discrete skills, but that they can deploy them simultaneously. They can dribble with their heads up; receive the ball while aware of where to run to receive the next pass; run off the ball to provide space for a team-mate while figuring out where to retreat to if possession is lost. World-class players have all the time in the world, not because they are faster than their rivals, but because they are multi-taskers. When a ball is hurtling towards Iniesta, for example, he is not just computing its speed and angle; he is also integrating information on the position of team-mates and defenders, and where to move next. His brain is projecting into the future even as it handles the present. Isn't this what game intelligence, that elusive concept, ultimately means?

To put it another way, skill is gestalt. This is the notion that has already started to drive the training of high-velocity pilots, special operations soldiers and innovative surgical teams. They are placed in 'decision-rich' environments, so that they are constantly challenged to solve complex problems under pressure of time.

The problem is that when I watch youth training, I see a lot of blocked drilling. Young people learning to dribble, for example, by running in a line across the pitch, eyes down. There is nothing wrong with this, up to a point. Drilling has its place. But there is a danger that, taken to extremes, it undermines the holistic conception of the game.

My hunch, too, is that players who develop skills in a discrete way are more likely to freeze in big competitions. Under pressure, they revert to focusing on one thing at a time, receiving the ball but struggling to pass, or executing a pass but not noticing a possible interception. I wonder if this is what has bedevilled England over the past two decades when blocked drilling was so popular with coaches. It would certainly explain why players have seemed so uncomfortable on the ball.

The key point, however, is that game intelligence is coachable. The brain is highly adaptable, and it develops ever more powerful and intricate connections when placed in the right context. Some will say, rightly, that coaching in this country has already moved in this direction, but the crucial point is that we need far more testing and trialling of different methods to see what works and what doesn't. Coaches should not be focused on copying rival nations, but innovation and boldness.

England have always had the potential to win the World Cup. By positioning the game as 'intelligent', and by encouraging coaches to see it in this way (as they do in Germany), we are far more likely to develop intelligent players. This is where the future lies. Youth coaching used to be about finding big, burly players who were good with their heads. It should always have been about developing players to become adept with their minds.

The Paradox of Time
7 July 2014

Lionel Messi has great ball control. He has a wonderful first touch. His feet are quick and he can get up to speed in the blink of an eye. But the secret of this most captivating of modern-day sportsmen is about something quite different. Messi has become clairvoyant.

This was the lesson of the Argentina captain's mesmerising performance against Belgium in the World Cup quarter-final on Saturday. There were moments when he was confronted by Marouane Fellaini, the ball stationary between the two men. The Belgian enforcer seemed unsure, hesitant; he was loath to try to steal the ball from his illustrious adversary. And with good reason, for the instant he plunged forward, the ball vanished.

Messi seemed to know what Fellaini was going to do before the Belgian did. Messi was not reacting to the lunges of his opponent but anticipating them, caressing the ball away from the incoming boot before it had moved, tap-dancing around the thrusts of the Manchester United player that, over the ninety minutes, became ever more frantic.

When Messi was on the run, the same principle applied. People talk about his control, the way the ball sticks to his feet as he runs forward. But the crucial quality when Messi is moving at speed are the little, almost imperceptible caresses around the lunges of opponents, the way he can anticipate the intentions of defenders even as they are being formed.

In his 1966 bout with Cleveland Williams, Muhammad Ali provided a similar lesson in clairvoyance. Ali connected with 100 punches and was hit by just three. Before Williams – a fine boxer, with power in both fists – launched into a hook or jab, Ali was on the move, swaying from the waist in what seemed like slow motion. It was languorous, almost lazy. Williams missed by an inch so often that, at times, it seemed like the entire bout had been choreographed in advance.

There was a moment in Saturday's match when Messi was all but surrounded. There were three Belgians in his path, each determined to take the ball, all adamant that he would not go past them. As each attempted to tackle him, their feet hit thin air. The ball was on string, each movement small and precise, their boots missing the ball by millimetres. Messi knew their minds: he could read their intentions. It was football as clairvoyance.

Psychologists talk about the time paradox. This is the well-versed observation that the greatest of performers seem to play at a different tempo to everyone else. Roger Federer, in his pomp, turned one of the fastest sports in the world into a kind of ballet. In the later rounds of his bout with Marvelous Marvin Hagler, Sugar Ray Leonard was fighting at what seemed like half-speed.

This paradox has been well studied by cognitive psychologists and there is nothing mystical about it. It emerges from a highly sophisticated form of perceptual awareness. Great sportspeople are able to 'read' the subtle cues of their opponents, extracting information about their intentions through early-warning signals (postural orientation, tiny alterations in body language, etc). When you know what an opponent is going to do before he actually does it, you have all the time in the world.

Messi has started basking in this capacity during this World Cup. He takes the ball, and literally stops. He stands there, like a mongoose facing a snake, daring his opponent to take a bite. These are fascinating moments in the game because they demonstrate that almost all the important action is going on not in the feet, but in the brain. The ball is stationary, the players are stationary; Messi's eyes are trained on his opponent, scanning and rescanning, picking up on clues that nobody in world football is able to see. Then his opponent lunges at the empty space where the ball used to be. It is beautiful and revelatory.

There is an argument that Messi must win a World Cup, or dominate a World Cup, before he is acknowledged as one of the greatest players to have kicked a ball. But these debates are sterile when set against the sheer joy of watching a sportsman at the peak of his powers, redefining the game he plays. When he is basking in the full force of his confidence and self-expression, he is, to my mind, the most mesmerising athlete on the planet. No player in history has quite dared to play the game as he.

Argentina are by no means a one-man band, however. Gonzalo Higuaín scored with a fast, almost instant, shot in the first half against Belgium (after a lovely cameo by Messi that took two defenders out of the game). Ángel di María has played well, too, and it is a great pity that he may not play any further part in the World Cup. Ezequiel Garay has produced some excellent performances in defence.

But it is the diminutive No. 10 who provides the magic. It is not just the mongoose-like skills that make him so invaluable. Every now and again he looks up, computes the spatial possibilities and slots a pass that unlocks the opposition. He can slow the game down, or speed it up, almost at will. Then there is the fear he creates in opponents, causing them to surround him in numbers, freeing up time and space for his team-mates. He is worth an extra man for that reason alone.

He has been voted Man of the Match in most of the games he has played so far in the World Cup, and he has already scored four goals. But these statistics fail to do justice to the sheer pleasure he has provided over the course of the past few weeks. He is the magician with the fast feet, a man who defies logic with almost everything he does with the ball. Most of all, he demonstrates the incalculable power of refined anticipation. He is football's clairvoyant.

The Collective Zone
21 October 2015

Serenity: that is the hallmark of the zone. The sense that everything is happening automatically, almost effortlessly. This is not to say that the mind is doing nothing at all: that would be to confuse the zone with Zen. Rather, it is that the vast subconscious machinery has everything covered – reading one's opponent, gearing up for the next shot, integrating the movement of the racket with the trajectory of the ball – leaving the conscious mind a bit like the surface of a rippleless pond.

It is, of course, beautiful to behold. Sampras, Roger Federer in his pomp, perhaps, or a young Muhammad Ali dancing around the fists of an opponent. Mihaly Csikszentmihalyi, the psychologist, talks about the state of 'flow'. 'The emotions are not just contained and channelled, but positive, energised, and aligned with the task at hand,' he has said. Let us call it the state of oneness between an artist and his art.

But there is another kind of zone that is more revelatory and, to my mind, even more beautiful. It is the state of flow acquired not by an individual, but by a team. Let us call it 'the collective zone'. This is where a player is anticipating the pass of a team-mate, even as his team-mate is anticipating, in turn, his run into space. It is where the individuals are not just co-ordinating actions, but harmonising them.

One thinks of Barcelona at their best, creating a unified dance that, almost incidentally, delivers the football into the back of the net. One thinks, too, of the Barbarians try scored by Gareth Edwards against New Zealand at Cardiff Arms Park in 1973, perhaps the most beautifully co-ordinated sporting movement of all (hymned by the incomparable Cliff Morgan).

And this brings me to the performance of the All Blacks against France on Saturday. There were moments, particularly during the second half, when this remarkable ensemble of men inhabited the collective zone. Despite the intensity and the collisions, there was an invisible seam connecting every New Zealand player, one to the other.

The majority of the astonishing nine tries scored during the game, particularly the first by Julian Savea, exuded a deep collective intelligence.

It is noteworthy that teamwork of this kind has the property of being recursive. None of the actions of the individual make sense without each of the actions of the whole. The run into space must be timed to coincide not just with the pass of one team-mate, but with the simultaneous movement of a different team-mate, now blocking the incursion of an opponent, and a third and fourth team-mate, creating yet more possibilities.

In short, this is not a set of sequential actions, but a unified and intricate web of human interaction. The nature of the collective zone is now the subject of serious psychological study – and one of the prime vehicles for its understanding is improvised jazz. This is where a group of musicians spontaneously create new music. It is fascinating to psychologists because, like sport itself, the outcomes are unscripted. The group are not playing from a piece of notated music. Rather, they are 'freewheeling'. Yet – and this is the key – none of the notes played by the saxophonist, or pianist, or the bass player makes any sense unless they harmonise with the rest. As Frank J. Barrett, an expert in military systems, put it in a marvellous essay on the subject: 'Although there are many players known for their soloing, in the final analysis, jazz is an ongoing social accomplishment. What characterises successful improvisation, perhaps more than any other factor, is the ongoing give and take between members. Players are in continual dialogue and exchange with one another'.

In his landmark study of jazz, David Bastien, the organisational psychologist, found that beneath the veneer of spontaneity was a network of hidden mastery and mutual understanding. One player might use a hand sign – four fingers – to indicate a change from 4/4 time to 4/2 time. Another might signal the end of a solo by resolving the chord. 'These behavioural norms and codes are designed to create clear communication while remaining unobtrusive to the audience,' he writes.

Above all, there is a need for empathy. I do not mean this in a soft and fluffy way, but in the razor-sharp sense of the willingness to subordinate one's own ideas and interests to those of the collective. This is the hallmark of great teams, in music, sport or life: they have a shared mental model. They begin to see the world through the same set of eyes, opening up new seams of possibility.

With this in mind, let us return to that Barbarians try in 1973. This was a group who exuded empathy and mutual trust: six of the seven players who touched the ball on its journey across the turf at Cardiff Arms Park were from Wales.

As Derek Quinnell took the ball a few yards past the halfway line, Edwards called over, even as he was darting into space. 'I remember shouting to him, in Welsh as it happens, just to give him an indication he had support,' Edwards said.

I found my eyes watering while watching the footage yesterday, not just because it is a beautiful try, but because it is a metaphor.

It reveals a truth that transcends sport: that we are capable of infinitely more together than we are alone. This is as true of organisations and nation states as it is of sports teams. 'You play at a level outside the conscious when everything is instinctive and sport achieves an art form,' Carwyn James, the Lions coach, who addressed the players before the match, said. 'The try was a demonstration of a game at that almost super-conscious level.'

Allow me to leave you with the commentary. I suspect that you will be able to see the actions in your mind's eye, and hear the tenor of Morgan's rich voice as it slowly builds. It was the greatest try ever scored, an insight into the beauty and incalculable power of the collective zone.

'This is great stuff. Phil Bennett covering. Chased by Alistair Scown. Brilliant! Oh, that's brilliant! John Williams ... Bryan Williams ... Pullin. John Dawes, great dummy. To David, Tom David, the halfway line! Brilliant by Quinnell. This is Gareth Edwards. A dramatic start! What a score!

'If the greatest writer of the written word had written that story, no one would have believed it.'

III
On Beauty

One of the most striking things about sport is that amid the Darwinian battle for supremacy, individuals and teams slugging it out to be the best, we witness a rare and powerful beauty.

This beauty takes different forms. In this section, we look at the elegance of Roger Federer, whose game takes an almost poetical form, and the development of Barcelona FC under the leadership of Joyan Cruyff. Both men were ferociously competitive, but in striving to be the best they created a kind of art.

We look at the embrace between Andy Murray and Juan Martin Del Potro at the Olympics, an embrace that spoke volumes about humanity and mutual respect, and at the life-affirming role of domestiques in road cyling – isn't there rare beauty in the self-sacrifice of these riders, a metaphor, perhaps, for the cooperative instinct that explains the success of our species?

We look, too, at how the beauty of sport is shaped by narrative. Contests, whether between England and Australia at cricket or Liverpool and Manchester United at football gain their meaning not just through the spectacle on the pitch, but against the backdrop of a complex history.

By exploring these themes, we will gain a wider handle on the nature of greatness, too. For true greatness is not just about winning and losing, it is also about the way that these contests and champions inspire, move and enthral us.

Inspiration

17 June 2015

Every morning at about 11 o'clock, a lovely woman called Deni would come into the office where my mother worked at Prospect Park Hospital, in Reading. Deni was in charge of mental health assessments and my mother worked as a personal assistant to one of the consultant psychiatrists. They would talk, share stories. After a few months, they became close friends.

They had a great deal in common. My mother had spent much of her adult life mentoring two table-tennis-mad sons. She had driven us to every practice session, every tournament. She shared our triumphs and offered consolation after the many crushing defeats. Table tennis was as much her life as it was ours. She called herself our taxi driver, but the commitment went much deeper.

The irony for parents is that they care as passionately as the children they are supporting, but always at one stage removed. They have to offer support without smothering, love without pressurising, consolation without ever appearing patronising. It is a delicate balance, which, as my mum tells it, you learn as you go along.

It is also gruelling. We had competitions every weekend, in all parts of the country. The Cleveland Three Star one weekend, the Cotswolds Select the next, the Essex Ranking tournament the week after. We practised every afternoon at the local club and mum was always there, in the background, the person who had to balance the huge cost of supporting a sporting career with the high probability that we would never make it to the top.

Deni was travelling the same road with her daughter, Fran, a football-obsessed youngster. Deni loved her professional work, and was a superb mental health professional, but her daughter's football career was always uppermost in her mind.

'It was her life,' my mum said. 'I have seen a lot of committed sporting parents, but Deni had this extra spark and passion, which was infectious. She would talk about how training had gone the day before or about how Fran had played in her latest match. Her eyes sparkled. Fran was only nine or ten when I first got to know Deni, so it was very early in her career. But Deni took incredible pride in everything her daughter achieved.'

As the friendship became closer, their chats became more involved. Deni was keen to give Fran every chance to make it to the top. She wondered about how she could secure a trial at Arsenal, about how to support her daughter when she became injured, about how to advise Fran about finding the right balance between her sporting passion and her school work.

'Fran's biggest ambition was to play for England and Deni was wise enough to know that it might never happen,' my mum said. 'But she clearly had huge ability. I remember Deni coming in one day and talking about a hat-trick that Fran had scored. It was so vividly described that it was as if you were there in the stadium. That is what Deni was like.'

On Saturday, seven years after my mother's final conversation with Deni, Fran Kirby scored for England on her full World Cup debut. It was a must-win match against Mexico and the tie was goalless as the clock ticked into the seventieth minute. The ball was played towards the 18-yard box and ricocheted into the path of Kirby. The twenty-one-year-old controlled the ball, went past two defenders and steered it into the left corner.

Inspiration

Her face was a picture of pure joy. Kirby threw her arms in the air and ran towards the dugout. England won 2-1; if they defeat Colombia this evening, they will qualify for the round of sixteen. Kirby received the Player of the Match award, as well as many accolades from Mark Sampson, the England head coach. 'She is our mini-Messi,' he said. 'Special players step up in special moments, there's more to come for her.'

Her father and brother were in the stands, but her mother did not see this wonderful moment. In May 2008, Deni passed away, suddenly and unexpectedly. She complained of a headache in the evening during a feedback session with Fran and her coaches at her club, Reading, then leant forward to put her head on the table and later lost consciousness. She had suffered a severe brain haemorrhage. She was rushed to hospital but died in the early hours of the morning.

Kirby was so close to her mother that, at first, she was not told. At the hospital the next morning, her father, uncles, brother and other family members knew the truth, but nobody could bring themselves to tell the young woman, just fourteen at the time, who looked to her mother for support, love, friendship, passion, and who had shared her football journey. When she heard the news, she sank into the arms of her friend, sobbing, disbelieving, unable to take it in.

She went to school the next day, tried to block it out, but ultimately sank into a deep depression. In 2011, Kirby stopped playing football, stopped school, stopped everything. The days were black.

'When I turned seventeen, that's when it all got a bit too much,' she said in a recent interview. 'I decided to stop doing pretty much everything. I quit football, I wouldn't get up in the morning, I wouldn't go out of my room, I was very depressed.'

It wasn't until she turned eighteen that she decided to return to football – not least because she realised that it was what her mother would have wanted her to do. At first, she played in a Sunday league, then rejoined Reading. They are a second-tier club, but she was around familiar, supportive faces. Last season, she scored twenty-nine goals in all competitions, and dedicated every one to her mother.

On 28 May, she posted this on Instagram: 'Seven years ago I lost my best friend, my biggest fan! The woman who would stand and watch me play no matter the weather; the woman who would drive me to training every night and never once complain. You never appreciate someone until they're gone, and I'm sorry I never appreciated you at the time but now I have so much respect for you.

'You had the brightest smile, and the most caring and loving heart. Not one day goes by where I don't think about you . . . I miss you so much, and always will miss you. You're my main motivation, and I love you so much. Rest in peace Mum.'

The Kirby story is powerful for many reasons, but it seems to me to express so much of importance about life. It is about love and loss, the two constants of the human condition, and the process of grieving and acceptance that underpins any quest for meaning. Football is a mere subplot in this deeper story: the vehicle for a shared journey between a mother and her beloved daughter, and the route through which a remarkable girl is paying homage to the woman who brought her into the world, and whose love continues to surround her.

'I shed a tear when she scored,' my mum said yesterday. 'I was so pleased for Fran, who has put so much into her football, and endured so much. Most of all, I shed a tear for Deni.

'I thought back to all those long conversations; all the hopes and dreams that she had nurtured for her daughter. She would have been proud beyond words. She was a truly inspirational woman.'

A Beautiful Mind

30 January 2013

I met Acer Nethercott only once, but he shone so brightly that I never forgot him. He died on Saturday at the age of thirty-five from an aggressive form of brain cancer after a glittering career in rowing: he won the Boat Race twice, in 2003 and 2005, and a silver medal at the Beijing Olympic Games. Sir David Tanner, performance director of British Rowing, described him as the 'the top British cox of his time'.

But Nethercott was so much more than that. In a world of artificially narrow horizons, particularly among professional sportspeople who focus on performance to the exclusion of all else, Nethercott's life presented a different vision. He was a dedicated sportsman, rising early, pushing himself to the limits and ensuring that no detail was left to chance. Even amid the ferocious work ethic of rowers, he had a reputation for vigilance.

Yet his life was never shackled to rowing alone. When he left the boathouse, Nethercott would immerse himself in the other great love of his life: learning. He was a brilliant scholar at Oxford, winning the Gibbs Prize in Philosophy. 'Life is not just about the body, but also about the mind,' he told me before the 2004 Boat Race. 'Philosophy was an escape from the rigours of rowing and vice versa.'

As an approach to life, this attitude was evocative of Ancient Greece, as Nethercott well knew. The original custodians of the Olympics celebrated the feats of great athletes, such as Milo of Croton, who won six wreaths.

Songs were sung about his achievements and lyric poets hymned his muscularity. But the Greeks also recognised the synergy between body and mind. Plato, whose philosophy changed the world, was so named because of his prowess at wrestling ('*Platon*' meaning broad-shouldered). The gymnasium and the academy represented complementary facets of man, each to be valued, rather than mutually exclusive pursuits.

It is a tragedy that this uplifting and humane vision has all but disappeared from modern sport. At football academies, the very idea that players should be striving for success at school is anathema. For the vast majority of coaches, stimulating one's mind is a distraction from the imperative of physical perfection. You can see this attitude in certain Olympic programmes, too. Dedication is thought to be synonymous with monomania. When I was invited to Balliol College, Oxford to study PPE, the national table-tennis coach warned that a university education was incompatible with elite sport.

But this is a stifling as well as a mistaken conception of human development. As Nethercott pointed out, sportsmen can benefit from the joys of intellectual stimulation just as academics can benefit from the liberation of exercise. Nethercott was, indeed, rather severe on Wittgenstein, his intellectual hero, arguing that he never quite grasped the role of sport in a rounded life. 'Wittgenstein held the view that sporting activities are inherently frivolous, which, to me, implies that he never understood their true meaning,' he said.

The disservice we are doing to aspiring sports stars, in particular, is profound. It is not just that many athletes are missing out on the joys of learning; they are also missing out on the opportunities afforded by a rounded education. Hundreds of professional sportspeople get to the end of their careers and are left on the scrapheap. They find out too late that a wonderful forehand topspin is of little use in the job market.

Top athletes who do study hard are often met with mockery or suspicion. I remember being jeered at when leafing through a copy of Hume's *Enquiry* on the team bus at the Barcelona Olympics. Reading was regarded as alien and pretentious. But perhaps this shows a deeper anti-intellectualism that has come to dominate our culture. We rightly celebrate top sportspeople, but we all but ignore our pioneers of the mind. John Gurdon and Andre Geim, our recent winners of a Nobel Prize, are almost unheard of. There is no more dangerous trend in British cultural life.

Nethercott is, in this sense, an important role model. Like Sir Roger Bannister, who combined pioneering work in neurology with a brilliant career as a runner, his life evokes the harmony between the physical and intellectual. Bannister once told me that 'my love of science and my love of athletics went hand in hand'. I can almost see Nethercott nodding his approval. In different ways, they are among the most inspirational sportsmen I have met.

Up in the French Alps, near Mont Blanc, is a chalet administered by University College, Nethercott's alma mater. Situated on a small plateau at altitude, it nestles in a wood and it is there for one reason: for students to enjoy 'classical reading parties'. The blurb says: 'Generally one day is spent reading and the next walking. Students can enjoy the twin benefits of exercise and learning.'

Unsurprisingly, Nethercott loved that place. Even after he had cancer diagnosed, he was a regular visitor. In his final e-mail to Daniel Crewe, his dear friend from university, he wrote: 'I think it's going to be quite difficult this year, but when was hiking easy?

'And isn't this what the doctors used to prescribe, back in the day: a good remedial stint in the clear and cleansing alpine air? I'm mightily looking forward to it, and the beautiful reminder that I am still alive (and what a wondrous and beautiful reason that is to give thanks for!) . . . I can think of nothing more nourishing to my spirit and soul right now than ten days out there.'

Nethercott passed away only a few months after that final trip, despite assiduous treatment from his doctors. But his friends and family will doubtless take comfort from his never ceasing to gain inspiration from the exercise of body and mind. His was a beautiful life.

The Invisible Men
3 November 2014

If I asked you to tell me the most brilliant moments in football, you wouldn't have to think for long. You might talk about the Cruyff turn, Pelé's famous dummy around the keeper, Gordon Banks's save against Brazil in 1970, or perhaps, to bring things up to date, that exquisite strike by Oscar on Saturday, the Brazilian using the outside of his boot to curl the ball around Robert Green.

These detonations of genius are part of what makes the game so beautiful. They are the stuff of dreams and inspire conversations on the way home after the match. They are dramatic, vivid and often scorched in the collective memory. But how often, when thinking about what matters in football, do we talk about the moments that we don't see? How often do we focus on the invisible?

Take Peter Shilton, one of the finest keepers to have drawn breath. Every now and again, he would pull off the most blinding save. And he could also perform spectacular punched clearances. These were the moments that ensured that he featured on Match of the Day and was name-checked in the next day's match reports.

But now think about how often he would go an entire ninety minutes without seeming to do very much. This was not coincidental. His positioning was so immaculate that attackers would shoot wide, which meant he didn't even have to make a save. Often, he would be off his line so early that a chance would be foiled before it materialised. He policed the penalty area with such authority that the usual mêlées simply disappeared.

Let us call this 'invisible genius'. It is an important concept because, to my mind, we tend to overlook it in this country. When it comes to defenders, for example, we love the last-gasp lunge that denies the opposition a goal. This is an art form in which John Terry, in particular, excels, and it is for this reason that he is so widely admired. His skill is highly visible and, in many ways, highly emotive. We can see with our own eyes how, with his heroic tackles, he is foiling the opposition.

But now think of the great German and Italian defenders. They engaged far less in last-minute challenges for a simple reason: they didn't need to. They possessed invisible genius, halting attacks not with spectacular lunges, but with brilliant positioning and organisational intelligence. They prevented attacks before they reached the moment of crisis. They also combined effectively, creating an invisible genius that emerged not from the individuals, but the whole.

Isn't this what success in football is ultimately about? Barcelona, at their best, had oodles of invisible genius. We often emphasise the dribbling of Lionel Messi, but if you examine how the Spanish team broke opponents, it was the less eye-catching stuff that mattered most. It was about short passes, controlled possession and slow strangulation. It was about the brilliance of Xavi Hernández and Andrés Iniesta, players who were rarely showy, but whose quiet authority provided the foundations of Barcelona's (and Spain's) success.

The idea for this piece was occasioned by watching Nemanja Matić over recent weeks. He will never be garlanded like Eden Hazard (the Fred Astaire of Chelsea) or Oscar, but he lends an understated presence to the heart of Chelsea. In many ways, he is a throwback to that other midfield patroller, Claude Makélélé. These are players whose genius is manifested, not in creating eye-catching moments, but in preventing them. The better they play, the less we see. You might even describe their *raison d'être* as invisibility.

The importance of the invisible has a mathematical aspect, too. In baseball, as everybody who has read *Moneyball* will know, scouts in the past overvalued the grandiose and the vivid. They liked players who could hit the ball out of the park. This is the baseball equivalent of the Cruyff turn or the Beckham goal from the halfway line: it is the aspect of the game that gets spectators excited.

The problem, of course, is that these highly visible qualities became hugely overvalued.

This is an issue that transcends sport. Banks like to sign star traders, newspapers like to sign star columnists, political parties like to fawn over the latest superstar MP. In doing so, they neglect the most important thing of all: the people behind the scenes whose invisible contribution is keeping the organisation alive. These are the sub-editors who correct howlers that might otherwise undermine the credibility of the title; the back office staff who realise the star trader is about to bankrupt the company; the night lawyers who prevent a libel action before it has even happened.

In a way, the neglect of the invisible is perfectly understand-able. We are bound to take greater account of what happened than what could have happened, but didn't (the counterfactual). Intelligence officers regularly thwart terrorist plots that would have killed and maimed on a large scale, but we don't hear about this because, well, the attacks didn't happen. These heroes prevent rather than create headlines. I am not comparing counterterrorism to sport, of course, merely pointing out the importance of these undervalued roles.

In football, at least, there has been a slight change in emphasis, with fans beginning to value the likes of Makélélé and goalkeep-ers like Edwin van der Sar, who could go an entire month performing quiet miracles without once finding his way into a match report. But it would be good for football, and the rest of the world, if this tendency became more widespread. Until we learn to value the invisible, the world will be a distorted place.

There was a lovely moment in the first half between Chelsea and QPR when Matić anticipated a crossfield ball that might otherwise have led to a dangerous attack. Nobody applauded and few people noticed. But I suspect that, down on the touchline,

The Embrace

José Mourinho experienced a little shudder of pleasure. The reason is simple: the success of the Portuguese has been founded, above all else, upon a deep appreciation of the invisible.

The Embrace
16 August 2016

At the end of the match, Andy Murray and Juan Martín del Potro embraced. Almost exactly four hours after they had first started taking chunks out of each other in the Olympic Tennis Centre, the Argentinian placed his head on to the shoulder of the Scot, angled to the side, offering whispered congratulations to his conqueror.

Murray, for his part, placed his right arm around the shoulders of his opponent, comforting him, as he took in the acclaim of a marvellously engaged crowd. Up in the commentary box, Simon Reed said: 'These two men will for ever share a special bond.' I suspect that people up and down Britain, and perhaps in Argentina, too, were shedding tears.

The longer I live, the more I recognise the triviality of sport. Hitting a tennis ball is not like inventing a vaccine. If sports scientists and athletes found a way of improving the world record for the discus by a few inches, it would not have a knock-on effect in the way of, say, a cure for cancer, a technology to improve communication, or a new kind of energy supply.

And yet it is precisely because sport is trivial that it enthrals us. No other branch of human activity more precisely dramatises the human instinct to win, to measure oneself against others, to dare to take on the world, and to learn more about oneself in the trying.

I have watched in amazement these past ten days as my three-year-old daughter has become a devotee of the Olympics. The gymnastics, the diving, the cycling, you name it. She has been transfixed by the drama of sport, the will of the athletes and the shocking realisation that it is possible to fiercely seek to deprive your opponent of that which they most desire, and yet to embrace them in the aftermath, in a spirit of mutual respect.

'Why are they bending over?' she said at the end of a judo bout, having watched Britain's Sally Conway and Bernadette Graf, of Austria, attempt to throw each other to the floor. 'They are bowing,' I said. 'It is a bit like hugging. They are telling each other that they are still friends.'

'So you can be friends when you are trying to beat someone?' she said, almost confused. I felt like saying: 'Yes, this is why our species has achieved so much. It's what makes us human.'

We witness Olympic Games with our lives happening concurrently. Perhaps we are having problems at work, in relationships, with a family illness. Somehow, however, this timeless drama retains its capacity to transport us from these everyday concerns, however serious, and provides solace, even inspiration. I have never been quite so transfixed by any sporting competition, not even London 2012.

Yes, there are drugs. Yes, there are cheats. Yes, there are those who seem to take delight in the negative aspects of sport. And yet when you witness Max Whitlock, the new double Olympic champion, turning a pommel horse into an extension of his body, when you see Jessica Ennis-Hill running her heart out in the 800 metres of the heptathlon, so vainly, so beautifully, when you watch Laura Trott turning her bike into Pegasus in the omnium, almost taking off from the track on the final bend, how can you fail to be moved?

I have been moved more times than I can remember during these Games. When Murray won, perhaps because of the late hour, my mind flitted to his mother, watching at home in a village in Scotland, doubtless reflecting on the sacrifices she made to help a small, rather shy child develop into the most formidable of champions. 'Warrior,' she tweeted at the moment Murray found renewed energy to close out the match.

I was moved, too, during the men's team pursuit final, one of the most dramatic sporting events of my lifetime, four British cyclists coming from seven-tenths of a second down to win gold, even as we feared they had left it too late.

I reflected upon Bradley Wiggins and the astonishing achievement of winning a fifth gold medal, and an eighth overall, by this lad who grew up in a council flat in Kilburn, and who was bullied so badly that cycling became an escape. Last December, I watched him training to his physical limits at the velodrome in Derby. 'This is all for one day,' he said. 'We live in the shadow of that one day.'

In a column written twenty-four hours before travelling to Rio, Constantine Louloudis, a rower who struck gold in the coxless four, wrote elegantly about the pressure of competing in the Olympic Games. 'It is exhilarating and terrifying. Those few minutes of such intensity and consequence that they will echo through a person's entire life.' He is right, of course, but it is not just success and failure that reverberate down the years. It is also how you play the game, the humanity you display.

Consider that Justin Gatlin was booed when introduced for the 100-metre final. The audience in Rio, like the watching public around the world, could not warm to a man who has tested not once but twice for banned substances. So fiercely did the American want to win that he lost sight of the meaning of sport. Del Potro, on the other hand, was embraced by the world for his courage and class in defeat. He left that stadium as the loser, but with his reputation infinitely enhanced. Isn't that part of the meaning of sport, too? The grace we show in adversity?

Yes, sport is trivial. Yes, it is inconsequential. But at the same time, it has such rare and beautiful depth. We have witnessed courage, with Becky James winning keirin silver in the velodrome after years of tribulation, Fran Halsall daring to take on the world in the 50-metre freestyle in the pool, losing out to the winner by just six-hundredths of a second, Jason Kenny, one of the finest British athletes of this or any other era, redefining man's relationship with two wheels.

The Olympics reveal the best and the worst in human nature. They are corrupt, have been tainted by drug-taking (organised, in the case of Russia, at the highest level of the state) and are run by cowards. And yet we should never allow these defects, these problems, to blind us to why these invented games matter, why they inspire, and why our children watch in wonder, as we once did.

'I did it,' Murray said after victory in the early hours of Monday morning. 'The feeling is just incredible.' He was talking about the emotion of winning a four-hour match, duelled for its duration at the apex of skill and intensity. But, somehow, he was speaking for us, too.

Perfect Timing

21 January 2015

Roger Federer recorded victory number 1,001 of his career at the Australian Open on Monday night. Like the vast majority of the previous 1,000, it was a mesmerising performance.

The Swiss always seems to create a memorable highlights reel. In the second set against Lu Yen-hsun, of Taiwan, Federer was pushed into the wide backhand and glided into position, just beyond the tramlines. He then guided the ball, ferociously, gracefully, around the net and on to the sideline.

Later, after a gruelling baseline rally, Federer made to hit a drive, then, at the last moment, cut underneath the ball for a delicate drop shot. The ball seemed to pause on impact, floated over the net, then died. The Taiwanese player dropped his shoulders, partly in disbelief, partly in supplication.

Perfect Timing

Federer is surely the most beautiful sportsman of our time. Some will point out that he has a losing record against Rafael Nadal (10-23) and others will argue that, on his day, Novak Djokovic plays a harder, more emphatic form of the game. Perhaps so. What few will dispute, however, is that when it comes to aesthetics, the Swiss is incomparable. He is the Michelangelo of tennis.

And my growing sense is that the aesthetic dimension is not incidental to Federer's achievements; on the contrary, it is fundamental to it. It is possible that he may have lost by the time you read these words (his second-round match was played overnight), but that does not really affect my argument. My point is that the elegance of tennis's most prolific champion is an integral feature of his success.

After all, beauty is rarely trivial, in sport or life. In nature, evolutionary biologists are continually discovering the mechanisms that explain beauty in human beings. Most of us tend to find symmetrical faces attractive, for example. But this is not for purely subjective reasons; rather, it is because symmetry is an indicator of health and a strong immune system. Likewise, aspects of body shape reflect other factors associated with biological 'fitness'.

Even the extravagant tail of a peacock can be encompassed within the intricate and complex structure of evolutionary theory. A male who can carry such a large and otherwise pointless appendage must be strong and virile indeed. The tail is beautiful to peahens because it provides a vital clue as to the male's reproductive value.

And so to Federer. With each aspect of his craft, there is an equally deep connection between beauty and 'fitness' (in this case, the propensity to win tennis matches). Striking the ball at the precise moment when the racket has reached maximum velocity, as the Swiss does with unerring regularity, represents perfect timing. The stillness of his head at the moment of impact vastly improves the sweetness of the stroke, as well as its precision.

The lack of superfluous movement on his volleys, serve and groundstrokes (this was once referred to as Federer's 'minimalism') improves accuracy and tempo. And the way he glides across the court (at Wimbledon last year, John McEnroe compared him to Rudolf Nureyev) preserves energy and allows him to sustain balance when moving at speed, something of vital importance, particularly on grass.

The same kind of truth can be glimpsed in other sports. Take Michael Phelps, and how he glides so magnificently through the water. It looks effortless, almost languorous, but it is underpinned by ferociously effective engineering. The hydro-dynamic efficiency of the stroke, with just the right amount of vertical and horizontal propulsion, is synonymous with its beauty. It is certainly more elegant than the thrashing around you might see at my local pool.

Or take Muhammad Ali, a boxer who had poise, balance, timing and who, in his time, evoked the same kind of thrill as Federer. He is widely regarded as the greatest boxer to have laced a pair of gloves. Even with a game such as darts, there seems to be a close connection between the fluency of a throwing action and its success. It is no coincidence that Phil Taylor, the most prolific champion, is also the most aesthetically pleasing.

Of course, beauty is not the aim of sport – winning is. Federer, a ruthless and entirely unsentimental athlete, is not interested in plaudits for artistic merit, he is solely interested in winning grand slams. But that is the point. In the same way that physical beauty emerges as a by-product of natural selection, so the technical efficiency of top athletes emerges from the rigours of competition.

Perhaps the same is true of team sports, too. Is it a coincidence that two of the finest football teams in history, Barcelona circa 2011 and Brazil of 1970, were also among the most captivating to watch? Patrick Barclay, my former colleague, joyfully admitted that watching Barcelona's victory over Manchester United in the 2011 Champions League final was an aesthetic experience rather than a sporting one. 'I felt like I had died and gone to football heaven,' he said.

I am not suggesting that this is an iron law. There is no disputing the brilliance of somewhat inelegant sportspeople such as Lee Trevino, Paula Radcliffe and Mahendra Singh Dhoni. And it is certainly true that beautiful players lose to less beautiful players all the time. But I would suggest, nevertheless, that there is a correlation between elegance and sporting success, for the simple reason that efficiency has a particular beauty. A cheetah, for example, is the fastest land animal and also the most graceful when running at full tilt.

In the third set against Lu, Federer stepped around to hit a forehand, dispatching the ball past his opponent in the blink of an eye. I have seen him hit the same shot hundreds of times, but I could not stop myself squealing with pleasure. You probably know what I mean, because when Federer is on top form, his elegance appeals to pretty much everyone, regardless of whether they are into tennis. It even beguiles his opponents.

This is not, then, a subjective thing, but an engineering one. It is about beautiful design and ruthless efficiency. If Steve Jobs had designed a tennis player, he would probably have looked like Federer.

The Story
6 August 2014

Kelly Sibley won a bronze medal in the mixed doubles table tennis at the Commonwealth Games on Saturday, alongside her partner, Danny Reed. I caught it on the telly and, as the final point was played, found myself overcome with emotion.

On Beauty

My wife, watching alongside me (somewhat reluctantly, it has to be said) was rather surprised by my reaction. 'It's only bronze, and it's only the Commonwealth Games,' she said. It was a justifiable response, but it caused me to understand something about sport that had never fully registered before.

I first met Sibley at the England team training centre in Nottingham. This is where the senior and junior teams trained, lived and slept and, even as Sibley arrived as a thirteen-year-old, there were raised eyebrows. She was way off the pace compared with her peers, in the England team and abroad. The women's coach told me: 'I know she's not the best, but I like her attitude.'

Back then the women and men played in different halves of the hall, separated by small barriers, but I kept noticing this small, determined girl, the youngest in the group. Her warm-up was different from everyone else's; she seemed to give it her all, sweating even before she made it to the table. The intensity that she put into her drills was quietly but emphatically different, too. She was reserved and gentle off the table, but, over time, it became clear that her determination was implacable.

Her form remained a problem, however. I watched her one afternoon doing multiball training. Every time the ball was placed wide to her forehand, she struggled to get in position. Again and again she failed, the coach advising her on balance and the pattern of her feet, to which Sibley would nod, smile and carry on. The sweat was dripping from her brow. All the other players had gone off to shower and have dinner. But still Sibley continued: trying, failing, trying again.

Her results in international competitions were invariably below par. At that level, the women's scene is dominated by China, who have the best players, coaches and system. They have won pretty much every international competition for the past thirty years. The players on the Continent are pretty good, too. Sibley would lose in qualification or the first round, time and again. But the improvement in her game was gradually becoming visible.

I got to know her parents, Lynne and John, a little. They were like so many of the parents of children who go on to excel in sport: devoted, gentle and proud. They watched her lose, sometimes they watched her win, and they would congregate with her afterwards to hear about how her training was going. They would have been proud if she had lost in the first round every week, but they took particular joy in those occasional successes.

Slowly, almost imperceptibly, Sibley moved up the rankings. She made it into the senior team, then into the lower echelons of the world rankings. She was not England's best or most exciting player, but her attitude never changed. 'It's a joy having her in the squad,' the women's coach told me last year. 'She has been a joy to have in the squad since she arrived at thirteen,' I replied.

The final points in that bronze-medal match were nothing less than enthralling. Sibley and Reed were playing Zhan Jian and Feng Tianwei, of Singapore, ranked more than 100 places higher in the world. Sibley and Reed lost the opening game but roared back into contention. As it reached the climax, I found my hands gripping the edge of my seat.

To my wife, this was a table-tennis match. To the other viewers on BBC One, it was a table-tennis match. To those who knew Sibley (or Reed), however, it was the final paragraph of a story that had been unfolding for more than fifteen years: a story of hope, tenacity, dreams, desire, a million training sessions, a hundred thousand sprints; of a homesick young girl in Nottingham staying after practice, night after night, to get her footwork right.

The final moment was beautiful, almost beyond words. As they won the decisive point, Sibley jumped into the air, embraced her partner, her eyes so alive with wonder and joy and vindication that they projected through the screen. The camera shot to her parents, jumping into the air; her coach, lips trembling; to supporters embracing each other. I could feel the tears welling, the drama of a decade, the fragmented memories of watching this girl's development, crystallising in my mind.

A few years ago, I took on a kind of unofficial role as chief sports interviewer of this paper. It was, to a point, a nice gig. I travelled to various locations speaking to top footballers, golfers, tennis players and the like. But after a while I questioned the value of these interviews. These athletes were great sportspeople, to be sure, but they rarely said anything of great philosophical or life-changing value. Why did our readers care about what they had to say?

Watching Sibley, it clicked into place. It is about narrative. We want to know these athletes, we want to understand their journeys and back-stories. If we are going to invest in them, if we are going to be inspired by them, we have to be able to place their games in the arc of a richer, more human story. The matches we watch on television are not 'sport'. Not really. They are just the final paragraph, the flourish of trumpets at the end of a concerto. Sport, in its fullest sense, is the whole thing: the moderato, the adagio and the allegro.

Sebastian Coe battling Steve Ovett in 1980 was more than a race. Muhammad Ali taking on George Foreman in the former Zaire forty years ago was more than a bout. Liverpool defeating AC Milan in Istanbul in 2005 was about more than football. These collisions evoke themes that are as rich and vital as any that exist. To watch them in isolation, without any attempt to see the wider canvas, is like trying to understand Shakespeare via a single paragraph or Bach through a single bar.

This is just as true of every match witnessed at the Commonwealth Games. It is true of Sibley winning the bronze medal in table tennis, of Nick Matthew winning gold in the squash, of countless other memories that followers, in different ways, will cherish. They were contests, but they were also culminations of essentially human stories. They were sport at its most profound.

Beauty v. Winning

28 March 2016

Johan Cruyff was, to put it mildly, successful. As a player, with Ajax he won the European Cup three times and the Dutch league on eight occasions. As a coach, he won La Liga four times with Barcelona, the Cup Winners' Cup in 1989 and the European Cup in 1992. That is the definition of success. Winning matches; winning trophies.

And yet there is a deep irony in Cruyff's life. He was not motivated primarily by winning. In an interview in 2011 with Matt Dickinson, my colleague at *The Times*, he said that what mattered most was the way a team played. He was interested in philosophy, expression. 'Winning is just one day, a reputation can last a lifetime,' Cruyff said. 'Winning is an important thing, but to have your own style, to have people copy you, to admire you, that is the greatest gift.'

It hardly needs stating that this is an inversion of the way we typically think about football, and life. In the conventional perspective, sport is about winning and everything else is subservient to that. In much the same way, business is about profit and all else must be shoehorned into this objective. This is what you might call instrumentalism: defining the bottom-line goal and then working towards it.

But Cruyff's success hints at a psychological truth that we overlook at our peril. Few of us, whether fans or athletes, are inspired solely by the bottom line. We want to embrace a wider ideal, a deeper meaning.

Let us move beyond football for a moment and consider a study by Teresa Amabile, a professor at Harvard Business School. She recruited a number of artists and selected ten of their works that had been commissioned (i.e., created for money) and ten noncommissioned works (i.e., created for love of the work itself, out of a desire for self-expression). She then asked a group of influential artists and curators to rate them.

'Our results were startling,' Amabile wrote. 'The commissioned works were significantly less creative than the noncommissioned works, yet were not rated as different in technical quality. Moreover, the artists reported feeling significantly more constrained when doing commissioned works than noncommissioned works.'

In a different study, researchers interviewed art students to see if they wanted to become artists to earn money or to express themselves in some more vital way. Twenty years later, they caught up with them to see how they were getting on as full-time artists. They found that 'those artists who pursued painting and sculpture more for the pleasure of the activity itself than for extrinsic rewards have produced art that has been socially recognised as superior'.

This finding is now so familiar that it has its own expression; what the author Daniel Pink calls the 'paradox of creativity'. We find our deepest inspiration when we are motivated by something other than winning, but that, in turn, makes us more successful. As the researchers put it: 'It is those who are least motivated to pursue extrinsic rewards who eventually receive them.'

When you look at the teams masterminded by Cruyff, both as a player and coach, this truth shines through. Winning was a big thing; but it wasn't the only thing. And this is why their performances were infused with such imagination and flair. He regarded the pass not as a functional aspect of the game, but as a thing of beauty. Even at thirty-seven, he was altering the dimensions of the game; hitting '30-metre passes so surprising that the TV cameras of the day sometimes missed them', as Simon Kuper put it in the *Financial Times*.

This is about more than football, or even art. Businesses rarely inspire their people with an emphasis on profits, or beating the competition, or ever larger bonuses. Indeed, these carrots and sticks often drain us of inspiration and obscure the meaning we seek in our jobs and lives. Truly visionary leaders never forget the bottom line, or the importance of paying a fair amount, but they inspire precisely because they articulate an ambition that transcends the profit and loss.

When Steve Jobs, of Apple, tried to lure John Sculley away from an executive role at Pepsi, for example, he did so not with a fat pay cheque. 'Do you want to sell sugar water for the rest of your life, or do you want to come with me and change the world?' he said. Jobs may not always have been admirable in his personal dealings (nor, incidentally, was Cruyff), but he made billions precisely because he was driven by something more than money.

And that is why Cruyff's greatest gift to football was to bequeath to Barcelona an understanding of this paradox. The 'more than a club' tag sometimes grates on fans, but there can be no doubt that Barcelona believe that they are about more than winning matches. This idea of a mission, a way of playing, infuses the way they think and act, both in the first team and at the academy. And this is one crucial reason why they have become so successful.

'Cruyff painted the chapel, and Barcelona coaches since merely restore or improve it,' said Pep Guardiola, who played under the Dutchman and learnt from him as a coach. Joan Laporta, a former president of the club, said: 'As a player he turned football into an art form. Johan came along and revolutionised everything. The modern-day Barça started with him, he is the expression of our identity. He brought us a style of football we love.'

After his death, I read many tributes to Cruyff, all deeply personal. But I was struck by one similarity: they articulated the importance of the Dutch master not in terms of his success, but in terms of how he made us feel. 'This was football from another planet, football as reimagined by a master choreographer assigned to strip it down, discard the rusted and outmoded components and reconstruct it in a way that was not just more aesthetically pleasing but more lethally and unanswerably efficient,' Richard Williams wrote in the *Guardian*.

In the *FT*, Kuper wrote: 'It was as if he was the lightbulb and Thomas Edison in one.' Dickinson, reflecting on speaking to the great man under the shade of a tree in the Catalan capital, wrote: 'It felt like a religious sermon from the pope of football. Winning is not everything. Beauty matters. I had marvelled at Cruyff the player, admired the coach, but what I came to love most in Cruyff was the idealist, the self-proclaimed romantic. Football has so very few of them.'

And that really is the point. Van Gogh, perhaps the most creative Dutchman of all, who earned not a cent while revolutionising art, said: 'For my part I know nothing with any certainty, but the sight of the stars makes me dream.' It was while reaching for the stars, for something beyond conventional success, that Cruyff became the most successful individual in football history.

Perfect Harmony
3 December 2014

Eight minutes into extra time in the memorable FA Cup semifinal replay between Arsenal and Manchester United in 1999, the ball is rolled back to David Beckham, who is midway in his own half, on the right side. He hits it first time to Paul Scholes, who is in the centre circle, who in turn hits it to Nicky Butt, ten yards away, who returns the favour to Scholes, who is already running on to the return, as if linked to Butt by telepathy.

Scholes controls the ball, turns and, without looking, hits a sideways pass to Butt, who is surging forward in anticipation. He, in turn, feeds it back to Phil Neville, coming up from the left. With one touch, Neville controls it and passes to Scholes, who has dipped back towards the halfway line and who, after a small interplay, hits an inch-perfect pass to Beckham, who has run into the Arsenal half on the byline. Beckham doesn't need to look up. He knows that Gary Neville is behind him, who takes it and chips it back to Beckham.

Twenty-seven seconds after the ball was first passed to Beckham, it has been touched nineteen times, seventeen of which were by the so-called Class of '92, players who grew up with each other in the United academy. United were down to ten men by that stage – Roy Keane, the captain, had been sent off – but at times, particularly when in possession, they seemed to have an extra man. They could anticipate each other's intentions, as if connected by a sixth sense.

On Monday, the three-man shortlist for the Ballon d'Or was announced. It includes Lionel Messi, who has been voted the world's best player five times, Cristiano Ronaldo, who won it last year, and Manuel Neuer, the Germany and Bayern Munich goalkeeper. It is a strong list and all are fine players. But I have to confess to a lingering unease about the award, and not just because it is selected by panel according to subjective whim.

My deeper objection is that the pomp and circumstance surrounding the Ballon d'Or detracts from an important truth in football: namely, that skill is not merely about the ability of an individual player, rather, it is about the interplay of a team. Players are not soloists, they are part of a symphony. When the team read each other, when they are able to anticipate each other's intentions, their skills compound. This is the joy and the meaning of the game.

Messi is a classic example. He is a brilliant player. He can dribble, shoot, take free kicks and, when he is in the mood, track back. But, while a fine performer on the international stage, he has not had the same impact for Argentina as for Barcelona.

Some pundits wonder if he feels the pressure rather more in national colours, or whether he is uncomfortable socially with his national team-mates. But these explanations, it seems to me, miss the point. For Argentina, the problem is simple: he doesn't have Andrés Iniesta and Xavi Hernández alongside him.

Watch Barcelona at their best and this truth is written through their play like a name through a stick of rock. The passing sequences are not dissimilar to that of the Class of '92 in that FA Cup replay. They share what psychologists call a mental model. The reason is not difficult to ascertain: Messi, Xavi and Iniesta came through the same academy, learnt the club's patterns and shapes and came to a mutual understanding of the way the game is played. They share a sixth sense.

Coaches talk about 'looking up' (as opposed to looking down at the ball) to find the right pass. Watch through-balls from Iniesta to Messi and you will notice that this is not strictly true. When they link up, there isn't even a need for a glance. Thousands of hours of collective practice have rendered this skill superfluous. There is just an instant, rapid, undefendable through-ball, with Messi bearing down upon goal. Their collective intelligence is thrilling to behold.

When Messi collects an individual award, then, my heart sinks a little. He is one of the finest sportsmen of my lifetime, but I always feel that he should be sharing the plaudits with team-mates who are integral to the expression of the very skills that have endeared him to fans around the world. An opera without a libretto has no meaning. A pianist without an orchestra cannot do justice to Sergei Rachmaninov.

Messi would shine for any club in the world. But his unique, once-in-a-lifetime genius only emerges in the company of the other two members of the Barcelona trinity. To his credit, he has often acknowledged this truth.

The Class of '92 also came through their club academy at the same time (Phil Neville came through a little later, but shared many of the training sessions). They could read one another like an ageing couple, where a mere glance is capable of conveying a depth of information that would take new lovers a week to communicate. A drop of the shoulder from Beckham, a swerve in the run of Ryan Giggs – these subtle movements could set in train events that no defender could anticipate.

It is noteworthy that Beckham came within an ace of winning the FIFA award in the 1998–99 season. Many pundits have shaken their heads at this, arguing that Beckham was not the second-best player in the world that season. They miss the point. In that team, Beckham was a cog in a machine of breathtaking orchestration (and willpower). He was sublime because they were sublime. As a group, they achieved greatness. Beckham's brilliance emerged, in part, from the players around him.

Players do not have to have grown up at the same academy to gel with each other. Alan Shearer and Teddy Sheringham, Gary Lineker and Peter Beardsley, some players share a mutual under-standing, as if by instinct. Others consciously work hard to build a shared mental model. But this aspect of the game is under-appreciated by many managers today. They assess and coach players as soloists rather than members of an orchestra.

It is noteworthy that Sir Alex Ferguson, among others, had a different perspective. He was highly attuned to how any poten-tial new player would integrate, how they might add to (or possibly subtract from) the sum of the parts. As Scholes put it, 'He always looked at players, not in isolation, but in terms of how their skills would complement the team.'

Awards such as the Ballon d'Or undermine this symphonic conception of football. Even a player with the individual mastery of Ronaldo is vastly improved when surrounded by team-mates with whom he shares a mutual understanding. It is never a criti-cism to say that a player is dependent upon his team-mates; it is no different from saying that John Lennon depended on Paul McCartney.

It is no coincidence that one of the finest teams, Brazil of 1970, contained one of the finest players. Pelé's greatness emerged from the team, just as the greatness of the team emerged from Pelé. Watch Carlos Alberto's goal in the World Cup final against Italy and you will witness the searing beauty of this recursive truth. Eight players, thirty touches, and arguably the finest goal ever scored.

Power of Narrative
1 April 2015

Bankruptcy is the greatest gift of capitalism. We should be far more relaxed when companies such as Woolworths and Blockbuster go under. This is the hallmark of competition, of the battle for market share. It is precisely because 5 to 10 per cent of companies go bust each year that free markets can create growth and prosperity. Joseph Schumpeter, the great Austrian economist, called it creative destruction.

Sport today enjoys a remarkably free market. This week on Sky Sports, I have watched the Netball Superleague and the National Badminton League. On Eurosport, there is ice skating, skiing and cycling. BT Sport has Ultimate Fighting Championship and MotoGP. Snooker and bowls are on BBC. Squash and hockey, too, have regular outings. These sports are battling each other for market share.

A quarter of a century ago, the terrain looked very different. Minority sports could not access TV coverage because there were only a few channels – it was impossible to break through. Administrators of games such as badminton often said to TV executives things such as: 'If you only gave us a chance, we would surprise you. Our sport is every bit as exciting as football, you know.'

This proposition is now being put to the test – and failing. Through enterprise of a kind that Schumpeter would have admired, Barry Hearn has carved out a lucrative niche for darts. Badminton has a loyal following on Sky Sports. Table tennis, too, secures a decent audience when it gets an outing on Eurosport. This widening coverage on television is a good thing for fans and for sport.

But there is no sign of any threat to the ascendant positions of football and, to a lesser extent, rugby union and cricket. These three sports dominated coverage fifty years ago, they dominated twenty years ago, and they continue to dominate today. Measured by TV output, newsprint, and the more ambiguous concept of cultural bandwidth, football remains king and rugby and cricket are princes. The second tier includes tennis, golf and motorsport. As for minority sports, they remain, well, in the minority.

This is unlikely to change any time soon. Netball is not going to knock football off its perch, as Delta toppled Pan Am or as Aldi and Lidl threaten Tesco and Sainsbury's. The basic structure is not going to be altered in any significant way, despite the destructive forces of capitalism that rage around it. And this truth, I think, tells us something important about the meaning of sport.

Economists often talk about incumbency advantage, and this has many aspects in conventional markets. Often it relates to capital spending. If one company has already invested, say, in an electricity grid, it becomes a huge barrier to entry for a competitor to build a parallel infrastructure. The incumbent may cut prices, turning the market into an attritional war for survival. This, in part, is what Middle East oil companies do to respond to the threat of fracking in the United States.

In sport, there is also an incumbency advantage, but it has nothing to do with technology or infrastructure. New rivals to football are not bothered by the number of football stadiums up and down the country. Instead, the incumbency advantage is about emotional rather than physical capital. The beautiful game has a weight of history, a surprisingly rich and deep storyline that connects the present to its past.

Think about a club such as Manchester United. When fans watch the team in action, they are not merely being entertained. Rather, they are evoking a rite in which parents and grandparents participated.

My brother-in-law, a United fan, has read biographies of Charlton, Best and Busby; he is viscerally aware of the tragedy of Munich; of the rebuilding of the club from the ashes of the runway; of Fergie's Fledgelings; of the Treble. United, to him, are not a product. They are a living institution with history and meaning. Watching United, like watching other clubs up and down the country, is about narrative. The top flight itself is a recurring confrontation between these clubs, these stories, creating its own narrative.

All fans know about the shifting dominance through the decades: of Arsenal under Herbert Chapman; of Tottenham Hotspur under Bill Nicholson; of Liverpool's glory days in the Eighties; of the modern re-emergence of Chelsea and Manchester City.

This is the stuff of emotional incumbency. It is the umbilical connection between fans and the game, and between the game and its past. The Surrey Smashers v. Team Derby in badminton may provide sport that is as compelling. Judged on its internal characteristics, it is no less entertaining than a game of football. But it does not reach into our shared emotional and cultural history. It is not underpinned by narrative – at least not one that is widely shared.

Look at other great sporting institutions and you will see this truth writ large. It is why the opening credits of Wimbledon, the Open, and the FA Cup always show the iconography and champions of the past. These montages evoke emotional incumbency, the sense that this year's event is not a product, but the latest stage of a journey. The meaning of Andy Murray's Wimbledon triumph in 2013 was built upon the pain of seventy-seven years. Thoughts flickered to the first-round exits of the past, of the cruel near-misses of Tim Henman, of decades of collective yearning.

Yesterday, I went on to YouTube to look at the opening credits for Australia's Channel Nine cricket coverage and found footage from 2008. It is beautiful. It starts with a ticking clock before cutting to grainy footage of Don Bradman and archive commentary. From there we see images of Dennis Lillee, of Steve Waugh, of Michael Clarke. This is not about cricket, the game; it is about cricket, the story. It is about cricket's place in Australia's national mythology.

These truths, with only a few rare exceptions, are evoked around the world. In the United States, for example, baseball, the NFL and basketball continue to dominate. Football is doing its best to break in, and has huge backers, but it struggles against the emotional incumbency of its rivals. All fans in the United States know about the Curse of the Bambino, the Dwight Clark Catch, the Michael Jordan Steal. No amount of capital spending, by football or any other sport, can purchase these wider cultural reference points. And that is why, more than twenty years after staging the World Cup, football is still in the second tier in the US.

Creative destruction is a marvellous thing. So long as it is managed properly, it benefits consumers. In sport, however, these destructive forces are held in check by the deeper truth of narrative. Sport, although enmeshed within the forces of capitalism, is not a conventional market. It obeys its own laws and evokes its own truths, many of which have more to do with culture and history than with orthodox economics. And that, I think, is ultimately why we love it.

Strength of Character
17 October 2012

In his new book *The (Honest) Truth About Dishonesty*, Dan Ariely, the renowned behavioural economist, investigates human deception. His method is simple. He gives a group a test consisting of twenty simple but time-intensive mathematical problems. Subjects have five minutes to solve as many as they can and are paid according to how many they solve correctly.

Ariely finds, perhaps unsurprisingly, that subjects tend to get better scores when they count their own results rather than having them counted by an invigilator. In other words, they lie a little. They score higher still when they are allowed to shred the test papers – i.e., destroy the evidence.

But they cheat most of all when they witness someone else cheating openly.

In one experiment, Ariely asked a student (actually an actor) to get up after one minute of the experiment and implausibly claim that he had solved all twenty problems. 'Watching this mini-Madoff clearly cheat and waltz away with a wad of cash, the remaining students claimed they had solved double the number of matrices as the control group,' Ariely writes. 'Cheating, it seems, is infectious.'

The infectiousness of cheating springs to mind whenever one looks at road cycling. Yesterday, Matt Dickinson recounted the scale of deception that has emerged in the wake of the Lance Armstrong revelations. There is insufficient room here to list all the riders who are known to have doped. It is almost everyone.

We often think of drug-taking as an ethical Rubicon and that those who cross it are either impressionable or downright evil (think back to the vilification of Ben Johnson). The findings of Ariely suggest that it is not quite so black and white. He finds that many people cheat when the context is conducive. In other words, when we think we will get away with it and, more importantly, when we think that it is normal.

When you read the memoirs and interviews of those who have fessed up to their doping past, one is struck by the psychological similarities of their excuses. Whether it is Floyd Landis, David Millar or Dwain Chambers, they each invoke, in different ways, the prevalence of cheating in mitigation. In an interview in 2005, Chambers said: 'Everyone else was doing it, so why not me? I knew that I would never reach my dreams without levelling the playing field.' Behavioural economists such as Ariely argue that, in order to cut the prevalence of cheating, you need to change the context: manipulate the psychological geography by hinting, for example, that deception is not as pervasive and normal as might be supposed.

It is about nudging people through the 'choice architecture'. And, at a broad level, these manipulations are undoubtedly effective. Perhaps sport could use some of these techniques in an attempt to reduce drug-taking.

But behavioural economics is also inclined to miss something important. By looking at average changes in groups and populations, it neglects to ask perhaps the most intriguing question of all: why are some people largely immune to the psychological context? To take the example of sport, why do certain athletes do the right thing even when they are immersed in a drug-taking culture, have team-mates who are doping, and who recognise that they won't win unless they follow the crowd?

Perhaps the most powerful example in road cycling is that of Christophe Bassons. The Frenchman was a rider for Festina in 1998 when a car-load of drugs was discovered during the Tour de France, triggering one of the biggest scandals in the sport's history.

Investigations uncovered an extensive and sophisticated doping operation encompassing almost the entire team. The sheer scale and orchestration was breathtaking. But one rider defied the social dynamic, not to mention team orders. According to Armin Meier and Christophe Moreau, two convicted riders, Bassons stood alone against the entire operation. It was not merely that he could not be nudged into cheating. He could not be cajoled or threatened, either. He was shunned by other riders and was not allowed to share in the team's winnings, as was customary. Eventually he was sacked. But he never budged.

Kirsty Wade, the British middle-distance runner, is another who stayed true to her principles. She competed at a time when drug-taking in athletics was rife, particularly in Eastern Europe. Many of her rivals had facial hair and astonishingly fast times. They were cheating just as obviously as the chap in the experiment who stood up after a minute and claimed to have solved all twenty problems. Wade knew that her only chance to win was to follow the crowd. But she didn't. She stayed clean.

There are many others in sport whose honesty was rewarded with little more than obscurity. You do not get a prize for coming seventh, even when the top six athletes are on drugs.

Perhaps that makes their probity even more intriguing and commendable. But what is fascinating about these athletes is that they do not regard themselves as morally courageous. Wade, Bassons, and almost every other resolutely clean athlete seem to have regarded the 'temptation' to take drugs as no temptation at all.

Here is Bassons: 'I don't think I was courageous not to take drugs. To me, courage is all about overcoming fear, and I was never scared. I was just lucky. I'd had a balanced upbringing, lots of love in my life, no void which made me want to dope. Refusing to take drugs was easy for me.'

Here is Wade: 'Doping never crossed my mind. It really didn't. To be honest, it was not even a temptation because it would have gone against everything in my character. I wanted to compete fairly and with a clean conscience. Chocolate biscuits are a temptation for me, not anabolic steroids.'

Many other clean athletes' interviews follow the same basic pattern. They did not weigh the chances of getting caught against the probability of winning gold, and they did not conduct an internal monologue comparing the benefits of doping with the loss to self-image of doping. They just didn't cheat, come what may. It would have gone against everything they believed in. Against their character.

This, it seems, is less about social psychology than about values. And it hints at a basic problem. We are all too often preoccupied with high-profile examples of extreme behaviour: why did Bernie Madoff defraud friends to the tune of hundreds of millions? Why did Lance Armstrong bully and deceive on such a vast scale? These instances of pathology are fascinating, independently of the value of the research.

But while these stories are important, they all too often crowd out the less sexy and eye-catching stories of those who behaved honestly. The athletes who regarded doping as not merely intolerable but inconceivable. The bankers who refused to take risks with their company's capital. The footballers who refuse to dive. Do we not need to know more about these people if we are going to get on top of cheating more generally? Do we not need to research their stories and motivations far more deeply than we have hitherto?

As Landis put it when told the story of Bassons: 'I'm impressed. I don't know how many guys would have the strength of character not to dope, but there's not a lot. I don't know Bassons. I would like to know him, though.'

Ageing Gracefully
21 July 2009

On a warm, rainy night in 1974, Muhammad Ali changed the world in the moment it took a gloved fist to swivel the previously impenetrable jaw of big George Foreman. The location of the contest was as improbable as the result, a jungle clearing in the former Zaire, a stone's throw from the Congo River, crocodiles looking on as the world's television crews jockeyed to record what continues to be regarded as the greatest sporting event of all time.

On Sunday on a small strip of links land on the west coast of Scotland, with television commentators conspicuously struggling to find the words to relate the magnitude of what they were watching, with fans and viewers rubbing their eyes and pinching their arms, with me begging my sister to put back our restaurant booking by another hour, Tom Watson came within a hair's breadth of creating a story to rival what occurred on that startling night in Africa.

The American golfer was not merely battling younger, fitter opponents as he made his way around the ancient course at Turnberry, he was vying with the ageing process itself. With mortality. With the Grim Reaper, scythe, cloak and all. For two hours on the inward nine, the fifty-nine-year-old, six weeks from his sixtieth birthday, more than three decades after winning his first Open title, looked as if he was going to subvert everything that we thought we knew about sport, about life.

His hitting was straight and clean, his strategy enlightened, his stroke-making flawless even as his joints were creaking. This was a man with a plastic hip, more wrinkles than a prune, and yet he had the glorious, thrilling, subversive impudence to believe that he could win the biggest prize in golf. Ultimately, he failed, an 8-foot putt for the championship on the seventy-second hole leaking to the right, but he had nonetheless succeeded in turning the world on its axis.

Competitive sport – at least at its highest level – is not supposed to be a place for the old or even the middle aged. I got out of international table tennis at the age of thirty-two, not because I had lost the will or the desire, but because I couldn't get my body to do the things that I asked of it. It wasn't just that

Ageing Gracefully

I was slower, a millisecond off the pace, but that I had lost the precision, the subtlety and the accuracy that ultimately separates the best from the rest. My opponents pounced like hyenas on a carcass.

At Turnberry on Thursday, 156 competitors took to the field, the vast majority in their twenties and thirties. Hyenas all. Voracious and motivated. Enough ambition to power a small town for a week. There was also a sprinkling of competitors in their forties and fifties. And then there was Watson, the oldest of all by more than six years, there by dint of the curious rule that permits former champions to keep coming back until the age of sixty, providing fans with the opportunity to salute the heroes of the past as they totter around the old course.

But Watson was not there for a ceremonial, he was not there for a regal wave or two, he was there to win the damn thing. The very fact that he dared to believe was thrilling enough, but to have held his game together as the pressure mounted – cumulatively, irresistibly, intolerably – over the final two days was more than heroic, it was revolutionary.

It spoke of indomitability and courage. It spoke of audacity. Most of all, it spoke of the curious things that can happen when we believe in the impossible. And for a few heady moments, Watson made believers of us all.

Some will argue that our admiration for Watson should be tempered by recognition that golf is a sport that suits the older man. But this is to misconstrue the thing. Had Watson triumphed, he would have been more than thirteen years older than any previous winner in the 150-year history of the event, an order of magnitude that speaks volumes. You may not need lightning reactions or raw power to win in golf, but you do require reserves of mental strength and stroke-making subtlety that, for whatever reasons, seem progressively to elude the ageing champions of yesteryear.

Golf may be sport's ultimate test of nerve. You have time between shots with which to hang yourself; minutes ticking away during which the mind can get up to all sorts of mischief.

Every year we see top players committing hara-kiri, hitting the ball out of bounds or going knee-deep into water, their minds mesmerised by the proximity of the prize. Volitional control of your own destiny as you stand above the ball: that is the most thrilling and the most terrifying thing about competitive golf. But Watson did not choke, even as we expected him to.

That, of course, was the unspoken assumption hanging over Turnberry all afternoon: that the old boy would melt away in the white heat of the closing holes. That is what always happens when an ageing champion is in the mix going into the final day. But Watson was like granite. If his iron to the seventy-second green had not shot forward off the turf, he would have triumphed. It was a glorious stroke, straight and true, homing in on the hole, until it jumped forward, through the green and into the fringe of rough at the back. He three putted from there. And a million hearts were broken.

It is easy for us sports hacks to exaggerate the importance of what happens on football pitches, in boxing rings, on cricket grounds and golf courses. Most of it is unremittingly trivial. But there are occasions when sport transcends the field of play; when it provides us with detonations of heroism that change the way we see the world.

Ali's triumph in Zaire was that of a former champion winding back the clock to defeat a young and seemingly invincible opponent; the triumph of a man who had come to symbolise the racial pride of a people; the triumph of a pugilist who was forced to absorb intolerable quantities of punishment about the ribs and kidneys before unleashing the iconic punch that he had saved for a career.

Watson's doomed tilt at history was so very nearly as intense, as moving and as momentous, albeit for very different reasons.

He came within an inch and a half of redefining everything we thought we knew about sport and the possibilities of age.

'Defeat tears at my guts,' he said afterwards. Ours too, Tom, ours too.

The Quiet Mind
13 June 2016

Andrés Iniesta already occupies a special place in the history of football, alongside the likes of Pelé, Diego Maradona, Lionel Messi and Johan Cruyff. But another superlative performance in France would, to my mind at least, take him clear of the field as the greatest player to have drawn breath.

It is not only the accolades that he has won at international level, but in club football, too. Since his debut for Barcelona in 2002, he has won La Liga eight times, the Copa del Rey four times, the World Club Cup three times and the Champions League on four occasions. Beyond his stellar statistics, however, Iniesta has another profound quality: he always delivers when it counts the most. He was an outstanding performer at the 2008 Euros, scored the winning goal (and claimed Man of the Match) in the 2010 World Cup final, and was voted Player of the Tournament (winning Man of the Match in the final against Italy) at the 2012 Euros. As Fernando Torres, the Atlético Madrid and Spain striker, put it: 'I've been playing with him since we were fifteen and I have never, ever seen him play badly.'

It is sometimes said, in the context of these remarkable achievements, that Iniesta has been fortunate to play in two of the best teams in history. To my mind, however, this reverses the direction of causality. Spain and Barcelona have been wonderful teams, in large part, because they have been constructed around the genius of this gentle midfielder who, by his own admission, 'cried rivers' when he left home to join La Masia, the Barcelona academy, as a boy.

In the ecosystem of football we tend to focus on the most colourful and extravagant flora. When we think of Messi and Cristiano Ronaldo, for example, we point to detonations of skill: extraordinary free kicks, mazy dribbles, leaping headers. This is why these figures have dominated the FIFA World Player of the Year award (in some cases, quite rightly). One can bring to mind their skill without even having to think (the so-called availability heuristic). Iniesta finds a different niche in the ecosystem. He is the soil that enables the flowers around him to grow and bloom. It is difficult to capture the totality of Iniesta's gifts in a single, symbolic moment, because they are so fertile and diffuse. You can only discern his skill by watching ninety full minutes, training one's gaze on how he receives the ball, opens up new vistas of space for team-mates, and, through immaculate control, retains possession. The effect of his contribution is cumulative and, by the end of ninety minutes, often decisive, but also complex and covert.

One of my favourite interviews involved Sir Alex Ferguson after Manchester United had been defeated by Barcelona in the 2009 Champions League final. I have to trust memory for the quotes because, despite persistent searching on YouTube, I have never found it. The interviewer was trying to needle Ferguson into admitting that United had underperformed, or that he had got things tactically wrong. The Scot cocked his head. 'We couldn't get the ball off them,' he said, simply. 'Xavi and Iniesta never lost possession. They are a better team than us.'

There is a well-established phenomenon in elite sport called the 'quiet eye'. This describes the finding that the very best sportsmen keep a perfectly still gaze for a fraction longer than their less illustrious counterparts, fixing on a part of the pitch (or ball, or bend on an F1 circuit) and thus extracting more information before they execute. Evidence suggests that when people are under pressure, or panicking, the eyes become 'noisy', flitting around without focusing sufficiently.

Iniesta doesn't just have a quiet eye, but a quiet mind. Amid the tumult of a modern football match, he can take a step back and calmly discern the threads, anticipate the problems, and decode the mysteries. 'He makes the team work,' Ferguson said. 'The way he finds passes, his movement and ability to create space is incredible.'

A feature in *The New York Times* attempted to deconstruct the genius of Wayne Gretzky. 'He doesn't look much like a hockey player,' it said. 'His shot is only average – or, nowadays, below average.' How, then, did he become the greatest performer? 'His gift, his genius even, is for seeing. To most fans, and sometimes even to the players, hockey frequently looks like chaos: sticks flailing, bodies falling, the puck ricocheting just out of reach. But, amid the mayhem, Gretzky can discern the game's underlying pattern and flow and anticipate what's going to happen faster and in more detail than anyone else in the building.'

Isn't this analysis equally applicable to Iniesta? Skill is not merely about what you are doing with your feet, but what is going on in your brain. The final product is often delivered by a team-mate, but Iniesta is an indispensable part of the accumulation of pressure that unlocks the defence. 'He is the most inventive player in Spanish football,' Luis Enrique, his Barcelona head coach, has said. 'He's like Harry Potter. One, two, three and whoosh . . . he's past the player. It's like he has a magic wand.' When Luis Suárez had his best season for Liverpool in 2013–14, pundits lined up to offer the view that the Uruguay forward was the 'third-best player on the planet after Ronaldo and Messi'. When Gareth Bale moved to Real Madrid, he was routinely described in the same way. The fact that Iniesta was not included in the discussion reveals, perhaps more than anything else, how his skills exist beyond the compass of the average pundit.

Nobody has played football with greater felicity, nor with such modesty and class. As no less a judge than David Silva, the Manchester City playmaker and one of Iniesta's Spain team-mates, put it: 'The press often ask me about whether Messi or Ronaldo is the best, but for me something is very clear: Andrés Iniesta is the number one. He is able to do even more difficult things on the pitch. He is magic with the ball.'

Loyalty

29 December 2014

There is a stretch of about thirty yards between the corner of the Ealing Road and the entrance to Griffin Park. I was striding up there with my father-in-law, Andy, in the autumn of 2010, for a League Cup clash between Brentford and Everton, when he was accosted by John, a friend he had not seen for more than thirty years.

'What the hell are you doing here?' he was asked. Once we got inside the gate, he met another old friend, then another. It almost felt like a reunion.

Andy has been an ardent supporter of Brentford since the mid-Fifties (he grew up in south Ealing), attending all the games for more than a decade and a half. But then life had taken him away from southwest London. He had found a teaching post in Wigan in the 1970s, then Derby in the 1980s. He had a family.

But the connection never wavered. For forty years, he kept in touch with the score every Saturday afternoon, first with the Green'un (the *Derby Evening Telegraph* football edition, published on Saturday evening at 6 p.m.), then Ceefax. Whenever he was in London, as he was that evening for the Everton game, he would always buy a ticket and enact the familiar rite once again.

Loyalty

I went to Griffin Park with Andy on Boxing Day. He moved back to London in 2012 to be closer to his grandchildren and has attended every home game since. He still sees people there who attended in the Fifties and Sixties, fans who provide continuity between past, present and, in the case of their children, the future. In many ways, this is the most profound aspect of fandom: the idea of a ritual reaching through the generations, an identity that transcends time. Andy has already bought my two children (a two-year-old girl and one-year-old boy) Brentford jerseys.

Brentford are having a pretty good season. They are sixth in the Championship, having ricocheted up and down the divisions over recent decades. There is even an outside chance that they will reach the Premier League, although a rather chastening 4-2 defeat by Ipswich Town on Friday and a 2-1 loss to Wolverhampton Wanderers yesterday put this hope into some perspective.

But if they go up, or down; if they plummet into non-League obscurity, or find a sugar daddy who can finance their ascent into the Champions League, it will make no difference to Andy and those of his ilk. They will celebrate, or commiserate, but they will not change their allegiance.

Up in the chief executive's office, the contradictory motivations of the modern-day club are ever-present. The yearning to get promoted is balanced by a concern about what it might mean for their traditional fan-base. 'It is a difficult balance,' Mark Devlin, the chief executive since 2011, said. 'We are really keen to get into the Premier League, but we have to recognise our responsibilities to our fans.

'It would be easy to jack up our prices, and to milk Premier League status for all it is worth, but that would alienate many of our most loyal supporters. It would be terrible for the club, not just in community terms, but in commercial terms too, if we priced them out for the sake of new "fans" who might desert us as soon as results turn against us. We have to be mindful of our traditions.'

Proposals to move away from Griffin Park are well advanced. The club have bought land half a mile away near Lionel Road (the cut-through between Chiswick High Road and the M4). This will facilitate an increase in capacity from 12,000 to 20,000, but it will also pose risks of scale and finance. Most fans are delighted with the move, due for 2017, but they are nostalgic too, about Griffin Park, which will be converted into social housing along with a memorial garden. 'This has been the ground since 1904,' Devlin said. 'It is not the most beautiful ground, but it has so many powerful memories.'

The history is so vivid at Griffin Park, you can almost smell it. The walls, the gates, the pubs on the four corners of the ground, the blistering paintwork, the old-style terrace to the right, the greetings that are enacted in the quadrangle of concrete inside the entrance as fans drink beer and eat meat pies: all of them speak of the rich and complex social role that football has played in this corner of southwest London for more than a century.

On Christmas night I asked Andy about his fondest memories of the club, and his eyes glistened as he moved seamlessly from a Brentford v. Leicester City match in 1954 (his first visit to Griffin Park) to a thrilling FA Cup tie against Middlesbrough in 1962. He talked about vicarious memories, too: the top-six finishes in the late 1930s, the victory in the London War Cup in 1942 and the heady days in the early Fifties when Tommy Lawton graced Griffin Park.

Most of all, he talked about Ken Coote, a defender who played for the club between 1949 and 1964, clocking up 559 appearances, most of them as captain. 'He wasn't the best player we have ever had, but he was the most influential,' Andy said. 'Above all, he was loyal.'

Loyalty is an underused word in modern football, but it represents the raw material of fandom. Statistics reveal a degree of fickleness when you look at the big picture. Crowds increase when a club are doing well and diminish when they are plumbing the depths. But this obscures a deeper and more vital truth: the hardcore fan who continues to watch, who continues to care, whose Saturday afternoons are defined by what is going on at the stadium, whether they are there in person, or waiting – anxious, fretful, cautiously optimistic – while living in exile.

Football is a sport, but it is also a rite. It is not just about the Premier League, glamour fixtures and slick analysis on Sky Sports. At its roots, it is about what happens in places such as Brentford and clubs up and down the country, in the Championship, in non-League football, on fields and pitches in long-forgotten corners, where the only cover for spectators is an umbrella and a long overcoat. Football is a community institution, a part of the social fabric that can be understood only in places where the indescribable thrill of identity and belonging has not been obliterated by what Marx called the cash nexus.

At half-time, I stood outside Griffin Park and peered down the Braemar Road. I looked in the window of the Princess Royal pub, then walked back to the gates to observe the hubbub. For a few moments, the image of Lowry's *Going to the Match* came into my mind: the excited chatter, the industrial backdrop, the angled stances, capturing both the excitement of attending football and the bitter cold. And suddenly I was hit by a realisation that this extraordinary sport should be celebrated, not just castigated, as so often happens. Its value and meaning should be recognised.

Andy left that afternoon chastened by the scoreline. No true fan is going to be happy about a 4-2 defeat, but he also left with a spring in his step. He walked out of the gates, as he had for the first time sixty years earlier, with a sense that he had been part of a social ritual that mattered, to him as well as to hundreds of thousands of others up and down the country.

He had been to the match.

Fearless

8 February 2016

In the 1890s, Max Ringelmann, a French agricultural engineer, asked his students to pull on a rope attached to a dynamometer. They were instructed to pull as hard as they could and, working alone, they pulled an average of 85 kilograms. He then arranged the students into teams of seven and asked them to pull again. What happened? The pull of each individual went down by 25 per cent.

This is still regarded as a seminal experiment for a simple reason: it challenged the seductive idea that teams invariably add up to more than the sum of the individual parts. In many contexts, they do no such thing. Instead, people slack. They make it look as if they are trying (in the rope experiment, individuals continued to grunt), but they are going through the motions, allowing others to take the burden. It is called 'social loafing' and you see it in many organisations, teams and sections of society.

You see it in sport, too. The egregious examples of defenders failing to cover, or of forwards failing to track back, are rare these days (although not unheard of). Instead, social loafing is more subtle. It is about the forward who tracks back, but without busting a gut, the defender who goes for a tackle but with 95 per cent commitment, the winger who spots danger when possession is lost but convinces himself that it won't materialise, thus sparing himself a 40-metre dash to help a team-mate.

These may seem like small things but, over time, they compound. Think about looking after your child: you cook for them, you chat, you go to the playground. Every interaction has power and meaning, love courses through your body. When you look after a friend's child, however, something is missing. To an observer, the activities look the same. But, almost without realising it, you are loafing. You are giving your time, but not your soul.

I was thinking of all this while watching Leicester City – a club that was bottom of the table eleven months ago, and playing in League One seven years ago – beat Manchester City on Saturday to become title favourites. They compete with skill, discipline and tactical coherence, but the most thrilling aspect of their play is the collective commitment. They run for each other, applaud one another (even when a pass goes astray), celebrate together, protect each other and, in a Platonic sense, appear to love each other.

I have never witnessed a team so thrillingly exceed the sum of their parts. Social loafing is not just minimal; it is non-existent. Every player is prepared to charge forward on the break, even if it is to cause a defender to swerve his run by a fraction, giving Jamie Vardy a few millimetres more space. Each player is prepared to expend energy to protect a team-mate, even if the danger is unlikely to materialise. Every player will throw his body into harm's way, even at the risk of injury. This is not teamwork in word, or even deed. It is a teamwork from the soul.

Would that Prozone could capture this magic in its data set, for it is the ingredient that so often drives collective greatness. It is the antithesis of social loafing. It is not about free-riding on the efforts of others, but adding to them. In every minute of every game, we have seen this, from victory on the opening day of the season against Sunderland, to the 2-1 win over Chelsea in December, to the brilliant 2-0 victory over Liverpool last Tuesday when many neutrals, perhaps for the first time, were forced to admit that this thrilling run is not about luck, but something infinitely more profound.

Against Manchester City on Saturday, a game that must rank among the most exhilarating in Premier League history, they reached higher still. A home team assembled at a cost of more than £220 million were outmuscled and outclassed by a team, the bulk of whom were playing in the Championship two years ago, and two of whom arrived on free transfers. More than anything, City were out-teamed. Riyad Mahrez is a magician and Vardy a striker of breathtaking industry and guile (one or the other must win player of the season), but the true magic of Leicester emerges from the collective.

In an outstanding feature last week, George Caulkin, my colleague, wrote about the vista from the rubble of the old ground at Filbert Street, past an outcrop of student flats, to the King Power Stadium a few hundred yards away. 'Walk closer and you can make out the piercing blue of the exterior, the word "Fearless" illuminated in white,' he wrote. '"Fearless" is daubed inside the dressing room, too . . . and if anything can encapsulate the club's blissful rise over the past ten months and how that growing confidence is mirrored in the city, perhaps it is this.'

This is the chemistry that, even now, social psychologists are trying to understand; the subtle factors that create shared endeavour – and eliminate the perilous temptations of social loafing. This is important not just for sports teams, but for corporations, military units, communities, and perhaps even nation states. But whatever answers ultimately emerge from this branch of psychology, we can be sure that its truths are being evoked, week in, week out, during this extraordinary run at the title.

Can Leicester sustain it? The bookmakers now have them as favourites, which creates a rather treacherous psychological dynamic. The plucky outsiders now have something to lose, the possibility of approaching the threshold of glory but falling just short.

Claudio Ranieri has been superb at setting a relaxed tone, making sure that his players compete not just with commitment, but also with joy. The trick in the coming weeks will be to sustain that approach, even as the pressure mounts, as it surely will, and as opponents target them with new tactics to cut off the supply lines to Vardy.

What seems certain is that neutrals across the country, across the world, will be rooting for Leicester as this most subversive of seasons reaches its climax. A group of decent individuals, who have grown to improbable stature as a team, are thirteen matches away from one of the most astonishing achievements in the history of sport.

The Domestique
23 July 2014

Yesterday, I fell in love with Bernhard Eisel. Observing this remarkable athlete from the back of the Team Sky car, watching him as he came to our window, leaning on to the frame as we chicaned up the slopes, exchanging crucial information with Servais Knaven, the sport director, as the sixteenth stage of the Tour de France wound its way near the Spanish border, was to understand finally the wonder of this unique event, and the heroism of its protagonists.

Eisel, a thirty-three-year-old from Austria who has been a member of Team Sky for three years, is a domestique, one of that curious breed whose participation is an exercise in self-sacrifice. His job yesterday was to assist Vasil Kiryienka, his Belarusian team-mate, to win the stage when they joined an early breakaway of twenty-one riders after the peloton had set off from Carcassonne, a beautiful, Neolithic town in the heart of Languedoc-Roussillon.

In the high-pressure moments leading up to the race on the team bus, he offered humour, encouragement and motivation. During the race itself, he was a revelation, constantly fetching water and high-energy drinks from the car, the sweat dripping down his brow as he reached through the window. It has not been the most successful Tour for Team Sky, but that was not going to deter Eisel or Kiryienka, or any of the rest of this team, back-up staff and all, from giving it everything.

At times during the course of this gruelling 237.5-kilometre stage, it was difficult to remember that they had started the over-all race almost three weeks ago. When Brazil were being thrashed by Germany in their World Cup semi-final, these cyclists were already on the fourth stage. By the time that Rory McIlroy had teed off in the first round of the Open Championship, they had powered their way through almost 2,000 miles. This isn't a race: it is an exercise in sustained, credulity-defying heroism.

Minutes from the start, one of the early leaders fell off his bike. As we whizzed past, we could see the blood streaming from his legs. He pulled himself to his feet, dusted himself down and jumped back on to his bike. Later, at the Col de Portet d'Aspet, we snaked past the bend where Fabio Casartelli, an Olympic gold medal-winner, died after a crash in 1995. That hints at the speed at which these guys career down the slopes. They talk about the importance of stamina in the Grand Tours. These guys also have dead-eyed fearlessness.

The scenery, at times, was breathtaking. As we reached the lower slopes of the Pyrenees, the vista opened up to reveal lush green meadows and snow-tipped peaks, and a path eddying ever higher, a steep precipice to one side. It was a view that the riders were not permitted to enjoy. They were nearing the fearsome slope of Port de Balès, the final climb of the stage, and the lactic acid was building again. Even the support staff, looking at the gradient, were awed. 'Can you make it back to carry another bottle to Kiri,' Knaven asked Eisel. There was a pause before a faint voice replied 'yes'. Moments later Eisel appeared out of nowhere. He took a bottle, then another and another. He had used all the storage room on his bike, so he stuffed the final bottle down his shirt. He was feeling it: you could see the anguish on his face, despite the attempt at a smile. One deep breath and he was off again, pushing up the slope to provide liquid to his colleague.

Could anybody deny that the role of the domestique adds a profound beauty to this extraordinary race? It is almost like a moral dimension, the sense that teamwork and altruism can coexist alongside the Darwinian imperative of competitive sport. Insiders might say that I am romanticising the case – after all, many domestiques receive a share of the prize money and some have ambitions one day to become a general-classification contender, the queen bee among the drones. But, for me, that should not detract from the symbolism of these remarkable men.

It wasn't until a third of the way up Port de Balès that Eisel was finally dropped. We heard over the radio that he was falling back and, a few moments later, we caught sight of him, still powering through those pedals, but without the same traction, the slope towering above him. Somehow, nothing I have seen in sport has looked so beautiful. We caught him, and as we came alongside, he shrugged and smiled. There was pride in that smile, and defiance. His gallows humour, such an important ingredient in sustaining the sanity of any team in this event, was still in evidence. 'See you at the finish, assuming you make it,' he said.

Now it was down to Kiryienka. The final part of the race down Port de Balès was not a descent in any normal sense of the word; it was a plummet of such speed that the cars struggled to keep up. Hunched low to maximise wind efficiency, taking corners with abandon, they reached the final, demented sprint. Kiryienka cycled well, but just fell short. Michael Rogers won the stage, with Thomas Voeckler the runner-up.

In the Sky team bus afterwards, Eisel took a well-earned shower. After that, he still found the energy to joke with the other riders. 'How can you still have that smile on your face after a marathon like that?' I asked. 'You have to keep smiling in this race or you will go crazy,' he replied. Eisel and his fellow domestiques symbolise much that is precious about this Tour.

They prove that glory, while important, is not everything. They prove that there is honour in being a foot soldier and nobility in contributing to a team effort. Perhaps, in that, they provide a lesson about life, too.

IV
The Political Game

In the centuries before Christ, the city states of antiquity would parade their triumphant athletes through the streets after festivals such as the Ancient Olympics. After all, if our boys can beat their boys at running, jumping or lifting, doesn't that show that our city is better than theirs in a more general sense? Sport, even back then, was highly politicised.

The importance of politics carries through to the present. In the period before the Cultural Revolution, Mao held up his world-beating table-tennis champions as icons of revolutionary virtue, Honecker sanctioned organised doping in East Germany as a key part of Cold War propaganda (a phenomenon that has resurfaced in Putin's Russia), while Castro explicitly argued that his gold medal-winning boxers demonstrated the superiority of the Cuban system.

In this section, we do not look merely at politics, but at the cultural context, too. We explore the nature of fandom and sexuality, hooliganism and terrorism. We look at the complex relationship between sport and racism. And as we further explore the nature of sport, we will get a deeper handle on the dynamics of greatness, too. For we will begin to see how the world's best athletes have not only impacted upon sport, but the wider world, too.

Cultural Revolution
17 February 2007

In October 1976, one month after the death of Chairman Mao, Zhuang Zedong was seized from his home and escorted by armed guards to an anonymous building in rural China. There the greatest sportsman in China's history was cast into a cramped room containing a single bed and a small reading lamp. For the next four years his only contact with the outside world would be at the hands of his interrogators from the Communist Party.

Such was the speed and secrecy of Zhuang's arrest that – to this day – he does not know the location of the building or whether it still exists. He was confined to his room, except for hour-long bouts of regimented exercise, and had no contact with other 'residents'. For more than two years his wife and two young children, who suffered terrible persecution because of their association with him, lived in the belief that he had been executed.

The only nod the party gave to Zhuang's illustrious sporting past was the privilege of being able to read books, which he devoured like a starving man. He credits Alexandre Dumas's *The Count of Monte Cristo* as having sustained his sanity and his life. 'It is a beautiful book,' he told me. 'Incarceration coupled with interrogation can play cruel tricks on the mind and many are driven to suicide. The book taught me to hope when I was living at my mental limits.'

How had it come to this? Just eleven years earlier, Zhuang had won an unprecedented third successive table-tennis world singles title, establishing his reputation as the most successful player in the sport's history. He had been eulogised by the political elite, revered by the masses and held up as an icon of revolutionary virtue by Mao Zedong.

The rollercoaster ride of the next decade, culminating in detention and exile, symbolises the brutal capriciousness of the Cultural Revolution. But was Zhuang just another innocent victim of that perplexing era, or a political criminal who got the punishment he deserved? Opinion in China, drawn from the labyrinth of rumour and innuendo constructed around its infamous past, is sharply divided. Here his extraordinary story is revealed in full for the first time.

I met Zhuang in a café at the Poly Plaza Hotel in an eastern suburb of Beijing and was immediately struck by his youthfulness. His boyish face and muscular upper body belied his sixty-six years and provided no visible manifestation of the incalculable trauma he has endured. His animated body language and ferocious assertiveness commanded attention, but his words would have enraptured an audience had they been spoken in a whisper.

'Everything changed in the spring of 1966 [the year after he had won his third world title] when we heard the shocking news,' he said. 'One day we were training at the national team headquarters without a care in the world, the next we received a letter from the Ministry telling us that sporting institutions were a bastion of anti-Maoist revisionism and were to be dismantled. China did not take part in international table tennis for the next five years.' The madness had started.

The official justification for the Cultural Revolution was to re-radicalise a society that was slipping into old capitalist habits. In reality, it was a naked attempt by Mao to eliminate all threats to his unbridled power. It began with a propaganda programme designed to create mass paranoia – pupils were incited to denounce their teachers and officials to condemn their superiors. It unleashed an epidemic of mutual suspicion that quickly gave way to a nationwide orgy of unspeakable brutality.

In the previously benign world of table tennis, the terror was just beginning. As rival groups vied for supremacy, Fu Qifang, Zhuang's coach, and Jiang Yongning, another member of the national team, were placed under house arrest by Red Guards, a radical student group. They were soon joined by Rong Guotuan, the first Chinese person to win a world title in any sport – at the World Table Tennis Championships in 1959 – and one of the country's most celebrated figures.

They were each condemned on trumped-up charges of spying and subjected to torture and public humiliation. Thrown into solitary confinement, they were forced to confess to imaginary crimes and to re-educate themselves by studying the supposedly infallible teachings of Mao. Slowly but surely, they began to lose their minds. In what is regarded as the greatest sporting tragedy of the Cultural Revolution, Fu hanged himself on 16 April 1968; Jiang took the same dreadful step one month later.

Rong, who had followed his distinguished playing career with an inspirational period as team leader and coach, was the last to break. A gentle and deeply principled man who had been revered by team-mates and officials, he hanged himself on 20 June. In his final letter he wrote: 'I am not a spy. Please do not suspect me. I am sorry to you all. I love my honour more than my life.' Although there is no evidence to suggest that Zhuang was implicated in the violence against his team-mates, his attitude provides a vivid insight into the mind control exerted by Mao's propaganda.

'At the time I felt miserable because I was close friends with those who were tortured to death,' he said. 'But on the other hand I had complete trust in Chairman Mao. It was he who started this campaign and I feel my belief in Chairman Mao is bigger than my feeling towards my friends. I still believe that Chairman Mao had the interests of China at heart.'

Zhuang has a habit of placing his hand on one's upper arm when he is saying something of deep meaning. His enduring faith in the wisdom of Mao is absolute, conveyed as much by the childlike appeal in his eyes as his words. When I confronted him with Mao's atrocities, his response was instant. 'There is no such thing as a perfect man, but there are great men,' he said. The former chairman could not have scripted it any better.

Zhuang's spectacular promotion after his seminal role in the 'ping-pong diplomacy' of 1971 took him even closer to his beloved leader. He retired from table tennis after being made sports minister and gaining elevation to the Central Committee, the innermost sanctum of the Communist Party and the font of political power in China. It set the stage for arguably the most catastrophic fall from grace in sporting history.

'It was a huge honour to be a member of the Central Committee, but it carried huge risks,' Zhuang said. 'It was like being taken to the top of a mountain only to find a steep precipice at your feet [I later discovered that his wife had begged him not to take the position]. If one was going to survive, one had to form an alliance that would please the Chairman and offer oneself protection.'

Given Zhuang's impeccable Maoist credentials it was, perhaps, inevitable that he would gravitate towards the Gang of Four, the fanatical grouping led by Jiang Qing (Mao's third wife), who had been masterminding the Cultural Revolution on the Chairman's behalf. By giving them public and political support, Zhuang implicated himself in some of the worst excesses of the era.

Such was the closeness of his relationship with Jiang that rumours soon began to surface of an affair. Although Zhuang admitted to having been granted dozens of private audiences with Mao's wife, he denied that their relationship was anything more than political. 'She was like a mother to me,' he said. 'She lived a clean and elegant life and has been unfairly scapegoated for her role in the Cultural Revolution.'

But Zhuang was more than a mere cheerleader for his political overlords. He soon set about organising mass-denunciation meetings, in which perceived political opponents were beaten around the head, forced to utter self-criticisms and had their hair shaved off. He also ruthlessly disposed of opponents within the table-tennis community. Xu Yinsheng, the man with whom he had won the world doubles title in 1965, was publicly humiliated and exiled from Beijing.

Zhuang repeatedly refused to talk in detail about his crimes. His former assertiveness was replaced by lengthy pauses as his eyes drifted into the middle distance. For the first time, the years seemed to lie heavily on his powerful shoulders. 'I was on the wrong side,' he said at last, his face registering the kind of bewilderment only seen on fanatics coming to terms with their errors. 'I did many dreadful things that I now regret.' But his reign of terror was not to last.

In the power struggle that followed Mao's death in 1976, the Gang of Four was arrested, and Zhuang soon felt the dread hand of the state investigators on his shoulder. Of his four years in captivity, he said simply: 'I understand why they wanted to ask me questions. I had been a top political figure so I was a good source of information for the government.' His equanimity was shocking but sincere; he was thinking of the interests of the party even as he was being persecuted by it.

In the twenty-seven years since his release, Zhuang has endured the ignominy of being implicated in one of the most infamous atrocities of modern times. His name and reputation are familiar to virtually every citizen in the People's Republic. He spent the first few years after his release in exile in Shanxi province, but for the past two decades he has been in Beijing, involved in low-key table-tennis coaching. Only in the past few years has he received official invitations to sporting events, including the thirty-fifth anniversary of 'ping-pong diplomacy' in 2006.

It is unlikely that he will be fully rehabilitated in his lifetime. But how will he be judged by history? The more one immerses oneself in the moral confusion of the Cultural Revolution, the less one is inclined to issue absolute judgements. Villain or victim? The answer is strange but simple and applies to many of those who put their faith in the monster that was Mao Zedong. He was both.

Glorious Amateurs

5 March 2007

Three days into his desperate attempt to cross the Florida Straits, Euclides Rojas confronted the realisation that his decision to defect could end up killing his family. One of the most formidable baseball pitchers in Cuban history, Rojas had boarded a makeshift 15-foot raft along with his wife, his two-year-old son and assorted friends from downtown Havana. They were equipped with nothing more than ham, cheese, bread, lemons, water, and the inextinguishable hope of a life of freedom.

The extraordinary risks to escape Cuba taken by Rojas – and dozens like him – provide a chilling counterpoint to the propaganda put about by Fidel Castro that athletes are the living embodiment of the revolutionary ideal. Time and again the 'Maximum Leader' has boasted about the supposed willingness of sportsmen to turn down the multimillion-dollar contracts of foreign capitalists. But with Castro on his deathbed and the battle for his legacy under way, it is time to expose the cruel myth of Cuba's 'sporting nirvana'.

'We navigated by the stars and the rising and setting of the sun,' Rojas told The Times. 'But when we saw other raft people rowing furiously in the opposite direction on the third day, we began to doubt our calculations. There were thirteen of us on the small raft: five men, four women and four children. We did not speak of it, but we became gripped by fear. The children were crying, the women were trying to comfort them and the men were exhausted because we were taking turns to row in two-hour shifts. We ran out of water but managed to swap food for water with other boat people.

'It was not until the fifth day that we were picked up by the US Coast Guard and taken to Guantanamo to be vetted for entry in the United States. That night there was a fierce storm at sea. When day broke there were bodies of fellow Cubans floating in the water. Had we not been picked up that afternoon, we would be dead.'

In 1995, one year later, Rojas – a sensitive and thoughtful man, who is a master of the breaking pitch – won a contract with the Florida Marlins.

Rojas offers a damning characterisation of the system he had escaped, one that the regime likes to describe as 'glorious amateurism'. 'We were nothing more than slaves,' he said. 'I played a number of seasons in the National Series in appalling conditions: for the last few months of my career, I earned 231 pesos per month [about £4.50]. The success of the national team [Cuba won gold at the Olympic Games in Barcelona, Atlanta and Athens] was achieved in spite of the system rather than because of it.

'Baseball is hugely popular and, even though the conditions for players were bad, they were better than for many ordinary citizens. That is why the team was able to recruit the cream of the nation's sporting talent.'

Baseball is more than a sport in Cuba: it is a facet of national identity. Imported by American sailors in the 1860s, it was initially played as an act of defiance against Spanish colonialism, until locals realised that they loved the sport for its own sake. Teams were established in the communities around American-owned sugar mills in the early twentieth century, and by the 1950s Cuba had established a hugely popular professional league.

But within three years of Castro riding into Havana with his guerrilla army in 1959, he had abolished the old system and replaced it with what he called 'revolutionary baseball'. Like every other dictator in modern history, Castro understood the propaganda potential of sport and immediately set about transforming the sporting apparatus into another arm of the Orwellian state he was constructing. But Castro had another, more personal reason for shaping Cuban baseball in his own image. The leader is a lifelong fanatic who ordered players to play with him in night games for his own amusement. Although the tale of him being offered $5,000 to join the New York Yankees in 1949 is apocryphal, there is no doubt that his passion for baseball transcended the boundaries of conventional political expediency.

'He would arrive, form two teams and they'd start playing,' Panchito Fernández, who umpired some of the games, said. 'Sometimes he'd pitch three innings, sometimes seven, sometimes he'd bat, sometimes he'd play first base. But he was tireless. There was one game when we were playing until after three a.m. When we reached the ninth inning, the score was 2-1. But the Commander said there was no time limit because he was losing. In the eleventh inning, it was a draw and we played on to the sixteenth inning. He was in the lead and said: "It's all over now." He hated losing.'

Until illness last year caused him to cede temporary power to his brother, Castro regularly delivered the ceremonial first pitch at televised games and continued to acclaim the ideological purity of baseball in communist Cuba and the ending of what he described as the 'exploitation of professionalism where athletes were bought and sold like simple pieces of merchandise'.

However, the much-proclaimed abolition of professionalism is a sham, with players benefiting from what is known as *licencia deportiva*, in which they are granted time off from their official jobs to play baseball. Special rewards are handed out at the whim of the oligarchy, something that has created an insidious form of corruption. Gambling at baseball games is commonplace, allegations of match-fixing rife and selection for the national team made increasingly on the basis of political affiliation.

As Roberto González Echevarria, the author of a history of Cuban baseball, said: 'The regime dances to the tune of its own contradictions. Cuban players must play for the squad in the district where they reside or not at all. They have no unions and no agents. And, like ordinary Cubans, they are not allowed to make critical remarks about the government to the foreign press and are subjected to preventive arrest. It is naïve to think that Cuban players mean it when they say they would rather play for Castro than for millions of dollars. All one has to do to be disabused of the notion is compare the statements made by players before and after they defected.'

The increasingly desperate attempts of the state to crack down on defections have failed spectacularly. The wave of departures that started in earnest during the Mariel Boatlift in 1980 continue to this day, and make a mockery of Castro's protestations that sportsmen are loyal to the regime. The hypocrisy of the hierarchy was in graphic evidence again last year when the country sent a team to the World Baseball Classic in the US. The propaganda machine eulogised the players as heroes of the revolution while locking them in their hotel rooms and confiscating telephones and televisions. For once, Castro allowed the players to keep the prize money (the usual practice was to force them to hand it to the regime).

But the twin techniques of terror and bribery have been self-defeating. 'The more Castro tightens his grip on the players, the more they will slip through his fingers,' Rojas, who is now an assistant coach with the Pittsburgh Pirates, said. 'We all know the huge risks we are taking when we try to leave Cuba. It is a treasonable offence and it means we will leave our friends and family behind. But many of us would rather risk death than live a life under the tyranny of Castro.'

Although there have been dozens of defections (foremost that of Orlando Hernández, who escaped on a small fishing boat in 1997, almost immediately landed a $6 million contract with the New York Yankees and then pitched his team to victory in three successive World Series), few have articulated the cruel ironies of sporting life under Castro as poignantly as Rojas.

'Even during the difficult six months at Guantanamo, I did not once regret my decision to leave because I knew that it was the waiting room for life as a free man,' he said, his voice faltering with emotion. 'Eventually, we were sent to Miami and I had the opportunity to earn my living in the American leagues.'

The despotic nature of Castro's regime has robbed hundreds of talented sportsmen of their right to self-determination. Cuban sport is not the success story that its apologists pretend. Like almost every other area of Cuban life, it is a living hell sugar-wrapped in the make-believe narrative of a dying tyrant.

The Little Girl
25 July 2008

In July 1979, Heidi Krieger received the letter she had been longing for – an invitation to join the fabled Dynamo Sports Club and Boarding School in East Berlin. For a thirteen-year-old who had recently fallen in love with shot-putting at her local athletics club, it was a dream come true.

The Little Girl

She arrived at her new school four months later, full of hope, and was inducted into a schedule of two school periods and two training sessions per day. Towards the end of her second year, her coaches informed her that she was to be put on a course of bright blue pills. They told her that they were vitamin tablets that would keep her healthy and protect her from the sometimes chill temperatures during training.

Krieger was grateful for the concern of her coaches; she took it as solid evidence that they were pleased with her progress. Almost immediately, her body began to change. Her muscles expanded and her face, nose and hands started to enlarge. Her mood, too, went haywire. One moment she was afflicted with depression, then, in an instant, she would be overwhelmed with feelings of aggression. Her girlfriends also found strange things happening to their bodies and minds: hair sprouted across their bellies and faces, their voices became deeper and their libidos swung violently.

But the coaches and doctors soothed the concerns of the girls and their parents, explaining that the strange alterations were a consequence of extra training and would be short-lived. Anyone who voiced doubts or concerns was told that they would be punished if they persisted with questioning the wisdom of their coaches. This was East Germany at the apogee of communism: citizens, young and old, did as they were told.

Slowly the number of blue pills increased so that, after a few years, Krieger was being fed five or six tablets a day and given regular injections of what her coaches told her was glucose. The teenager seemed, even to herself, a different person: aggressive, depressive and with anatomical and facial characteristics almost unrecognisable compared with the slight girl who had arrived at Dynamo with such high hopes.

But while Krieger's life fell apart, her shot-putting soared. At the European Championships in Stuttgart in 1986 she reached the pinnacle of her career, winning gold with a putt of 21.10

metres. It ought to have been a moment of celebration, a vindication of her many years of hard work.

But it was not. Krieger was in despair, out of sympathy for herself and her body, unable to cope with crippling mood swings and chronic pain. She retired in 1990 to join the ranks of the unemployed, a broken woman.

It is a beautiful midsummer's day in the eastern German town of Magdeburg, and in an army surplus store on the high street a middle-aged man is standing behind the till. Business is slow and the man exudes a faint but unmistakable air of loneliness. He is tall, with a large, round face, powerful forearms and huge hands. His dark hair, brushed back from the forehead, is thinning a little; his four-day stubble is shaped in a goatee.

His face brightens as I come through the door and he bounds across to shake hands, his face breaking into a wide smile. He is friendly and tactile, with a deep, booming voice and a surplus of boyish charm. At the back of the shop is a small kitchen and he gestures me through to join him for a coffee. The room is full of stock, but he is not trying to sell anything. Instead he goes to the cupboard under the sink and heaves out a red crate. It is full of medals, images and other sporting mementoes. He pulls from the pile a large photo of Heidi Krieger being presented with the European Championships gold medal in 1986 and grins as he examines it. I look from the face of the man to the face of the woman in the photograph and the truth is strange but indisputable: they are one and the same person.

It took many years for Andreas Krieger – the name Heidi chose after her sex-change operation in 1997 – to discover what had been perpetrated at the Dynamo Club. Top-secret documents relating to the sporting system in East Germany were uncovered only after the fall of the Berlin Wall in 1989, and it took almost a decade to excavate the full, mind-bending story.

At the heart of the story were those bright blue pills. Krieger discovered that they were not vitamin tablets but androgenic-anabolic steroids called Oral-Turinabol, powerful prescription drugs that built muscle and induced male sexual characteristics.

'We did not question the pills because in GDR times you were expected to trust your coaches,' Krieger says. 'Nobody thought, "Is this dangerous for me?" The coaches said the pills were important to keep us fit and healthy. I did not even consider the possibility that they might be harmful. We were doing incredibly tough power training, so I thought that was the reason I was growing more muscles and strength.'

Krieger was not alone in being fed the blue pills. According to the secret files, more than ten thousand athletes were doped with Oral-Turinabol over a twenty-year period. Extensive experimentation by East German doctors revealed that the steroids had the greatest impact on the sporting performance of women, who naturally lacked androgens (male hormones).

Between 1968 and 1976, East Germany leapt from nine gold medals to forty at the Olympic Games, propelled by the unprecedented success of their female athletes. 'You could train without limits,' Krieger says. 'We were able to do heavy weightlifting for hour after hour without feeling tired or having to take a long time for recovery. Over the course of one week I estimated that I lifted more than a tonne.'

The political establishment kept a lid on the pervasive doping programme by forcing coaches and sports doctors to sign confidentiality agreements, and through the active involvement of more than three thousand moles who reported dissent to the Stasi, the East German secret police.

But concealing the damage inflicted on the athletes was not so easy. In his regular reports to his Stasi handler, Manfred Höppner, the chief sports doctor, documented cases of extreme clitoris growth, severe acne and hair growth. So deep were the voices of the top female athletes, he decreed that they should not give television or radio interviews. He also documented potentially fatal damage to the liver resulting from steroid use.

Krieger, who has liver complications, says: 'They did not care at all about the dangers or the damage. We were the guinea pigs in some huge experiment that was undertaken to build the prestige of the political classes and the communist system. It is almost unbelievable that they were prepared to sacrifice so many of the young and vulnerable for their own ends.'

By the time Krieger arrived at the Dynamo Club, the doping officials – intoxicated by the success of their athletes – had taken steroid violations to scarcely believable levels. An average teenage girl produces about half a milligram of testosterone per day. Krieger, by the middle of her career, was being fed 30 milligrams of anabolic steroids each day, far in excess of Ben Johnson, the Canadian sprinter, at the height of his drugs programme.

State scientists also developed STS 646, an anabolic steroid that caused male characteristics in women at a rate sixteen times that of Oral-Turinabol. It was distributed to coaches, even though it had not been approved for human use, not even in stage one clinical trials. Even Höppner expressed his doubts, telling the Stasi that he was not willing to be held responsible. But Manfred Ewald, the president of the sports federation at the time, insisted that they were necessary and ordered an additional 63,000 tablets. Krieger was probably one of the recipients.

Although Krieger's unease over his sexual identity pre-dated the doping programme, he says that the androgenic abuse left him with little choice but to have a sex-change operation. 'I had no sympathy with my body, it had changed beyond all recognition,' he says. 'It was as though they had killed Heidi. Becoming Andreas was the next logical step.'

Krieger had surgery in 1997 – then prayed for justice to take its course upon those who had wreaked havoc on his life.

On 2 May 2000, Höppner and Ewald, the masterminds of the doping programme, were brought before a court in Berlin to face charges of actual bodily harm. Court documents revealed that former athletes had a range of medical complications ranging from cancer to psychological trauma, and from liver damage to pregnancy complications. More than 140 East German athletes lined up to testify, hoping to gain closure on one of sport's most sinister episodes.

For Krieger, however, the trial set the stage for yet another chapter in his tumultuous life. For on the other side of the public gallery was Ute Krause, a talented female swimmer, who was also there to testify about her suffering at the hands of the East German sporting system. As their eyes met across the packed courtroom, the world moved.

'I saw Andreas in court and it was, like, wow,' Krause tells me when the three of us meet for dinner in the evening. 'At the end of each day the athletes would get together in small groups to talk about what we had seen in court. I immediately clicked with Andreas. We shared similar experiences and could empathise with each other. We talked and talked. I knew he was the man I wanted to spend the rest of my life with.'

Tall, with piercing eyes and a warm smile, Krause also suffered horrifically from the effects of Oral-Turinabol. 'I was very good at swimming at school and was invited to join SC Magdeburg in 1973,' she says. 'The coaches were very happy with my progress and in 1977 started to give me the blue pills. I put on fifteen kilos in weeks. I thought it was because I was eating too much and I became bulimic. I felt like I was living in somebody else's body.'

After a suicide attempt in 1983, when she woke in a pool of vomit after an overdose, Krause managed to escape from swimming, finding a new job as a trainee nurse. It was there that she learnt the shattering truth.

'I was looking in on a patient and saw those same blue pills. I could hardly believe my eyes,' she says. 'I had been told they were vitamins, but I discovered they were powerful prescription drugs for patients recovering from chemotherapy. It was unbelievable. When the call came to testify against the leaders of the doping regime, I knew that I wanted to be there to tell my story.'

Krieger and Krause have mixed feelings about the sentences handed down to Höppner and Ewald – the latter was given a suspended sentence of twenty-two months and the former eighteen months' probation. 'It was not as severe as the athletes had hoped, but it was enough that they were convicted,' Krause says. 'It provides at least some comfort that they did not evade all responsibility for their actions.'

After the trial, Krieger moved to Berlin to live with Krause and her daughter from a previous relationship. 'We married at Hundisburg Castle [near Magdeburg] in front of seventy guests,' Krause says, glancing with a warm smile towards Krieger. I ask if she still struggles with depression. 'Since meeting Andreas it has got less and less,' she says. 'With his help I will overcome it.' Krieger invariably refers to Krause as 'my wife', as though he has long wished to use those words and has yet to exhaust the novelty factor. 'All this gold,' he says, pointing to his many medals, 'has no meaning. They are doping medals, not sporting medals. This gold,' he says, caressing his wedding ring, 'means more than all those medals put together.'

Krieger requires regular injections of male hormones to maintain his stubble and other male characteristics. His wife – who administers the injections – comments wryly that Krieger receives male hormones voluntarily, having previously been duped into taking them. The irony is not lost on Krieger, who responds with a huge belly laugh.

It is, perhaps, the ultimate twist in one of sport's most mind-bending stories.

Football and War

21 November 2012

The long-range rockets continue to fly across Israel from bases in Gaza. In Jerusalem, Hillary Clinton, the US Secretary of State, has arrived to head off a potential ground invasion. Meanwhile, Tony Blair, the Quartet envoy, has pointed to the terrible suffering in Gaza as an already terrorised community suffers bombardment.

And in Tel Aviv, the Israeli capital, a city that has hitherto been out of range of rockets fired by Hamas, Hezbollah or Islamic Jihad, Robert Earnshaw, the Wales striker who is playing for Maccabi Tel Aviv on loan from Cardiff City, goes through his paces in the build-up to a league match this weekend.

'On Sunday morning, we were just coming out of the dressing room when it happened again,' he said in a fascinating interview yesterday. 'The sirens, and the shouts to find shelter. We heard the sound of two missiles being launched. We watched them go up – really high – and then they sort of disappeared. Then all you heard was this enormous boom, when they took the rockets out. It's not something you ever think will happen to you. It's not something I expected to find myself in, in the middle of a war.'

Sport and war. There has always been something jarring and philosophically disconcerting about their juxtaposition. Earnshaw's interview conveys, above all, the surrealism of preparing for a game under the cloud of an existential threat. 'They are certain the interceptors protect them,' he said of his team-mates. 'They've got faith in Iron Dome (the Israeli missile defence system) and the army . . . But it's different if you're not used to it. It has been really difficult, and you can't help but be a little shaken up.'

If Earnshaw decides to leave Tel Aviv, he will garner great sympathy. Football must seem rather unimportant while bombs are flying overhead. But one of the most curious facts of military history is that football has often thrived during periods of great conflict. For those who, through choice or necessity, are stuck in a war zone, football (and sport more generally) seems to take on a particular significance. And it is worth asking why.

Perhaps the most famous episode of football during conflict occurred during the First World War. Amid the Christmas truce of 1914, *The Times* reported a game between the Royal Army Medical Corps and the 133rd Saxons who, according to David Goldblatt in his book, *The Ball is Round*, 'sang "God Save the King", drank the monarch's health and then beat the English 3-2.' This game took place in the context of unimaginable horror. Otto Dix, the German expressionist artist, described the trenches as places of 'lice, rats, barbed wire, fleas, shells, bombs, underground caves, corpses, blood, liquor, mice, cats, artillery, filth, bullets, mortars, fire, steel: that's what war is. It is the work of the devil.'

Yet, in that small window of peace, and amid the carnage of a conflict that would produce more than two million corpses in its first two years, a Scot provided a ball in the space between the fortified ditches and 'this developed into a regulation football match with caps casually laid out as goals.'

Twenty-seven years later, two years into the Second World War, football took centre stage in a slightly different context. This time it was civilians who were mesmerised by its promise, despite the unfolding apocalypse. As Simon Kuper, the football writer, has observed: 'On 22 June 1941, the day the Germans invaded the Soviet Union, the decisive act of the entire conflict, 90,000 spectators watched the German league final in Berlin. What were they thinking of?' Perhaps – like the combatants in Flanders – they were seeking to escape the horrors of war, an emotional breathing space provided by a game with a ball and twenty-two men.

Maybe this also explains the astonishing boom in football in the immediate aftermath of the two world wars. The Norwegian Cup final, played in the summer of 1945, received 158,000 applications for only 35,000 seats. After the First World War, according to Goldblatt, attendance at games across Europe 'grew almost exponentially'.

That need for escapism also rings true in Israel. In *When Friday Comes*, a trek through Middle Eastern war zones by the journalist James Montague, football provides both a common language and a shared meaning. Making his way along the Allenby Bridge crossing, one of only two corridors available to Palestinians seeking to get out of, and back to, the West Bank, he was stopped by a rather severe Israeli female border guard. The area was in a state of high alert and the atmosphere tense. Montague, who had recently received an Iranian stamp on his passport, feared an interrogation.

Only at the mention of football did the female guard crack a smile and engage in banter that would otherwise have been inconceivable. 'I'm going to see Maccabi Haifa's first match against Maccabi Netanya in—' Montague explained, but didn't quite get a chance to finish his sentence. 'Maccabi Haifa, they're my home team!' the guard interjected. Her excitement was tangible. 'Who is your favourite player?' 'Well, I like Yaniv Katan but Yossi Benayoun is my favourite,' Montague replied.

So two strangers on the edge of war found themselves in a solemn discussion about the merits of Benayoun's stint at West Ham United. For a precious few moments, the shelling was forgotten.

This, I think, is why the juxtaposition of football and war offers such a powerful contrast. The usual thesis is to say that war makes a mockery of football. Why would one wish to indulge in the triviality of kicking around a pig's bladder when bombs are dropping? The truth is quite the reverse: football makes a mockery of war. Some wars may be just and morally necessary. But the act of playing and watching football, along with enjoying the many other gifts of life, rebukes the devastation of war.

That is why football thrives in the most desperate of circumstances, often against overwhelming odds. People reach for the little things that give life meaning when life itself is in the balance.

From the drill squares of the First World War to the prisoner camps of the Reich, and from the killing fields of Flanders to the streets of Gaza, where a thirteen-year-old boy was killed this month having a game with friends near the Israeli border, this truth has been affirmed and reaffirmed.

Football is sometimes not simply a means of expressing a tribal allegiance or passing an enjoyable afternoon. It is also a reminder – along with myriad other things – of why life is precious.

Today, in the context of a six-decade-old war that has claimed thousands of casualties and where the combatants have become, by degrees, inured to the devastation, that is worth remembering.

The Reserve Law

3 December 2012

It didn't seem particularly significant at the time. It did not make headlines and aroused little comment. But the appointment of a silver-haired, forty-nine-year-old New Yorker to a backwater administrative job in baseball in 1966 could legitimately be regarded as one of the most significant watersheds in twentieth-century sport.

His name was Marvin Miller, a labour economist who died of liver cancer last week. His job was as head of the baseball players' union and he started out with little more than a rusty filing cabinet and a kitty of $5,400. By the time he left his post in 1982, sport had changed to such an extent that, in obituaries on both sides of the Atlantic, he was proclaimed alongside Babe Ruth and Muhammad Ali as among the most influential people in sporting history.

The reverberations of his tenure as executive director of the Major League Baseball Players Association can still be felt today. From the astonishing salaries of John Terry and Wayne Rooney, to the cosmopolitanism of the Premier League, and from the lingering tensions in the Association of Tennis Professionals to the present lock-out in the National Hockey League: these things would not have been possible, perhaps not even conceivable, without the transformations pioneered by Miller.

If there was one achievement to be written on his tombstone it would be the abolition of the infamous reserve clause. This was the cornerstone principle – familiar in all team sports in the middle part of the twentieth century – that tied a player to a club even after the expiration of their contract. When an agreement had run its course, clubs could simply dictate new terms, safe in the knowledge that players could not enter into negotiation with rival clubs.

For Miller, a unionist who had cut his teeth in steelworking, this was nothing less than blatant restraint of trade. But he knew, given the curious status of sport on both sides of the Atlantic, that it would not be easy to repeal.

For many in the political and legal establishment, sport was exempt from the usual rules of the economic game. The US Supreme Court judgment in 1922 that decreed that baseball was an 'amusement' and therefore not subject to anti-trust laws was still setting the agenda into the 1970s.

Miller began a patient campaign to destroy the reserve clause as soon as he started in his post. He negotiated baseball's first collective bargaining agreement and obtained the right for players to take disputes to an arbitrator. Then, in 1974, he saw his big chance. A test case based upon the reserve clause was taken to the new arbitrator.

When the arbitrator found in favour of the players, the guiding economic principle of baseball was, at long last, under threat. When this decision was upheld in the federal courts, the reserve clause was obliterated. Other American team sports soon followed suit. As one observer put it: 'Miller was the Moses who led baseball's Children of Israel out of the land of bondage.' As players started to exercise their newfound freedom, wages exploded.

The average salary in baseball when Miller started as union leader was $19,000 and many players had to take on a second job to make ends meet. When Miller left in 1982, the average salary had leapt to $241,000. Today it is $3.4 million. The abolition of the reserve clause also conferred economic blessings on the sport as a whole, with major league revenues growing from $50 million in 1967 to $7.5 billion this year.

The willingness of the players to flex their collective muscle under Miller, such a contrast from their former docility, can also be seen in their willingness to withdraw their labour. According to *The New York Times*, 'the players went on strike for thirteen days in 1972; they were locked out of spring training for almost a month in 1976; they struck for the final eight days of the 1980 exhibition season; and staged a fifty-day strike that began in the middle of the 1981 regular season.'

From a situation in which baseball was dominated by powerful owners and administrators, players were now banging the drum. Unsurprisingly, athletes from other sports, witnessing Miller's pioneering work from afar, started to agitate for reform. The genie was finally out of the bottle. 'Anyone who's ever played modern professional sports owes a debt of gratitude to Marvin Miller,' Chris Capuano, of the LA Dodgers, has said. 'He empowered us all.'

It took until 1995 for the Bosman ruling to shatter football's equivalent of the reserve clause, but the balance of power in the Premier League, Serie A, etc., today is largely defined by the framework created by Miller. Fans may not like the big salaries and footloose tendencies of modern sport, but they will also acknowledge that the quasi-cartels of the past were a serious drag on progress. What is certain is that economic freedom and player power is here to stay.

So, when Rooney banks his next weekly pay cheque for a reported £250,000, he may wish to look to the skies and thank the slightly built unionist who made it possible. Miller never played sport at a high level, and never managed a full game of baseball, but he transformed the economic basis of all sport.

On Masculinity

28 June 2007

Word is that Tony Blair may pass up the tradition of bestowing resignation honours, fearful that it would send the wrong signal while some of his friends are under the cosh in the 'cash for honours' scandal. It is a pity because one suspects that the most intuitive politician of his generation would otherwise have bestowed a parting knighthood upon the man who was so glaringly overlooked in the Queen's Birthday Honours – Mr Posh Spice.

When details were leaked a few weeks ago that the erstwhile England captain might be in line for an award that eluded the late Bobby Moore, there was something close to outrage. How, it was argued, could someone who lacked any significant international success as a sportsman be given one of this nation's highest honours? How could someone who bombed out in the quarter-finals of the World Cup be considered worthy of an award that has escaped the majority of those who triumphed in 1966?

The problem with this argument (notwithstanding the fact that David Beckham has won six Premiership titles, two FA

Cups, one Champions League, one Spanish league title and 96 caps for England, 58 as captain) is that it assumes that a sportsman's contribution is measured solely in terms of medals. It assumes that one could come up with a formula that awards points to sportsmen and women – ten for an Olympic gold, perhaps, three for a Premiership winner's medal, etc – and then bestows awards mechanically.

The point about Beckham, however, is that he deserves a knighthood precisely because his influence has been exerted in a sphere that cannot be measured; that he has transcended his sport and touched lives in a way that cannot be formulised; that he has had an impact upon the public consciousness in ways so subtle, but at the same time so powerful, that it is only after he has disappeared from our public space that we will fully comprehend the measure of his achievements.

The full scale of Beckham's influence struck home during a conversation with John Amaechi last week. The former basketball star – who came out this year, the first NBA player to do so – made the startling observation that Beckham had made it easier for homosexuals to come out. 'Beckham has made it possible to be a real man and gay,' Amaechi said. This from a 6ft 10in sportsman who understands how stereotypes – 'all gays are pansies' – can stigmatise and blight lives and how counter-cultural icons can help to change all that.

Beckham has been the single most significant catalyst in the metrosexual revolution, changing the contemporary notion of masculinity, softening it, smoothing it, widening it, diversifying it. He has not only made it possible to be a real man and gay. He has also made it possible to be a real man and sensitive; to be a real man and concerned about one's appearance; to be a real man and to cry in public; to be a real man and to wear dresses and high heels.

It is not only the sarong and the fact that Beckham has embraced being an icon of the gay community. It is not only the fact that he wears earrings and his wife's knickers. It is not only his palpable sensitivity and the fact that he is so visibly in touch with his feminine side. It is – much more importantly – about the things that can be measured only in the hearts and minds of those who have been confronted by his new slant on maleness. It is about the little things that have, in their way, helped us to embrace a new vision of tolerance.

Beckham has undergone so many personal reinventions and image changes that he is a walking tribute to cosmopolitanism. He is someone who would be as comfortable in Soho as in Solihull, someone who could as happily spend his day pumping weights as prancing around the shops of the fashion district, someone who is as revered by heterosexuals as by homosexuals. He is someone who has changed the face of masculinity – and not only with his moisturisers.

No British sportsman of the past half-century has exerted a more powerful or benign influence on Britain's consciousness. While Blair was softening majority attitudes through the statute book – enacting civil partnerships, scrapping the 'section 28' prohibition on promoting homosexuality in schools, equalising the age of consent, reclassifying cannabis, opening the doors to immigrants from Eastern Europe – Beckham was softening those same attitudes through the potency of his persona.

The fact that Beckham embraced the New Age philosophy instinctively – without the merest hint of political correctness – made it that much more powerful. Members of the British public have never taken to those who preach at them.

Many will pillory Beckham for having become the visible embodiment of a superficial celebrity culture – but this seems overly censorious. One can hardly blame the man for the obsession that he inspires in magazine and newspaper editors and their readers. Any criticism of Beckham's superficiality reflects more upon those who gorge upon the tittle-tattle of his private life than upon the man himself. One ventures to suggest, indeed, that Beckham is a deep person; certainly someone who has handled fame and infamy with rare courage and grace.

A knighthood would have been an appropriate gift from the outgoing Prime Minister to a man who has symbolised the vast stride into modernity that has occurred over the past decade and that has left the nation more at ease with itself than ever.

Beckham was, in many ways, Blair's soulmate: the New Man who was the cultural embodiment of Blair's political liberality. To say that he has not won a World Cup winner's medal is to miss the point. Rarely has a knighthood been more conspicuously merited.

Discrimination
27 July 2013

In September 2007, I experienced the most pulsating week of my journalistic career. In seven scorching days in Manhattan, I was lucky enough to interview Jake LaMotta, the boxer immortalised by Martin Scorsese in the film *Raging Bull*, Billie Jean King, the feminist tennis icon, and Marty Reisman, the legendary table-tennis hustler who dominated the underground gambling scene of the Lower East Side, who died in December 2012. However, the most fascinating interview – as well as the most poignant – was never written or published.

Emile Griffith, the former welterweight champion, whose trilogy of bouts with Benny 'Kid' Paret remain among the most infamous in boxing history, was already suffering from pugilistic dementia when we met in east New York – where he died this week – but was nevertheless able to recount the many episodes of his extraordinary life. All except one. One secret he wished to take to his grave.

Discrimination

Griffith, who was born in the US Virgin Islands but moved to New York in his teens, was a beautiful boxer, if such a term can be used for this most brutal of sports. His skin was smooth, his body perfectly proportioned and his fists animated by some kind of magic, so fast did they move.

When he took up the sport in 1957, Gil Clancy, his trainer, spotted immediately that he had a unique athlete on his hands. 'He combined elegance and power in perfect proportion,' Clancy said.

When I met him, Griffith still had his looks. He was sixty-nine, but appeared younger, his eyes and face shining as we discussed the contests that had made him a staple of the *Friday Night Fights* programme on ABC during the high-water mark of the 1960s. 'I liked boxing, but I am not a violent man,' he told me, slowly and with many pauses. 'It was more like a job.'

Alongside Griffith at the interview was his adopted son, Luis Rodrigo. They had met in 1979 when Rodrigo was in his late teens and Griffith was working as a corrections officer at a juvenile facility in New Jersey, and they became firm friends. Griffith eventually adopted Luis, and cared for him. As Griffith fell into the grip of dementia, the roles were reversed. Rodrigo became his carer and companion.

Many of the obituaries that have been written about Griffith have focused on his final bout with Paret, on 24 March 1962. It remains among the most controversial contests in boxing. Griffith had been taunted by Paret in the build-up because he did not conform to the stylised machismo that was conventional in the Mob-infested fight game. He was gentle and softly spoken. He worked as a hat designer before taking up his gloves. He liked flowers and art.

It was all too much for Paret, who, according to Norman Mailer, the novelist and boxing aficionado, said: 'I hate that kind of guy. A fighter's got to look and talk and act like a man.'

At the weigh-in, Paret, who was Cuban, escalated the tension by calling Griffith a *maricón*, a Spanish epithet for homosexual, and then patted him on the behind. Griffith was angry and humiliated. 'It got to me,' Griffith said. 'I got more and more worked up.'

His anger would have tragic consequences. In the twelfth round, with Griffith ahead on points, he trapped Paret on the ropes and caught him with a concussive hook. The legs of Paret sagged, indicating a loss of consciousness, but his right arm caught on the ropes, holding him upright as Griffith launched a blistering sequence of punches, almost every one of which landed flush on the chin.

To watch the sequence now, with the foreknowledge of what ensued, is to experience something close to nausea. Mailer, who was sitting in the second row at Madison Square Garden, wrote: 'He hit him eighteen right hands in a row ... the right hand whipping like a piston rod which has broken through the crankcase, or like a baseball bat demolishing a pumpkin.'

When the referee, Ruby Goldstein, stopped the bout belatedly (he never refereed again), a blood clot had already formed on the brain of Paret. He was taken to hospital as his pregnant wife, Lucy and young son, Benny Jr, travelled over from The Bronx, but the Cuban never recovered consciousness and was pronounced dead ten days later. It was the first televised championship fight that led to a fatality and caused widespread revulsion. Boxing all but disappeared from the networks for a decade.

Paret's young family never fully came to terms with their loss. Perhaps unsurprisingly, his opponent, who had regained his title, never came to terms with his victory. 'I didn't mean to kill him,' Griffith said when we discussed the bout forty-five years later. 'I am so sorry it happened. I wake up at night. I have nightmares about it.' When Griffith met Benny Jr in 2005, he wept as the two men hugged. 'I didn't go in to hurt no one,' he said.

But this tragedy, which haunted a sensitive man for the rest of his life, was not the principal reason why I travelled out to meet him. The deeper story, the story that tells us most about the trials he faced as a boxer and a man, only came to light in 2005. Griffith was bisexual. In an interview with *Sports Illustrated*, he said: 'I like men and women both.' To me, he said: 'There is nothing wrong with liking men. I know right from wrong.'

For years Griffith had lived with the secret, frightened to tell the truth, paranoid about the effect it would have on his reputation and career. His handlers created a fake persona, insinuating that he was a woman's man, with photos taken surrounded by Swedish blondes. At a time when homosexuality was considered a disease, it would have been impossible to come out and continue as a professional boxer.

As Neal Gabler, the historian, put it: 'The very idea back then was just unconscionable. How could you ever think of an athlete who was homosexual? It was oxymoronic.'

Griffith married in 1971, but the marriage didn't last. In 1992, he was attacked as he left a gay bar in New York and spent four months in hospital as doctors battled to save his life. 'It was an incredibly difficult time,' Rodrigo told me, eyes welling up. 'We were not sure he would pull through. The attack was savage. They wanted to kill him.'

As the interview progressed, and I watched the interplay between Rodrigo and Griffith, it slowly dawned on me that the deepest secret of all remained intact. This was not a father-son relationship, as both men publicly claimed. It was a romantic one. The adoption had not been about conferring legal status on a paternal friendship; it had been about concealing the true reason why two adult men had decided to live together in a small New York apartment. They were lovers.

Rodrigo confirmed the nature of their relationship when I put the question to him, but asked for it to remain a secret, as did Griffith and Ron Ross, his long-time friend and biographer, who was also present. They worried about the effect it would have on Griffith's reputation if it emerged he had had an affair with his adopted son. That is why the interview was never written up.

But with Griffith's passing, it is surely time to place the relationship into proper context, without any prospect of recrimination. In many ways, the concealment was just another consequence of the anti-gay sentiment that stalked the era. They did not feel able to acknowledge their love, at least not in the media. It was easier to create a fictitious relationship to justify their shared life.

'It is OK to write about it now,' Ross told me by phone on Thursday. 'It's time.'

Griffith's health deteriorated sharply in his seventies and he spent his last twenty-four months in a vegetative state in a health facility. Rodrigo, according to Ross, was by his side until the end. 'He finished work in the afternoon and went over the nursing home every day,' Ross said. 'He was there till late at night, caring for him, right until the end. The bond between them could not be broken.'

Griffith remains among the most fascinating sporting figures of the last century. His life symbolises much about the angst and lost innocence of 1960s America. He was a star with a secret, an immigrant who never reconciled the liberalism of underground Manhattan with the bigotry of Main Street. That he never came to terms with the death of his most famous opponent demonstrates the scale of his empathy. The discrimination he faced is measured by the fact he could never publicly acknowledge the love of his life.

Thought Control
18 February 2015

I have been thinking a lot about tyrants these past few weeks. It was occasioned, in part, by watching the wonderful documentary series *The World at War*. It is being rebroadcast on BBC Two and via the immaculate narration of Sir Laurence Olivier it pierces through to the underlying motives of one Adolf Hitler.

What were his motives? Well, they were just the same as all other tyrants through history, and are reflected in the various totalitarian ideologies doing the rounds today, whether of Kim Jong-un, the Taliban, al-Qaeda, Isis, the Ayatollah Khomeini or even the pseudo-democratic fascism of Vladimir Putin.

It is about control. Tyrants and tyrannical ideologies seek to control human beings. The more people they can control, the better – this is why they seek power. They exert control through legal prohibitions, threats, arbitrary punishments and, very often, the use of terrorism. The ideal society for a dictator is everyone behaving in precisely the way he wishes.

But there is one thing that tyrants cannot control – and it drives them crazy. No matter how much power they obtain, no matter how much terror they inspire, no matter how aggressively they control behaviour, they cannot control thoughts. What goes on in the little cavity in people's skulls is their business. I like to think that this keeps Kim awake at night: the notion that for all the public adulation, many of his subjects despise him. Even as they chant, many are mocking him. And the Islamic fascists on the streets of Tripoli, Ar-Raqqah and Mosul are driven half-crazy by the knowledge that – as they maim and kill – they will not terrorise people into believing in their grim version of Islam.

That brings us to sport. Tyrants, in general, are not keen on sport (except as a projection of fascistic power). The Taliban, for example, banned it in Afghanistan. They took the view that there were many more serious things to do, such as chant the name of the Chief Mullah. For many years after they gained power in 1996, it was illegal to play football, cricket, kabaddi and the other frivolous games that provide meaning for many.

But no matter how much they tried, they couldn't kill the instinct for sport. They could ban the governing bodies and close down the stadiums, but they couldn't eradicate the longing to play.

Just as human beings want to love and be loved, they also wish to throw and catch balls. According to Neil Faulkner, the archaeologist, there are few surviving manuscripts from any time in history that lack descriptions of sporting contests. The human desire for play cannot be censored, even by religious decree.

This is why Afghanistan has proved to be an interesting experiment in the limits of totalitarian control. Through the first few years of Taliban rule, there was no sport. Kabul's Ghazi Stadium was used not for hosting sporting events, but for executions, beatings and mutilations carried out by the Taliban. According to one source, its 'playing field was so blood-soaked that even grass would not grow there'.

Games would keep reappearing, though, despite the prohibitions. Children would play in their homes. They would throw and catch balls, like my young children do every day. They would create makeshift games on the streets.

The religious police gradually realised that no matter how much they tried to shut down sport, it would emerge in new, often informal ways.

That is why, even before the United States-led invasion in 2001, a twelve-team football league was taking place in Kabul with the unofficial but implicit consent of the Taliban. It was male only, and the players had to wear long shorts and socks, but it was competitive and, according to insiders, rather splendid. Music, television and cinema were still banned, but not sport.

Meanwhile, cricket was being played by Afghan refugees in the Kacha Garhi camp outside Peshawar. Sport doesn't stop when there is poverty, either. By 2000, the Taliban had lifted the formal ban on cricket, making it the only officially sanctioned sport. But this was not really a victory for cricket as much as for the human spirit. It was an implicit (and, to many in the Taliban, deeply resented) acknowledgement of the inherent limits of totalitarian control. Through the US-led invasion, and the many indignities of a renewed civil war, cricket has endured. The national team cannot play matches at home (it is too dangerous), but they have competed valiantly around the world.

Children learn their craft on dusty streets using tennis balls wound together with tape and, when they are elevated into more formal teams, they take their verve and spirit with them. The only player to have hit a six off his first innings in first-class cricket and his second is an Afghan: Mohammad Nabi. In the early hours of this morning, Afghanistan, led by Nabi, played Bangladesh in the World Cup.

The quality of the Afghanistan team is such that they have rocketed up the world rankings to eleventh. They are the top associate nation and have qualified for three World Twenty20s.

They will also play against Sri Lanka, Scotland, Australia, New Zealand and, finally, England during these group stages.

How have they achieved so much in the teeth of so many obstacles? According to one former editor of *Wisden*, it is a consequence of 'enthusiastic hunger', a phrase that captures just the right note. For a nation divided tribally and ideologically, cricket has become a unifying phenomenon. There were spontaneous celebrations across Afghanistan last October when the team defeated Kenya to qualify for the World Cup. Even some of the militants have come to love the game, occasionally handing out awards at competitions. The religious police feel relatively at ease with the modest white dress.

It is not all good news, however. Women's sport is still virtually non-existent. In April of last year, Diana Barakzai, the founder of the national women's team, resigned after receiving threats from the Taliban.

Nasimullah Danish, chairman of the Afghan cricket board, has also been subject to intimidation. In a phone call, he was warned: 'Do not develop women's cricket, it is not in Islam, it is not in Afghanistan culture. If you do so, we will not be responsible for your players.'

But Danish remains optimistic. He has publicly stated that he wants Afghanistan to become a full member of the International Cricket Council by 2025, something that is contingent upon the nation having a women's team. He is likely to be vindicated, despite the present, admittedly fierce, resistance. Women long to play sport, too.

Many people are rightly fearful about the rise of fundamentalism around the world. But my conviction is that the fascists will lose. The curious desire to control other people will have its day. They will lose partly for reasons of realpolitik (the West has superior military power), but also for more subtle reasons. The fascists will realise, through bitter experience, that no matter how hard they try, they will never be able to control people's thoughts. They will never police desires and instincts.

The presence of Afghanistan in the World Cup is a testament to the heroism of a swashbuckling group of young men. But their most profound message is to the fascists: for all your warped hatred, you are fighting a battle that is ultimately unwinnable.

Subliminal Racism
21 May 2014

Donald Sterling is, we can probably all agree, a bigot. The owner of the LA Clippers basketball team was covertly taped berating his girlfriend for posting a picture on Instagram with Magic Johnson. 'It bothers me that you want to broadcast that you're associating with black people,' he said. 'You can sleep with [black people]. You can bring them in, you can do whatever you want, but the little I ask you is . . . not to bring them to my games.'

Subliminal Racism

The furore has dominated the media on the other side of the Atlantic, but I have to confess that it leaves me cold, and not just because the information came via a sting. No, what worries me is that this ludicrously overblown focus on one octogenarian is obscuring the real story when it comes to racism. It is a bit like the overhyped focus on Jeremy Clarkson for allegedly using the N-word: it represents an almost criminal distraction from the big picture.

You see, the problem of race in most of America and the UK is not people such as Sterling or, for that matter, Clarkson. Sterling represents a tiny fraction of the American population, a fag-end demographic who are nostalgic for Jim Crow. We should censure them when they are nasty (Sterling has been banned from the NBA for life), but we should do so with a sense of proportion. Those who really matter when it comes to racism are not people such as Sterling, but people such as me.

If I was the chairman of a football club, I am just the kind of person who might overlook the credentials of a talented black manager. If I was the owner of a club, I might easily pass over a black candidate for chief executive. I hate to admit it, but that's the way it is.

How do I know this? Well, for starters, take an experiment in which researchers took a group of students and asked them to make hiring recommendations for prospective white and black job candidates with either strong, weak, or marginal credentials.

These were nice college kids, not the kind of people to use the N-word. They are like the people who read *The Times*, and who write for it. When the black candidates had strong credentials, they were recommended for the job. Of course they were. The students were not racists, for heaven's sake. The same thing happened for strong white candidates. But what about when the candidates had marginal CVs; when there was wriggle room?

You guessed it: the white candidate was significantly more likely to get the nod over the black.

There are dozens of studies of this kind: evidence that reveals how decent, progressive folk (of all races) are unconsciously influenced by stereotypes. It is precisely the same effect that occurs when you are walking down a dim alley and see someone coming the other way. If it's a black person, your heart rate and blood pressure are likely to rise more than if it were a white person of the same build. This is not a conscious choice; it is a subliminal effect of stereotyping.

It is evidence such as this that makes a mockery of those clever dicks who rush into print whenever racism in football is debated. They marshal all their tedious arguments as to why John Barnes should have been sacked from Celtic, why Chris Hughton wasn't up to scratch at Norwich City, why Chris Powell had to go from Charlton Athletic, why it was perfectly reasonable to sack Paul Ince from Blackburn Rovers.

Enough already. We get it. Decisions on managers are ambiguous. There are arguments on both sides. Somebody has to make a call.

But now, take a step back and look at the big picture. There are 92 football league teams. The number of black managers? Zero. The number of black chief executives? Zero. There are a few ethnic minorities here and there, but no blacks. You would have to be a fool, or a senior figure in the FA, to think that this is coincidental.

But people are stubborn. They say that you cannot prove racism unless you have two candidates for a job with identical CVs, and the black one is ignored.

Well, consider that two American economists drafted 5,000 CVs and placed archetypal black names such as Tyrone or Latoya on half and white names such as Brendan or Alison on the other half. A few weeks later the offers came rolling in, and guess what? The black candidates were 50 per cent less likely to be invited to an interview.

Subliminal Racism

The employers were not racists. They were not like Sterling. But, with limited time on their hands, they used the stereotype 'blacks are, on average, less educated than whites' and proceeded to ignore an entire racial group.

And it has recursive effects. Why would a black footballer bother to get his Pro Licence if it is unlikely to lead anywhere? As Andy Cole put it: 'I started doing my Uefa B three years ago. But I told myself last year that it just wasn't worth it. What's the point? I honestly don't think there is going to be anything there for me when I finish.'

You could blame him for being lazy, except that, as team-mates testify, he has a ferocious work ethic. His problem is not laziness, but a pathway blocked by people who don't even realise they are erecting the barriers.

Getting on top of this subliminal bias, which is entrenched by poorly constructed institutions within sport and beyond, is hard work. It takes stamina and sensitivity. The Rooney Rule – which requires at least one minority candidate to be interviewed for management roles, and has been successfully trialled in the NFL – would help.

It is not a quota; it is not tokenism. It merely requires football clubs to interview a minority candidate and, as a temporary measure, it could make a difference. As Brian Collins, a lawyer, put it: 'A decision-maker harbouring unconscious bias is forced to confront his own partiality by meeting face-to-face with a candidate he might never have considered.'

The profound irony is that sport has long been an oasis for blacks. The lack of ambiguity acts like a magnet. Nobody can fail to select you for the football team if you are running rings around the opposition. Nobody can deny you a place on the badminton team if you are beating the white boys. This objectivity is one reason why sport has proved a popular career for minorities. It is why my dad, who suffered terrible discrimination at work, pushed me into sport: 'They can't thwart you if you keep winning,' he said.

It is the non-sporting world, the world of ambiguity, which we need to tackle today. This is far more difficult than having an orgy of outrage over an eighty-year-old bigot or the mumbled words of a TV personality.

In short, we have to get away from the Jim Davidsonisation of the race debate, where a risqué joke at a football club dinner dance is given more airtime than the chronic lack of blacks in senior positions of the game.

Of course, there are problems beyond subliminal bias, not least the corrosive subcultures of certain minority groups, as President Obama has identified. But let's please move away from Sterling and Clarkson, if only for a minute or two. It has become a dangerous distraction.

Terrorism

13 January 2010

The conjunction of sport and terrorism, as witnessed so tragically in Angola last week, stirs many thoughts and emotions. Our horror at the ordeal endured by the Togo football team; our empathy with the families of those who lost their lives; our wonderment that anybody could suppose that the murder of innocents might provide moral succour for a cause of any kind, let alone one of territorial advantage.

But perhaps uppermost is the thought that sport, while very jolly in its way, can never be worth any loss of life. That these invented worlds of bat, ball, shuttlecock, puck and the like, which get so many of us so very animated, are, when all is said and done, rather trivial.

We may even find ourselves indulging an inner shudder at Bill Shankly's famous line that football is more important than life and death. Surely he was joshing, we reassure ourselves

– because nothing that happens on a football pitch can ever have value of existential proportions.

But here's the thing; while this viewpoint is natural and, in its way, commendable, it is, I think, misguided.

Sport matters. It matters so much that it is worth staging even when there is a real danger of fatalities, whether to players or fans. This may seem a strange, almost jarring assertion, but it is surely the only viewpoint worth having.

After all, why do we want to live in the first place? The answer is because of the things that make life worth living. And it is hardly a perceptive observation that sport is one of these things. It is certainly something I value deeply: as a sportsman, as a television viewer, as a spectator through the turnstiles. Alongside love and art and friendship and merriment, sport is an essential ingredient of what Lucretius called the *praemia vitae*, the gifts of life.

This, of course, is one of the reasons why terrorists, particularly of the nihilistic perspective, are keen to target sport. They see in its innocence a profound and offensive frivolity. By targeting grand sporting occasions, they seek not only to secure a global platform for whatever maniacal cause they endorse, they also strike a blow against the *praemia vitae*. They take a little away from what makes life valuable and, therefore, meaningful.

That is why if you were to say that there was a chance that a spectator would die during the London Olympics as a result of terrorism, most of us would want to make our way to the stadiums nonetheless. And if you told athletes before 2012 that one of them would likely die as a result of a suicide bomber, few would decline to participate. We may revise our thoughts as the risks escalate, but in no circumstances would we wish to spend our lives cowering in the ramparts, for that would be no life at all.

We all make choices. Every time we step out of the front door we are asserting the primacy of living over the imperative of not dying. We are taking a risk, however small, in the pursuit of something that makes the journey of life worth the price of the ticket.

Such choices are, in an important sense, individual, which is why no athlete (or fan) should be placed under political pressure to attend a sporting event. But it is also why many accept the risks of the modern world with equanimity.

None of this is to deny the importance of security and the responsibilities of organisers for the safety of competitors and spectators. Nor is it to diminish the horror of what happened to Togo's players or the need to assess the adequacy of security and the reasons for taking the Africa Cup of Nations to Angola in the first place.

But it is to say that, in a world in which it is impossible to offer copper-bottomed guarantees about safety, we can nevertheless have urgent reasons to stage, to play, to watch and to revel in sport.

Perhaps that is why the Togo team wanted to return to Angola. They wanted to do the thing they love, the thing their fallen comrades loved, even in the teeth of murderous intentions.

There was probably defiance in this stance, a feeling that they should not give in to the fanatics, along with an admirable sense of duty to their deceased colleagues and a desire to honour their memory. But even stripped of any political or fraternal veneer, the desire to play and watch sport expresses a powerful, and life-affirming, imperative.

We all know that, however well the London 2012 Games are secured, there is a risk that fatalities will occur as a consequence of terrorism. Does that mean we should stop construction and pack up tools? Does it mean we should raise the white flag?

The answer hardly needs stating. Even as we attempt to minimise the risk of atrocities, to prevent the nightmare of mass murder, we also accept, at some profound level, that sport is worth pursuing despite the possibility of death and heartache.

In a recent newspaper article the artist David Hockney wrote: 'Given the choice of fifty years as a free person or seventy years as a slave, I would choose freedom. I suspect there are many like me, as most people seem to go for quality of life, not quantity. Time, the great mystery, is elastic. Watch the kettle boil and it takes "a long time". Ten hours in a police cell might seem like ten months.'

I sometimes wonder if the primary goal of terrorism is to turn life into a prolonged futility; to compel us to live lives of such trepidation that we turn our backs on the things that make time, that great mystery, fly. We must not allow that to happen, now or in the future, not just because to do so would be to excite more terrorism, but because a life stripped bare of the *praemia vitae* is no life at all.

Dictatorship
20 July 2016

There is probably, somewhere, an equation that traces how political leaders reach for expensive vanity projects at precisely the time they foresee a looming crisis of legitimacy. The Romans (simplifying a little) went for bread and circuses, other tyrants for grandiose buildings and cathedrals. Since the beginning of the twentieth century, the chosen vehicle has been competitive sport.

I visited East Germany before the fall of the Berlin Wall to play a table tennis competition and was shocked by the economic malaise. Queues everywhere. Factories crumbling. Fear in the eyes of everyone who walked the streets, including the interpreter (probably a member of the Stasi) who was looking after our team. Just over a wall, their brothers and sisters were enjoying an economic boom, growing living standards and political freedom.

And yet there was one area in which East Germany was punching way above its weight. Huge subsidies, coupled with a vast state-sanctioned doping regime, had propelled a relatively small nation to near the top of the Olympic medals table. The calculation of the leadership was not difficult to decipher: one way to distract our people from the unfolding social and economic disaster was the sight of blue-clad athletes winning the javelin, the 200 metres and the shot.

Could such a crude tactic work? Did it really add momentum to the propaganda machine? I suspect that, for a time, it probably did. I remember talking to an East German table tennis player and broaching the subject of politics. 'You say that East Germany is backward,' she said in surprisingly good English. 'How then do you explain why we are so many places above Britain in the medals table? That must tell us something about our two systems.'

Chairman Mao reached for legitimacy through a more fringe activity: table tennis. At the very moment when the Great Leap Forward was decimating the lives of millions, the Great Helmsman was orchestrating China's rise to supremacy in a sport that didn't exist in China until Ivor Montagu, an aristocratic British film director and communist intellectual, convinced him that it could prove a useful tool of propaganda.

Between 1958 and 1961, the rural economy of China was collapsing. The sheer scale of the suffering has yet to be fully explored, but commentators estimate that about 30 million people died during the attempt to increase production through the pseudo-scientific means. And yet at the very same time, the propaganda vehicle was proclaiming a triumph; that of Rong Guotuan at the 1959 World Table Tennis Championships in Dortmund. 'China top of the world', trumpeted the newssheets.

Dictatorship

Again, could such a contrived tactic work? Could victory in an invented game involving bats and balls really be taken as a sign of political and moral strength as people were dying en masse? I went to China in 2007 to speak to historians, as well as to Zhuang Zedong, who won three successive world table tennis championships in the 1960s, directly after Rong. 'We believed in Mao,' Zhuang said. 'I still believe in Mao. The Communist system may not have been perfect, but it had huge strengths. You do not dominate a world sport without a strong system.'

There are numerous other examples of sport used not so much as a projection of soft power, but as a diversionary tactic. Fidel Castro reached for legitimacy through his victorious amateur boxers as the Cuban economy was falling apart (partly, but by no means exclusively, as a result of western sanctions), while Leonid Brezhnev sought to bolster the legitimacy of the Communist ruling cadre through the prism of Russia's triumphant Olympians. In each case, the record shows that the policy, for all its grotesque charlatanism, worked.

This is why one of the seminal lessons of the twentieth century is, as Orwell perceived, the scope for mass brainwashing provided that the state commands a monopoly of information. Sport was so obviously a fig leaf. It was so blatantly a political ruse. The success of athletes revealed almost nothing about the economic, moral or scientific vitality of the nation they represented. And yet dictators successfully used them, again and again, to bolster their legitimacy. 'If we can defeat our rivals at running, jumping, even ping pong,' they insinuated, 'then our system must be strong, and our leaders wise.'

I would suggest, however, that in the modern age of telecommunications and social media, this technique has limitations. That is at least one of the lessons of the most recent episode involving state-engineered success. The Russian economy under Vladimir Putin is in deep trouble. Real incomes dropped by more than 4 per cent in 2015. Real wages dropped by 10 per cent. The number of Russians living below the poverty line increased by 3.1 million.

The more his policies have failed, however, the more he has reached for sport (among other things) as a fig leaf. The staging of the Sochi Olympics came straight out of the old playbook, as did the hosting of an F1 grand prix in the same city and the bid for the 2018 World Cup. Bread and circuses. And yet somewhere in the political firmament was recognition that the mere staging of these events, and shots of Putin flanked by athletes, wasn't enough.

The state-sanctioned doping regime – explored in a shocking Wada report – took this exercise to its logical endpoint. Putin's state had already engaged in deceit, with officials for the 2018 bid destroying computer discs the moment allegations of corruption surfaced, and with huge kickbacks alleged in the infrastructure development for the Sochi Games (critics claim that between $25 billion and $30 billion were stolen by oligarchs and companies close to Mr Putin). The tampering with urine samples was merely the next line to cross. After all, when it comes to the exercise of political power, the end justifies the means.

But the miscalculation, even abstracting from the moral effrontery, is now evident. Despite Putin's best endeavours, most Russians now know about the chicanery surrounding Sochi. The democratisation of information has even taken credible allegations of millions of dollars held by Putin in offshore accounts into the ears of the public. And now, thanks to a whistleblower, Russians know that the state engaged in systematic cheating. The exquisitely manufactured tapestry of propaganda is falling apart before our eyes.

Putin will try to spin this as a western conspiracy, and the organs of state control will engage in the usual techniques of misinformation. Perhaps this might even work for a while, at least with certain demographics. But the idea that Putin has benefited, politically and personally, from his audacious foray into sport is unsustainable. If the International Olympic Committee has the balls to ban Russia from the Rio Games, which it should, he will look even more foolish and venal.

Perhaps this is one blessing that will ultimately emerge from this otherwise sordid episode.

Hooliganism
15 June 2016

'I had not expected the violence to be so pleasurable . . . This is, if you like, the answer to the hundred-dollar question: why do young males riot? They do it for the same reason that another generation drank too much, or smoked dope, or took hallucinogenic drugs, or behaved rebelliously. Violence is their antisocial kick, their mind-altering experience.'

These words were written not in the aftermath of the grotesque scenes in Marseilles, but years earlier by Bill Buford, a *New Yorker* journalist, who spent eight years examining the phenomenon of hooliganism after witnessing mass violence on a train home from Cardiff in 1982.

Look at the pictures of the England fans throwing bottles, chanting abuse, and raising their arms in delirious provocation, and you will find yourself acknowledging Buford's perspective. This violence is not political. It is not caused, as some have imaginatively suggested, by the anti-immigrant rhetoric of Brexit leaders. It is not xenophobic: hooligans are more than happy to assault their countrymen if they think that they'll get away with it. No, this is about the intoxication of pure, anarchical violence.

Reflect on the French gangs who roamed the streets in Marseilles and, indeed, the Russian ultras who came out in organised force on Saturday night. 'When we are not technically at war we need some kind of conflict,' Vadim, a Spartak Moscow fan, told a journalist who studied Russian hooliganism. 'As we say in Russia, a voinushka – a "little war". Something to get the blood up. That's what football hooliganism is.'

Hooliganism is a thrill in search of an opportunity. For a long time in the 1980s, football was not only about the game, but the signal it sent to those titillated by violence. Thugs knew that stadiums offered a chance of a 'little war', something to 'get the blood up'. As a seminal article in the *Cato Journal* put it: 'Certain kinds of high-profile events have become traditional "starting signals" for civil disorders . . . People near a ground on game day know that mischief, possibly of a quite violent kind, is apt to occur. They relish getting drunk, fighting, enjoy the whiff of anarchy . . . Hooligans make a point of being where the trouble is likely to start.'

Why always England? The reason is simple: fans from this country represent a signal, too. Hooligans from around Europe know our reputation; that some England fans are 'up for it'. That is why they travel to challenge them, and anticipate, as Buford put it: 'the adrenaline-induced euphoria that might be all the more powerful because it is generated by the body itself but with, I was convinced, many of the same addictive qualities that characterise synthetically produced drugs.'

The more orgiastic the violence, the bigger the thrill, but also the higher the probability of getting away with it. A man who assaults another in plain sight is likely to get arrested. A man who does so alongside hundreds of others is rarely going to get detected, let alone prosecuted. When violence is perpetrated en masse, hooligans enjoy something close to de facto criminal immunity.

But this takes us to a deeper question: why always football? Why does this beautiful game have a longstanding, geographically dispersed problem of a kind that other sports do not? It is here, I think, that we need to confront hard truths and not merely indulge in grandstanding about the inadequacy of the authorities. For this is also about ordinary fans; those who condemn the hooliganism of 'a minority' without realising that they too are a part of the problem.

In the 1980s, New York had a crime epidemic. Mugging, rape, serious assault: all were at historically high levels. The city suffered from something else, too: graffiti, casual littering, shattered windows in social housing. In addition to a high-level crime wave, there was a low-level crime wave.

It took a famous essay by social scientists James Q Wilson and George L Kelling in 1982 to connect the dots. They realised that the 'norm-setting and signalling effect of urban disorder and vandalism' was 'directly causing serious crime'. Take a pavement. Some litter accumulates, then more; then people leave their refuse sacks. Finally, people start to break into cars. Serious crime emerges from the tolerance of low-level disorder, the steady attrition caused to good values and respect.

In football, there is a similar tolerance of low-level disorder. It is not a 'small minority' who indulge in the Munich runway song, who mock the tragedy of Hillsborough, who screamed sexual abuse at Eva Carneiro, who use homophobic epithets to impugn referees; it is a critical mass. This is the everyday. It has been going on for years, tolerated not only by the authorities, but – let us be honest – many 'ordinary' fans too.

It is part of the rough and tumble, people say. OK, so we're having a giggle about 96 innocents who died in terrible pain, but, hey, that's football. This mute acceptance is not limited to England. Read fan analysis from around Europe and South America and you see the same discourse legitimising abuse that would be anathema in any other context.

And that is why hooliganism is not confined to pitched battles in coastal France; it is about violence in youth football, where on one weekend in Surrey, 'a parent threatened to stab a referee, another headbutted a linesman and young players threatened to smash up a changing room.' It is about the vile nature of many fans' forums. It is about racism in stadiums around Europe, beatings outside grounds. These examples are merely illustrative. I could fill a dozen articles with the shameful behaviour incubated by football.

Conventional hooliganism has declined in England, but the game in this country, as elsewhere, still confronts a vast problem. When you merge the narcotic of violence with the sociological incitement conferred by the tolerance of casual abuse, you have a Molotov cocktail waiting to ignite. We do not wish to sanitise stadiums, but unless we crack down on low-level disorder, travesties of the kind that we saw in Marseilles will continue.

Experts disagree about the full significance of Rudy Giuliani's famous 'no broken windows' policy, but most concur that the 'zero-tolerance' approach to petty crime directly contributed to the unprecedented drop in serious crime in 1990s New York.

Fans should consider this the next time that they smile and shrug their shoulders when those around them are calling the referee a faggot or targeting a female assistant referee with graphic slurs. Football authorities must do more. But let's not pretend that they are the only problem.

Endurance

9 May 2012

To stand upon the slopes of Mount Kronos is to glimpse something significant not merely about sport, but perhaps also about life. Above is the summit upon which Zeus mythically wrestled his father for dominion of the world, while below is the lush sanctuary, bordered by the River Alpheios, which hosted the greatest festival in history. The running track is still there, an oblong metaphor to human achievement.

Yesterday, we were permitted to run its length, imagining the wall of noise as 30,000 spectators from across the Greek world cheered the athletic heroes of antiquity. Aristophanes, Sophocles and Plato all took the journey to the ancient Olympics, partly in pilgrimage to Zeus, but ultimately to indulge the universal instinct for sport.

As Lucian, the historian, wrote: 'Oh, I can't describe the scene in mere words. You really should experience first-hand the incredible pleasure of standing in that cheering crowd, admiring the athletes' courage and good looks, their amazing physical conditioning, their unbeatable determination and unstoppable passion for victory.'

Today, the Olympic flame will be lit from the rays of the sun and carried by Vestal Virgins through the crumbling remains of the temple of Hera to begin its journey to East London. The symbolism is powerful, but also indulgent. There was no torch relay in ancient Olympia. The ritual was invented at the behest of Hitler to exploit the majesty of the ancient Games for propaganda purposes.

And, in one sense, who can blame him? The scale of the ancient Games remains staggering. According to historians, they started in 776 BC and continued, without interruption, for almost 1,200 years. They survived famines, plagues, upheavals in the intellectual and moral climate, and an almost uninterrupted period of war. The Olympics were, in effect, the one interlocking theme connecting the classical and pre-modern worlds.

It hardly needs stating that the modern Olympics are in their infancy by comparison. Had they commenced in 1066 with the invasion of William the Conqueror, rather than in 1896 with the intervention of Baron Pierre de Coubertin, they would still have many decades to run before matching the epic scale of their ancestors.

The Political Game

How did the ancient Games survive without a single interruption (three modern Olympiads have already been cancelled because of war)? Historians remain befuddled. Perhaps part of the answer hints at the presiding power of paganism. The Games were held in honour of Zeus and were deemed necessary to placate his anger. His statue – one of the Seven Wonders of the Ancient World – stood just yards from the stadium, his eyes gleaming with menace.

Another reason hints at a simple political imperative. Athenian democracy had transformed the military basis of war, with the fighting undertaken – and funded – by the mass of voters rather than a paid army. Athleticism and physical strength developed at the various gymnasiums were partly about the body beautiful, and the prevailing culture of homoeroticism, but it was also about building a fighting force capable of dealing with the barbarians.

But, more than anything, the longevity of the ancient Olympics is a testament to aspects of sport that remain today. Competition. Heroism. Drama.

It is not just the poets who hymned the emotional intensity of watching the world's finest athletes compete for the greatest prize in sport; philosophers, historians and politicians were also blown away. As Apollonius of Tyana, a holy man, put it: 'By heaven! Nothing in the world of men is so agreeable or dear to the gods.'

From this vantage point, contemporary sport no longer seems a distinctively modern phenomenon. Stripped of its commercial paraphernalia and television cameras, it is merely the latest incarnation of a ritual stretching back to antiquity. Whatever else sport may be, it would seem that it is indistinguishable from what it is to be human.

And it is for this reason, perhaps more than for any other, that sport has been so consistently mythologised. Victorians argued that sport builds character; politicians of today claim that sport is a panacea for all manner of social ills. But nobody propagandised sport quite like the Greeks. Socrates argued that the discipline of sport created virtue. Plato argued that it hardened resistance to temptation. The evidence, or the lack of it, for these claims was as immaterial then as it is today. The moral, social and political significance of sport was, and is, a necessary myth.

It was Christianity that ultimately finished off the ancient Olympics. Emperor Theodosius I of Rome condemned the pagan symbolism and the festival was banned. The gravitational centre of the sporting world shifted from Olympia to Rome and the contests turned away from athletics to the more existential activities familiar in the Colosseum and Circus Maximus. Sport had taken a bloodthirsty detour.

But as you stride the sanctuary at Olympia, and inspect the archaeological remains, you can see the umbilical link connecting ancient and modern. At the entrance to the stadium, many of the greatest athletes are commemorated in statues. To win the Games was not merely to bring honour to oneself, but also one's home city. Victories became important tools of political propaganda, as they remain today. Many cities funded elite training camps to prevent that happening.

The inevitable result was professionalism. Just as the modern Olympic champion wins no cash prize, the ancient victor was presented with nothing more than an olive wreath. But the commercial ramifications of victory were immense. Winners could expect prizes from their cities and huge cash incentives from promoters to compete at lesser festivals. The adulation was unrivalled. When Exainetos of Akragas won his second sprint victory in 412 BC, he was escorted back to Sicily by 300 chariots and a section of the city wall was demolished for his entrance.

But with great rewards came great temptation. Although substance abuse did not exist then, cheating found its way into the ancient Olympics in many forms. Match-fixing was the principal cancer; the first recorded instance was in 388 BC, when

Eupolus of Thessaly bribed three boxers to throw fights against him. From that time onwards, cheats were levied with huge fines and the proceeds used to erect cautionary statues, many of which remain on the pathway as you enter the stadium. One warns: 'You win at Olympia with the speed of your feet and the strength of your body, not with money.' But there are also discontinuities between the ancient and modern Olympics. Perhaps the most obvious was the requirement that male athletes in Olympia perform nude (women were not permitted to compete, or watch). This was partly for practical reasons, to prevent runners from tripping on clothing, but ultimately expressed the culture of homoeroticism. Greek society encouraged pederasty, and older men stalked the gymnasiums looking for sexual conquests.

Nudity was also, in its way, an important nod to the democratic sentiment that waged a serial battle (military and philosophical) with conservatism throughout Greek history. Stripped of clothing and the other symbols of rank, the aristocracy competed with the lower classes in equality. Everybody was equal before the eyes of the judges.

But, as with the modern Games, the notion of meritocracy is easy to exaggerate. Only those who could afford to train full time had any chance of success. Although lucrative prizes could have changed this basic principle, it was a huge risk for the poor to take a sabbatical from work to conduct a period of intense training. In effect, privilege acted as an invisible barrier. The victory wreaths were dominated by the richer social classes, just as they are today – in almost all sports – by richer nations.

The lighting ceremony will culminate today with the flame being transported by foot to the Panathenaic Stadium in Athens, where the formal handover ceremony to London will take place in a week's time. Once it reaches the UK, it will travel – according to the publicity – within one hour of 90 per cent of the population, with thousands expected to line the streets.

Greeks are, of course, proud of their place at the epicentre of the Olympic movement. Many hundreds watched the rehearsal yesterday and thousands more are expected today. But they are also struck by an obvious and bitter irony. The IOC craves the symbolism provided by Olympia to connect the modern Games with the great civilisation that gave birth to it. Ancient Greece has an almost unrivalled significance to the world. Its association provides legitimacy and a powerful meaning to the modern Olympics.

And yet who would wish to be associated with the Greece of today? An economic basket-case teetering on a sovereign default that could plunge the eurozone into crisis, its attempt at a general election last week seemed more like a collective nervous breakdown. As one tour guide at Olympia put it yesterday, 'My job is to talk about the past glories of Greece. It almost brings me to tears that the future looks so dark. I am not sure that there will be any glories for a hundred generations.'

But even as Greece engages in a bout of national soul-searching, it would appear that the Olympics – one of its greatest inventions – is safe. The modern custodians of the Games have done much to tarnish their appeal, but they have nevertheless continued to grow in global scope and prestige. And even if the Games under the IOC were to falter, for reasons of incompetence or corruption or whatever else, the underlying ritual will surely remain intact.

If Olympia proves anything, it is that as long as there are humans, there will be sport.

V
Icons

Not all of the legendary figures interviewed or reflected upon in this section deserve the epithet 'great' – Lance Armstrong, for example, should properly be remembered for having swindled his way to glory, and for defaming his accusers until the last moment.

But all of these icons illuminate – in one way or another – themes touched upon in this book. From Roger Bannister to Michael Schumacher and Billie Jean King to Martina Navratilova we see, in their stories and achievements, qualities that underpin greatness: courage, resilience, determination, and, of course, the ability to compete under pressure.

Some of the characters are dark – Jake LaMotta was a sociopathic misogynist who raped a woman before becoming middleweight champion – but this reveals, perhaps more than anything else, that those who reach the top in sport are not always role models. The qualities they portray on the field of play do not always translate into their personal lives.

The final essay reflects upon the most famous athlete of all. In the extraordinary life of Muhammad Ali, the themes of the book coalesce. He was a great sportsman, but also a cultural icon who subtly altered the history and consciousness of the United States and the wider world. He touched us not merely through his endeavours in the ring, but through his moral courage, his many flaws, and through the backstory of a boy born into a small town disfigured by racial segregation, but who dared to 'shake up the world'.

He was, unquestionably, the greatest.

Billie Jean King

14 September 2007

As Billie Jean King observed in *Billie Jean*, her autobiography: 'Maybe all my life I've just been trying to change things so there would be someplace right for me to be.' She has been fighting battles for so long that she would find it difficult to drop her fists even if she wanted to. Her crusades against sexism and homophobia in the Seventies and Eighties were, in their way, as revolutionary as those of Muhammad Ali against racism and Vietnam in the Sixties and Seventies. Together they shook up the world.

It is a measure of how far things have moved on that King is not merely tolerated but actively embraced by the sporting and political establishments that once vilified her. 'The Billie Jean King National Tennis Center,' she says with a lovely grin when we meet in her suite at the Flushing Meadows complex that was renamed in her honour last summer. 'It has quite a ring, doesn't it?'

To meet King, sixty-three, is to encounter a human whirlwind. 'Why d'ya go into journalism?' she asks. 'Where d'ya go to college? Wotcha gonna do with the rest of your life?' Her questions come so thick and fast that I fear I may not get an opportunity to ask any of my own. When there is a pause I seize my chance, but she launches into an answer with such gusto I struggle to keep pace with my note-taking. 'Here, let me help,' she says, and starts to jot down her own quotes.

Icons

When I leave ninety minutes later, head spinning, she hands me a piece of A4 with line upon line from the BJK repository of wisdom: 'Don't take anything personally'; 'Always forgive'; 'Everything starts with integrity'; 'Never forget that 90 per cent of the media is controlled by men'.

It is the spring of 1981. Ronald Reagan is the new President, Tom Watson is the Open golf champion and King has just lost to Sue Rollinson in the first round of a tournament in Florida. At the age of thirty-seven and with brittle knees, the former world No. 1 is struggling to rediscover the form that won her twelve grand-slam singles titles.

King returns to her hotel room and notices a pink message slip. It tells her that a reporter from the *Los Angeles Times* has called to ask about 'a lawsuit'. King instantly realises that Marilyn Barnett, her former secretary, has acted upon her threat to go public with their five-year affair and to sue for palimony.

Two days later, King calls a press conference to admit that she has had a sexual relationship with Barnett. It is arguably the most controversial sexual revelation in sporting history.

'It was a nightmare at the time,' King says. 'Although there were lesbians on tour and doubtless in other sports, too, nobody had come out of the closet. It seemed that for weeks all anyone was talking about was my love life. I was still married to Larry King so that even those who were broadly sympathetic felt I had breached his trust – which I had. Much of America was shocked by the affair.'

This was a time when homophobia was not merely connived at but actively endorsed by the establishment. A few years earlier, the United States Supreme Court had refused to hear the case of a teacher from Washington who was dismissed because of his sexual orientation, and in 1978 the court voted not to interfere with the right of states to enforce anti-sodomy laws after a North Carolina gay man was imprisoned for a consensual sexual encounter.

However, King's press conference was not the liberal rallying call that many had hoped for. Although she admitted to a lesbian affair, she did so with a reluctance that appalled gay rights activists. 'I hate being called a homosexual,' she said. 'I don't feel homosexual.' King bitterly regrets her comments to this day, even if she has more than made up for them with her campaigning.

'You have to remember that, at that time, I was as homophobic as most other people,' she says. 'I was brought up in a household where homosexuality was rarely discussed, but when it was, my father made his views pretty clear. I was so messed up by it all that I went back to Larry for a year after the court case and continued to live a lie.

'For the whole time I was together with Marilyn, I was overwhelmed with guilt. I felt guilty because I was brought up to believe that what I was doing was wrong in the eyes of God. I felt guilty because I was cheating on Larry. And I felt guilty because I knew that if it got out it could jeopardise the women's tour that was still in its infancy. I wasn't just in the closet, I was at the back of the closet hiding in the corner. I was damn well trying to build a brick wall between myself and the closet door in case it slammed open.'

Do you feel at ease with your sexuality today? 'Yes, but it has been a lifetime endeavour,' King, who is in a long-term relationship with Ilana Kloss, a former tennis player, says. 'It was not until fifty-one that I fully accepted myself for who I am. I always understood rationally that there was nothing wrong with my sexuality, but it is not just about what you think but how you feel. It took thirteen years of therapy to get me there, but I am glad I made it. It just goes to show it is never too late.'

The ramifications of King's coming out were considerable. Within a year, Avon had dropped its sponsorship of the women's tour, and King estimates that over the next three seasons she lost more than $1.5 million in endorsements. Although her revelations marked a watershed in the public discourse on homosexuality, widespread prejudice remains to this day – as Graeme Le Saux's autobiography, serialised this week in *The Times*, piercingly demonstrates.

'Things are nowhere near perfect,' King says. 'To change the hearts and minds of people takes generations. We had slavery three hundred years ago and we are still dealing with the consequences today. We have won many battles against discrimination, but the war continues.'

Joe Frazier
8 November 2011

There is something both poignant and morally significant in the fact that Joe Frazier was determined to carry on. After fourteen rounds of the most pulsating action seen in the history of prize fighting, and with his rugged face disfigured by swollen mounds, Frazier heard the countdown to the start of the final round and made to stand up.

He had no chance of winning, despite the exhaustion of Muhammad Ali, the champion with whom he had shared a ring twice before. Frazier, who lost his battle against cancer at the age of sixty-seven today, could no longer see the punches coming and was hopelessly unable to defend himself. In the previous round he had stood in the centre of the ring, indomitable and pitiful, as Ali had thrown hooks like confetti. But pride and carefully nurtured hatred demanded that Frazier answer the bell for the fifteenth.

'I want to go out,' he said, as he felt the gentle hands of Eddie Futch, his trainer, on his shoulders, pushing him back on to the stool. 'I have to go out.'

'Joe, it's over,' Futch replied, sadly but firmly. 'You're taking too much punishment and I don't want to see you take any more.'

And with that, as Frazier bowed his head in obedience to a man who was more like a father than a coach, the greatest bout in boxing history came to an end.

'The Thrilla in Manila' was not the final contest in the career of Frazier, nor was it the most lucrative, but it formed the axis of his life. It was the contest that everyone wanted to talk about, the contest every documentary-maker wanted to deconstruct, the contest Frazier relived in his own mind over and over, and not just because of the punishment he took at Ali's hands.

More significant, and infinitely more attritional, were the taunts Frazier endured in the build-up to that extraordinary contest.

Of course, verbal sparring was a familiar feature of the pre-bout vaudeville of any fight involving Ali. In the build-up to their first contest, in March 1971, Ali had dubbed Frazier an 'Uncle Tom', a slur that sought to position Frazier as a stooge of the white establishment at a time when America was coming to terms with the ructions of Vietnam and the civil rights movement. The absurdity of marketing a bout between two black men as a proxy battle in the fight for racial equality did not seem to matter.

Frazier, for his part, was outraged at the way he had been pigeonholed by Ali and sought to convey his progressive credentials at press conferences and in television interviews. But he was hopelessly outmatched and out-talked. Only in the ring could he hope to match Ali's articulacy.

The fight itself was a classic, if lacking the sustained intensity that would characterise Manila four years later. Tickets were so much in demand that Frank Sinatra had to double as a photographer for *Life* magazine to get a ringside seat. Ali, who was coming back after a three-year layoff after his refusal to be drafted for Vietnam, boxed on the outside, while Frazier (who had won the title in Ali's absence) bulled forward. When Frazier put Ali on the canvas with a ferocious left hook in the fifteenth, the decision was no longer in serious doubt.

Frazier smiled at the climax, as if in the act of victory he had exorcised the demons. 'When he went down, we were both dead tired,' he said. 'And the only thing going through my mind when he got up was what was going through my mind all night. Throw punches. Let [Cassius] Clay [who changed his name to Ali in 1964] do the talking. All I had to do was punch.'

But in the build-up to Manila in 1975 (there had been a non-title fight in the interim, won by Ali), the marketing spiel became personal. Ali's poem had the press corps in hysterics – 'It will be a killer, And a chiller, And a thriller, When I get the gorilla, in Manila'. Ali even started taking a pocket-size ape to his training base each day to ridicule his opponent, and mocked Frazier as 'dumb' and 'unintelligent'.

'Joe Frazier is so ugly he should donate his face to the US Bureau of Wildlife,' Ali joked, with the contest less than a week away. But as the world laughed, Frazier became ever more withdrawn. According to those closest to him, the bout had become personal, and his animosity towards Ali almost obsessive.

'He will get an answer when the bell goes,' Frazier said with a smile, feigning indifference. 'He knows what is coming.'

Perhaps if Frazier had won in Manila, he would have found the emotional space to forgive Ali, but in defeat his grudge seemed to compound. When he was interviewed for a biography of Ali in the 1990s, his bitterness took Thomas Hauser, the author, aback.

'Twenty years I have been fighting Ali and I still want to take him apart piece by piece and send him back to Jesus,' Frazier said. 'He shook me in Manila; he won. But I sent him home

worse than he came. Look at him now; he's damaged goods . . .
He's finished and I'm still here.'

When I interviewed Frazier in 2005 to mark the thirty-year
anniversary of Manila, he talked about the importance of forgive-
ness, but as we discussed his inner feelings, he paused and
seemed on the verge of tears.

'There were bruises in my heart because of the words he
used,' he said slowly. 'I spent years dreaming about him and
wanting to hurt him. But you have got to throw that stick out of
the window.'

Frazier was a proud and decent man and always willing to
give interviews. He was also among the greatest of heavy-
weights, winning Olympic gold in 1964 and defeating Jimmy
Ellis to unify the world heavyweight title in 1970. But he will
always be defined by the rivalry with Ali, the pain they shared
in the ring, and the agonies they, in different ways, endured
beyond it.

Ali, for his part, apologised. 'I'm sorry if Joe is mad at me. I'm
sorry I hurt him,' he said. 'I couldn't have done what I did without him, and he couldn't have done what he did without me.
And if God ever calls me to a holy war, I want Joe Frazier fighting beside me.'

But the deepest tragedy of all is that the men who shared
sport's greatest and most enduring rivalry were never fully
reconciled.

Jimmy Connors

22 June 2006

'I *always* left my blood out there on the court. Whether it was
the first round at San Jose or the final of Wimbledon, I gave it
everything. My attitude to any match was, "Let's get it on. I don't

care if you have more talent, better shots, whatever. Let's get the result out there, one on one." God, it was good.'

Amid the torrid psyche of one of sport's greatest gladiators, one thing is eloquently clear: Jimmy Connors misses the thrill of competitive tennis.

The two-times Wimbledon champion, talking in that husky high pitch, like a baritone trying to imitate a contralto, lit up like a blowtorch as we discussed the battles that redefined the parameters of sporting courage.

'I can't say that I was my happiest on court, but I felt completely free,' he said. 'Free from family obligations, free from my own torment. In a real sense I was a different person. It was a place where I could not tolerate the idea of being beaten. I psyched myself up into a state where I felt something close to hatred towards my opponent, a state where I detested the idea of someone making his name at the expense of Jimmy Connors.'

In a world of cardboard cutout champions, Connors is a revelation. His attitude towards tennis is not merely passionate but something approaching metaphysical. 'I was in my element on court, measuring myself against someone else,' he said. 'I was not competitive for show. It came from deep within.'

Just how deep would be revealed later in the interview, when he opened up about his troubled relationship with his late father.

Connors's career is the stuff of red-blooded, blue-collared legend. Coached and guided by his formidable mother, he burst forth from East St Louis, Illinois, to win his first professional title in 1972. He went on to become world No. 1 for five consecutive years, winning eight grand-slam titles. In 1991, at the age of thirty-nine, he strung together a miraculous sequence of victories to make it to the semi-finals of the US Open, bringing a smile to the face of a nation.

His career record of 109 men's singles titles has not been equalled.

But there was one adversary he could not beat. 'I competed with three generations of players, from Laver and Rosewall, through Borg and McEnroe and finally against guys like Sampras and Agassi. I was afraid of no one,' he said. 'But there was one opponent that I couldn't contend with: age.

'That upset me more than anything. I knew that I was still capable of vying for titles, but my body was falling apart. If I played now against the new guys, they would win. But they would not be beating the real Jimmy Connors.'

Rage is a word that fails to do justice to the feelings Connors directs against the dying of the light. When, in 1999, he realised that his crumbling body was preventing him from competing effectively on the seniors tour, he disappeared like an apparition. For five years he refused to attend competitions, and when Wimbledon came on television he would leave the house. 'I could not bear these events being on and not being a part of them,' he said. 'Age had got me and I struggled to deal with it. I wanted to be out there, battling.' All of which poses an intriguing question: why? What drove Connors to give so much, so often? What was the 'torment' from which he felt compelled to escape?

Many have muttered about some deep and dark alchemy in his relationship with Gloria Thompson, his mother, coach and mentor. The man himself, however, paints a sympathetic picture of the woman who took him from toddler to temperamental champion.

'Despite the rumours, my mother was not overly pushy,' he said. 'She understood me and was there for me whether I won or lost.' They are still very close. Connors visits her (she is eighty-two and still living in Illinois) every ten days.

His relationship with his father, however, is more suggestive.

'He never came to competitions,' Connors said after considerable coaxing, his voice beginning to falter. 'He was not a part of what I did in tennis. He was a very proud man.'

Did he ever tell you that he loved you? 'No he did not – and that taught me a lot about parenthood. If a week goes by when I do not tell my son [a twenty-six-year-old graduate living in Los Angeles] that I love him, there is something very wrong.'

It is facile, perhaps, to surmise that Connors's preternatural drive for success was all about gaining the acceptance of an unloving father, but it was unquestionably part of the story. I asked if they were ever reconciled.

'We discussed a lot of things when it was too late, when he was on his deathbed,' he said.

'I was not looking for peace of mind and he was not looking to provide it, but I am glad that we had that conversation.'

Now fifty-three, Connors lives in Montecito, an hour's flight north of Los Angeles on the West Coast. He is married to Patti, a former *Playboy* Playmate, whom he met nearly thirty years ago at a party in the US. Although he said that he is at ease with his post-tennis existence (he talked about walking the dogs and 'doing regular things'), one can hear the faint but distinctive echo of emptiness. This, perhaps, is the inevitable consequence of losing something to which one has given so much.

His turbulent relationship with tennis was like a love affair. When he commentates, as he will for the BBC for a second time at Wimbledon this summer, he sounds like someone ruminating on a former sweetheart who has turned her attentions to younger men. His observations are raw, sometimes melancholic, but always compelling. You know that Connors would do anything to ditch the microphone and get back on court with a racket in his hand and the tumult in his ears.

'Nothing replaces the thrill of competitive tennis,' he said. 'But it is something you have to learn to live without because there is no getting it back.'

I asked if he finds any consolation in the pleasure he gave to so many during the glory days. He answered in the affirmative, but without conviction. Perhaps, for those who love too deeply, there is no lasting comfort.

Jack Nicklaus and Sir Jackie Stewart
22 May 2007

It was only in the final few minutes of an hour-long interview with Jack Nicklaus and Sir Jackie Stewart that the two great men became animated – to the extent that Nicklaus's agent, who was towards the back of his employer's suite at the Old Course Hotel in St Andrews, got to his feet to see what the commotion was about.

For the first forty-five minutes we had discussed triumph and adversity, love, marriage, fame and mortality. Both men had been as wise and warm as one might expect from two sixty-somethings with reputations for thoughtfulness and self-awareness. Nicklaus is like Gandalf sans beard: quietly assertive, humane and discursive. Stewart is quirkier, more combative, with a potent streak of mischievousness running through his wiry frame.

Both talked about the importance of family and their gratitude to their wives (both have been married for more than forty-five years). Both talked about the ethereal nature of fame and their belief that self-fulfilment is to be found in places beyond the sporting arena. Both talked with charming self-deprecation about how their post-sporting careers would not have happened had they not been superstars. 'I don't kid myself that I would now be designing golf courses had I not been such a successful player,' Nicklaus said. 'There is not a chance on this earth. The doors were open for me.'

But it was in response to what seemed a rather dull question about 'clutch putting' – 'Is it difficult to prevent the mind from worrying about the consequences of a mistake?' – that Nicklaus lit up like a blowtorch, as if he had been zapped with a thousand volts. Soon Stewart started to weigh in. For all their range of interests, these two are fanatical about one thing above all else: the art of winning.

'You should never think about the negatives,' Nicklaus implored, like an evangelist warning against the dangers of immorality. 'I didn't. I always looked at competition-winning putts as an opportunity, never as a threat. That is the mental trick that so many players are unable to make.

'Any time I had a six-foot putt to win a tournament I was happy because that is what I had worked for. I was excited and, man, that was fun. Give me that putt!' He almost got to his feet to hammer home the point. Stewart was nodding. 'It is about management of the mind,' he said.

'You have to shut out all the negative emotions because they can inhibit you when you get to the moment that determines success and failure. The key to winning is being able to stay in control when the temperature is rising. In motor racing there was an element of danger to think about as well. In 1968 we lost four drivers in four consecutive months.'

When I asked Stewart – the Scot who won three world championships – what had driven him to take such palpable risks in the pursuit of success, I was again taken aback by the vehemence of the response. 'Ninety-eight per cent of my ambition came from a need to prove myself because I had been a failure at school,' he said. 'School was a painful and humiliating time of my life. It was only when I was forty-two that I was diagnosed with dyslexia, after my sons had been tested for it and it was suggested that I should be. It was as if a weight had been lifted from my shoulders because I had always worried that I was thick.

'Once I was asked to read in front of class and I couldn't do it – the page was just a clutter of words. I started blushing and the other kids started to snigger. It was deeply humiliating.

'The desire to overcome that schoolboy insecurity drives me to this day. I still don't know the alphabet. I still can't read and write properly. I still don't know the words of the National Anthem. I still can't recite the Lord's Prayer. Being dyslexic has given me that extra drive to prove myself.'

But can ambition be indoctrinated? Can the skill to remain calm on the grid or when standing over a 6-foot putt be taught? Both men, who are global ambassadors for the Royal Bank of Scotland, lifted their eyes to the heavens. 'Psychologists! I laugh at every one of them,' Nicklaus said. 'What do they know? It is all theory to them. You are giving me routines from people who have never done it.

'How are they going to teach Tiger [Woods] and Phil [Mickelson] and Retief [Goosen] how to play? These are things you have to figure out for yourself.'

How does Nicklaus feel about Woods, the only man who can legitimately challenge his status as the greatest golfer? Does he secretly hope that his compatriot, who has won twelve major championships, will fall short so that his own record of eighteen will remain in place? Although Nicklaus had earlier said that records were there to be broken, he acknowledged that he does feel a sense of competitiveness with the pretender to his throne.

'Of course I would prefer that my record continues to stand,' he said, suddenly looking more like a grizzly than a golden bear. 'I do not celebrate when Tiger gets another win under his belt.' Like many great sportsmen, including Stewart, Nicklaus's fearsome competitiveness is matched only by his candour.

Martina Navratilova

2 July 2007

There have been so many trials and tribulations, so many injustices and tyrannies, so many radical life changes and personal reinventions, that it seems natural to regard Martina Navratilova's life as one of permanent revolution. Each year a new philosophy, each month a new challenge, each day a potential watershed.

Like the day in the summer of 1975, when an eighteen-year-old Navratilova is walking along the banks of the Berounka River in her home village of Řevnice, talking quietly to her stepfather, tears in her eyes, fear battling hope in her heart. Her blossoming tennis career is under threat from the communist-controlled Czechoslovakian tennis association and she is agonising over whether to defect to the United States at the forthcoming US Open.

The dice is cruelly loaded. Defecting might mean she never sees her homeland again, that her family might endure persecution, that she will be alone in a foreign country, fending for herself. Her stepfather advises her to go for it – it might be her last chance – but tells her not to breathe a word to anyone lest the secret police get wind.

A few days later, she is closeted on the top floor of the Immigration and Naturalisation headquarters in Lower Manhattan, signing the papers that will seal one of the most high-profile sporting defections of the Cold War.

Like the day in the autumn of 1975, when Navratilova finally gets a handle on her sexuality, waking up alongside a woman and saying to herself: 'OK, I guess I am gay. My life is going to be a lot more complicated. I may lose some sponsors. I may alienate some fans. But I am not going to deny myself, my true nature.' Six years later, she is outed by the *Daily News* in New York, something that threatens the viability of the fledgeling women's tour and outrages conservative America.

Like the day in 1981 when a twenty-four-year-old Navratilova decides to end her relationship with Rita Mae Brown, her third serious girlfriend and an author from Charlottesville, Virginia. They argue violently and, as Navratilova tries to speed off in her BMW, Brown reaches for a gun and pulls the trigger. According to reports, the bullet flies through the headrest of the passenger seat and shatters the windscreen. It is the moment when Navratilova learns that love can be as dangerous as it is intoxicating.

Like the day in 1981 when Navratilova falls in love with Nancy Lieberman, a former basketball player who takes her by the scruff of the neck and cajoles her to transform her training methods. 'Nancy pushed me harder than I thought possible,' Navratilova says. 'Meeting her changed everything. Until that moment, I had been going through the motions.'

Up until the age of twenty-five, Navratilova had won only two grand-slam tournaments. Over the next nine years, she would win sixteen grand-slam singles titles – including nine at Wimbledon – and redefine the nature of sporting professionalism.

And so it goes on, more watersheds than you could shake a racket at, each of which has contributed, in its way, to the fascinating, complex, warm, loving, radical, bright, passionate, charming, fifty-year-old woman I am sitting opposite on the roof above Wimbledon's broadcast centre.

And she is beautiful. Rarely has a person looked so different in the flesh as compared with how she appears on television. Her green eyes burst with life-force, her smile radiates humanity, her eyebrows convey all the wit of someone who has faced prejudice in all its guises. One wonders at the caricature of a harsh and forbidding woman who grimly monopolised tennis in the 1980s. How can we have got her so wrong for so long?

Navratilova giggles. 'The press have a lot of power over the way you are perceived,' she says. 'It is difficult to shake off a negative image. Even the pictures they would pick when I was in my playing days. I mean, I am quite photogenic, but they picked the worst shot on the cover of *Sports Illustrated*. There is Chris [Evert] smiling as she walks up the court and there is me yelling because there is one bad call, but that is the picture they show. They wanted Chris to be the all-American girl next door and they wanted me to be the muscular lesbian. And you have no control over that.'

Did she resent it? 'Yes. Because I am not like that. I remember asking Chris, "How come your image is so good and mine is so bad, so hard? How come the fans love you so much? What do you do with your fan mail?" She just giggled and told me that she chucked her mail in the bin. And there I am, paying a guy a lot of money to answer my fan mail. I am like, "What am I doing wrong here? Why don't they love me the way they love her?"' But they love her now. 'It took a while, but I got there,' she says. 'Now I can say almost anything and get away with it. It's pretty nice. I feel like I earned it, but it took a long time. I've grown as a person and I am definitely more lovable now than thirty years ago – but I was never the ogre they made me out to be.'

Earlier, I had sat alongside Navratilova in the TV commentary box as she called a match for the BBC. The booth is a small affair with an oblong window opening out on to Centre Court from its northwestern corner, level with the third row. It is like peering through a letterbox into an amphitheatre. Alongside her is Andrew Castle, the former Great Britain Davis Cup player, and Navratilova seems to be enjoying every minute. Half an hour after our interview, she will analyse the day's play for the BBC's highlights show.

I make the mistake of playing devil's advocate, asking whether it is sensible to spend one's life devoted to something as trivial as hitting a ball over a net. She laughs derisively. 'Oh God,' she says. 'I had a duty to be the best I could be, to see how far I could get. You will always regret it if you don't push yourself. That's the beauty of it. If you don't push yourself, you will never know where that limit is. Once I realised how good I could become, my question was: "How many titles can I win?"'

Does she get irritated by those who do not share that philosophy? 'I see players like Feliciano López [who beat Tim Henman last week], so talented but so lazy. He is a poser. You know he could be so much better. He's got the goods, he's got the talent, but he's not got the workrate.'

How about Serena Williams? 'I would not call Serena lazy exactly, because she is not that. She has been interested in too many other things and has not given tennis the priority. And you cannot underestimate how much the death of her sister has affected her. But I am telling you that it is a crime not to explore your limits.'

But was Navratilova not a perpetrator of that crime? 'Yes, until the day I met Nancy.' Love, more even than tennis, has defined Navratilova's being. It is not difficult to see why she has left a trail of lovers in her wake: she is a passionate, beautiful and vulnerable woman who yearns to love as much as she yearns to be loved.

'I always wanted a partner,' she says. 'I never wanted to be alone. I always thought I wanted to live my life with one person for ever and ever. Whenever there is anything great, it is in my nature to want to share it; the bad stuff I can handle alone. If there is an amazing mango, I want to cut it in half and share it. It's like, "I want you to taste it, too." If there is a beautiful sunset, I want to share it. Experiencing a sunset on your own can be the loneliest feeling in the world.'

Her relationships have never been anything other than intense experiences that have deeply affected both parties. Her first affair was with an older woman, who enabled Navratilova to understand her sexuality; later came Brown, who taught her to think more deeply about the world around her; then Lieberman, who transformed her attitude to tennis, paving the way to sporting greatness.

Then came Judy Nelson, a former beauty queen, who was married with two children when they met. They spent nine inseparable years together, but when Navratilova upped sticks, Nelson sued for $15 million (about £7.5 million) in palimony. The fact that Navratilova fought the claim angered gay rights campaigners, who believed that homosexual relationships conferred the same obligations as straight ones. Navratilova, however, remains unapologetic.

'It had nothing to do with being gay or straight and everything to do with the feeling that half of what I made should not be going to a person who had absolutely nothing to do with the fact that I was the No. 1 player in the world,' she says.

'I was the top player before I met her and continued to be after we split up. That's all it was. I feel the same way about straight couples. If kids are involved, you should make sure you take care of them. But when I made my fortune and she had nothing to do with it, you don't share half and half.' They eventually settled out of court.

Navratilova has been with her present partner for seven years and professes to be very fulfilled with love and life. Would she like children? 'I am too old to have my own biologically. I am going through the menopause,' she says. 'But some day, I hope to adopt a kid or two.'

Time has not entirely healed the righteous anger she feels towards those who hated – and still hate – her because of her sexuality. 'I grew up in a communist country where they locked up homosexuals,' she says. 'I never could understand that. And I did not even know I was gay then. I didn't think there was anything wrong with loving a human being, which is why I never apologised for it. And to this day it really baffles me why it is people's business to judge you.'

Michael Phelps

22 December 2009

It is strange, the moments that change history. In 1997, a shy, 'problem' schoolboy from a working-class family in Baltimore, Maryland, was told that he would 'never achieve anything in life'. It was the kind of throwaway remark that many school-teachers – overworked, overstressed, underpaid – make about disruptive students. But for Michael Phelps, at that time and place in his young, faltering life, it changed everything.

'I still remember the way I felt,' Phelps says during an end-of-year interview in Manchester. 'I had just started swimming seriously and those comments from my teacher seemed to burn deep inside. I was often made to feel like an outsider at school because I had Attention Deficit Hyperactive Disorder [ADHD] and struggled to fit in. But I thought to myself: "You can think whatever you want, but I am going to prove you wrong." I am not sure why it fired me up so much, but it did.'

From that day to this, Phelps's life has been one long sacrifice in pursuit of the impossible. His daily routine is so punishing and so neurotically relentless that it strays into the vicinity of masochism. He does not simply want to win, he wants to set goals that inspire incredulity and disbelief, as if revelling in an eternal cycle of proving people – anybody – wrong.

When Phelps announced in advance of the Olympic Games in Beijing that he was aiming for eight gold medals in the pool, Ian Thorpe, the Australian swimming legend, said (quite reasonably) that the American was unlikely to achieve his target. Phelps responded by pinning the offending remarks to his locker and staring at them every morning until the day he left for China.

'When people doubt me, it gives me huge motivation,' he says. 'It is like the negativity is the fuel that takes me through the water day after day.

'I want to show that I can achieve things they consider impossible. The first time it was the teacher at school, but now I trawl the internet looking for anyone else who doesn't think I am going to cut it. It can be competitors, journalists, whatever.

'The more negative they are, the more determined – and the more certain – I am to do it. And you know what? If I have an ambition in my mind, whatever it is, nothing is going to stop me. Nothing.'

He sounds almost pathological as he describes the nature and intensity of his ambition. But this, of course, is the stuff of greatness.

Phelps was born in the Lake Point area of Baltimore County in 1985. His parents divorced a few years later and his mother – whom the swimmer describes as an 'amazing woman: wise, tough and incredibly strong' – brought up her son and two daughters almost single-handed. But it was evident early on that the young Phelps had difficulty focusing on anything for more than a few moments at a time.

'As a very little boy, I was not just always on the go; I simply could not sit still,' Phelps writes in his autobiography. 'I would twirl pens and pencils between my fingers. I made faces at cameras. I climbed on everything. I never shut up. I had a question for everything, and wouldn't stop asking questions until I got the answer. If then.'

It was for this reason that he had so many problems fitting in with his class-mates and was considered unruly by his teachers.

Phelps was prescribed Ritalin in sixth grade to combat ADHD and, for a while, took the drug three times a day. But his ultimate redemption was to be found in the pool. 'What I discovered soon after starting to swim was that the pool was a safe haven,' he says. 'Two walls at either end. Lane lines on either side. A black stripe on the bottom for direction. I could go fast in the pool, it turned out, in part because being in the pool slowed down my mind. In the water I felt, for the first time, in control.'

I ask if the extent of his ambition – and the inspiration he derives from proving people wrong – is a consequence of his marginalisation at school. 'Yes, I think that is part of it, for sure,' he says. 'Proving yourself is a way of gaining acceptance and showing what you are really made of. Even when I was hugging my mom after winning my eighth gold in Beijing, my mind was flitting to that teacher and what she had said. God, it felt good!' Has he seen the teacher since he left school? 'No, I haven't, but it would have been a lot of fun if I had.'

Phelps's exploits in China transformed his profile around the world, with invitations to appear on *Saturday Night Live* and other top US television shows, but they also brought attention of a rather different kind. In January, the *News of the World* ran a front page story with a picture showing Phelps using a bong, a device used to smoke marijuana. Phelps admitted to 'behaviour that was regrettable and demonstrated bad judgement' and USA Swimming suspended him from competition for three months.

I ask if the photo was an unjustified intrusion into his private life or an inevitable consequence of his celebrity. 'I think the media has been this way for a long time,' he says. 'Sport has become more and more public and I think that once you have got to a certain level you have to accept that the press is going to be interested in your private life. Of course, that means you have to be more careful about the people around you and who you are going to trust. But it also means that you have to learn from your mistakes. I hope I have done that.'

Today, Phelps's eyes are set firmly on London 2012 and another tilt at history. He has already ditched the ultra-fast 100 per cent polyurethane suits that will be banned from next month, suffering a number of defeats as a consequence, not least in the 200 metres butterfly at the Duel in the Pool on Saturday. But this does not worry him. 'Everything that happens between now and 2012 is about giving myself the best shot at the Olympics,' he says. 'Starting as early as possible with the new suits was a no-brainer.'

When I ask if he has figured out his goals for the London Games yet, he smiles. 'Yes, I have worked them out and written them down,' he says. 'But I am not going to tell anybody what they are for a while yet. Not even my mother knows. The only person in the loop is Bob [Bowman, Phelps's long-time coach].'

Phelps continues to evoke the aura of the outsider, a man who is not altogether sure where he fits in. Perhaps that is his strength as a professional athlete, the reason why his competitors should be fearful of another bout of Olympic dominance come London. He seems to have no obvious comfort zone beyond the rigours of the pool.

I ask whether he ever doubts his own ability to achieve his exacting goals; that he might fail to prove his detractors wrong? 'If you are passionate about something, you are going to get there come what may,' he says.

'People say that I have great talent, but in my opinion excellence has nothing to do with talent. It is about what you choose to believe and how determined you are to get there. The mind is more powerful than anything else.'

Sir Roger Bannister
24 March 2012

To describe Sir Roger Bannister as a giant of the twentieth century is, in many ways, an understatement. His smashing of the four-minute-mile barrier in 1954 was, for complex reasons of psychology and history, a watershed in sport that captivated the world.

Sir Roger Bannister

He was voted the inaugural Sportsman of the Year by *Sports Illustrated*, and came to be hailed as one of a new generation of postwar British pioneers, alongside Lord Hunt, leader of the successful 1953 British Everest expedition, round-the-world yachtsman Sir Francis Chichester, and the like.

But Bannister was not really a sportsman – at least, not in the sense that we use the word today. In modern usage, sport is a profession, a relentless quest to improve performance, with nothing else getting in the way. To be a great sportsman is, in many ways, to have artificially narrow horizons.

Bannister was not like this. Even when he was training in the summer of 1954, weeks from breaking the world mile record, he continued to pursue his career in medicine. He was not merely representative of the amateur ethos, but of a conception of sport fundamentally at odds with the vogue today.

'It still seems strange to me that the intrinsically simple and unimportant act of placing one foot in the front of the other as fast as possible for 1,760 yards was heralded as such an important sporting achievement,' he writes in *The First Four Minutes*, his wonderful memoir. 'My achievements in neurology were far more important than anything I did as a runner.'

I meet Bannister, who turned eighty-three yesterday, in his garden flat in suburban Oxford. The sun is streaming through large windows and Moyra, his lovely wife of more than fifty-seven years, is pouring tea. Bannister is smartly dressed, complete with blazer and tie, and his eyes light up as the conversation begins.

Subjects pass like scenery on a train travelling through twentieth-century history: the Second World War, the age of amateurism, the founding of the Sports Council (Bannister was its first chairman), medical innovation, meeting Winston Churchill, conferences at Buckingham Palace, life in academia – the subjects are endless.

But it is when we turn to philosophical questions related to sport that Bannister is at his most fascinating. 'I sometimes wonder if sport has become altogether too extreme,' he says. 'It is marvellous to be involved in recreational sport, playing football or running a few times a week. It is very good for health and also for vitality.

'But professional sport is often quite different. It is inevitable, with the rewards on offer, that people will want to push themselves to the limits. And yet this is not always conductive to well-being. Intense training often leads to injury and illness. The immune system becomes depleted. You just have to look at professional sportspeople and the list of breakdowns to see the dangers.'

Bannister's passions have always extended beyond sport, and his life is a marvellous tapestry of interests. After the year in which he broke the four-minute mile, as well as winning the mile at the British Empire and Commonwealth Games and the 1,500 metres at the European Championships, he retired to focus on medicine. Alongside pioneering work in neurology, he later became deeply immersed in sports politics and, from 1985, served for eight years as Master of Pembroke College, Oxford.

According to Moyra, no day has passed when Bannister has not devoted a portion of his waking hours to learning. 'Even when we went on holiday as a young family to our modest cottage, Roger would spend the mornings in his study, reading and researching,' she says. 'He loves to learn new things. I think that is when he is at his most happy.'

Bannister says: 'I have always believed that humans are at their most fulfilled when they are engaged in interesting work. A life as a dilettante may sound rather wonderful, but it quickly becomes unsatisfying.'

Bannister's career in medicine is the stuff of legend. Over more than four decades he established a reputation as one of the most eminent neurologists in the world. He authored textbooks, published numerous papers and developed original research that pushed the boundaries of our understanding of the autonomic nervous system. In 2005 he was presented with a lifetime achievement award by the American Academy of Neurology.

'Neurology is, to my mind, the most fascinating branch of medicine,' he says. 'The brain and central nervous system link to all sorts of other things, like psychology and behaviour. At the beginning of my career, the bar was set high by colleagues. As a former athlete, I had to work hard to convince them that my true ambitions were in medicine. But I think I had convinced them by the time I made it as a consultant.'

It was while on secondment with the Royal Army Medical Corps in 1957, as part of his military service, that Bannister made his most audacious contribution to his subject. Posted to Aden, the seaport city in Yemen, his remit was to conduct research into why servicemen in the field were collapsing and dying of heat-related conditions. 'It was a desolate terrain, with temperatures up to 130°F and humidity of 60 per cent,' he says. 'It was one of the most trying climates in the world.

'I marched with the troops up and down jebels [mountains]. The research was important because we needed to understand the reasons for the illnesses and fatalities.'

When he returned to London, Bannister undertook an extraordinary experiment: he gave himself an injection of pyrogens to take his temperature to hazardous levels. 'To test my hypothesis, I needed someone to experiment on, so I experimented on myself,' he says. 'It was dangerous, but it gave me the chance to verify my theory, and save lives.'

Moyra says: 'When he arrived home after the experiment, I didn't recognise him. He was a deep shade of green.'

Since retiring, Bannister has lost none of his energy. He has taken up wood carving – a charming ornamental cat, a result of long and satisfying endeavour, is sitting on the mantelpiece. He is also a member of a walking group and, alongside other retired academics and their wives, a book club.

'We have just finished Burke's *Reflections on the Revolution in France*,' he says. 'The next book is one on global banking.'

Moyra is no less active. A tremendous source of support for Roger as they built a life together (he earned no money from athletics, so they have always had a modest existence), she helps her husband to reply to the fan mail that still arrives in the post and is also an amateur painter (her wonderful landscapes are evident throughout the flat). They have four children and fourteen grandchildren.

Although he never won an Olympic medal (he came fourth in the 1,500 metres in Helsinki in 1952), Bannister has colourful memories of when he volunteered as a teenager to assist the British *chef de mission* at the London Games of 1948.

With minutes to go before the opening ceremony, it was realised that Britain was the only nation without a flag to march under. 'I was dispatched in a Jeep to get the flag from the boot of the car of the *chef de mission*,' Bannister says. 'An army sergeant was driving and I was on the hooter trying to get through the traffic. We managed to find the car, but I didn't have a key, so I smashed the window. The traffic was so heavy going back that I had to get out and run, and I only arrived with seconds to spare. If you look at the video of the parade, you will notice that the British flag is smaller than all the others.'

After two hours of conversation, it seems as if we have barely scratched the surface of Bannister's extraordinary life. To meet him is to come face to face with a seminal figure in British history, but also to perceive a kinder, more civilised epoch. Bannister is an intellectual, a patriot and a man of tremendous honour. In every sense, a great Briton.

Tiger Woods
27 March 2012

A confession. I bought into the Tiger Woods shtick, hook, line and sinker. To me, in his pomp, he was representative of a new breed of sportsman: brilliant, audacious, hard-working, supremely composed and astonishingly handsome. I marvelled at his megawatt smile.

The family values stuff, I never really thought about. At least not at a conscious level. Of course, I read the affectionate tributes to his dad and mom, glanced at the soft-focus shoots with his wife and children, but thought myself above all that schmooze. That was not the reason I loved Woods.

It was his golf I loved. I was one of the millions of viewers who watched, riveted, when Woods was in with a shout during the final round of a major, and often switched off when he dropped out of contention. I even favoured him above my countrymen – the likes of Nick Faldo, Monty and, later, Lee Westwood and Luke Donald. Perhaps that is an unpatriotic admission, but it is true.

The storyline surrounding his colour was particularly rousing. A mixed-race kid, brought up in Orange County, California, was sending shock waves through the subculture of golf, with its arcane rules, stuffy etiquette and country club insularity. Gosh, when he was striding around the closing holes, fist pumping, putter swirling like a wand in his hand, Nike swoosh gleaming in the sunshine, it was almost subversive.

But are these memories merely a figment of my imagination? Did these things actually happen? Looking back upon the Woods phenomenon, I genuinely can't make sense of it any longer. I can't see the dividing line between appearance and reality. Can't distinguish between what I was watching, and what I thought I was watching. I feel deceived, but possibly I deceived myself.

My confusion is simple. Since the revelations about his private life, I see Woods in a fundamentally different light. I don't love him any longer, don't care about whether he wins or loses – at least, not in the same visceral way. I don't jump out of my seat when he nails a long putt, as he did so often on Sunday night while winning his first competition in two and a half years, teeing himself up nicely for the Masters next week. The sheen has gone.

But why? So the man had a few flings with a variety of cock-tail waitresses and sat with a fat cigar at the Bellagio, swilling champagne while hitting on passers-by. What's the big deal? The sex was consensual, he paid for the champagne and, as for infidelity, is that not ultimately a matter for him and his wife? Why should his private actions make any difference to the way we estimate him as a public figure? And why, for heaven's sake, should it matter to how we feel about him as a golfer?

Qua sportsman, nothing has really changed when it comes to Woods, except his form. But we did not stop loving him because he lost form or altered the geometry of his swing. We stopped loving him – at least I stopped loving him – at the moment his reputation for wholesomeness was shattered. I thought it wouldn't make any difference. But it did.

And this hits me hard every time I think about it – because it reveals that I am a sucker. The advertising industry and, in particular, his ultra-smart handlers at IMG, calculated that by positioning Woods as a family-loving, morally upstanding, all-American hero, he could become one of the most potent forces in global advertising. They told the story for all it was worth, down to the position of Elin's eyes on the soft shoots for the glossies.

Sophisticates among us knew what was afoot. I wrote a dozen articles about Woods as a poster boy for global capitalism and a conduit for new-fangled theories of consumer psychology. I could see inside the machine and comprehended the mechanics of how he was influencing consumers from Baltimore to Beijing. What I didn't realise is that I was one of the suckers. What I didn't realise is that I was putty in the hands of the global advertising industry.

For how else to explain the end of the affair? If my love for Woods all but disappeared with the revelations about his sexual indiscretions, my love must have been constructed – at least in part – upon the myth of his probity. Despite myself, it must have sunk deep, slipping past my conscious radar. The Woods Effect didn't merely work its magic upon Middle America; it worked on me and, possibly, you, too.

And not just in terms of pulling for him on the golf course. As I write these words, it occurs to me that I use Gillette. Not just the razor and the shaving gel, but those damned expensive blades you have to buy every few weeks (and which apparently cost only five pence each to manufacture, despite selling for up to £2.50). I have never really considered why I buy this brand, because there are dozens of less expensive alternatives that do just as good a job. But buy them I do, thoughtlessly, almost robotically. The ads involving Woods have sunk deep – and turned me into putty.

And when I play sport, as I do most weeks, I wear Nike. A Nike T-shirt is pretty much like any other T-shirt, except for one crucial difference: a swoosh that does nothing whatsoever to improve my performance, but causes me to reach into my pocket and pay a hefty mark-up. This is not just about Woods, of course. Other brand ambassadors such as Michael Jordan have also left their psychological mark. But the truth is pretty much the same. I am putty.

Woods was dropped by many of the multinationals for a simple reason: they knew that Middle America had stopped loving him. They will return just as soon as he finds atonement, in whatever form that takes. Winning the Masters would help, particularly in a culture that has a weakness for redemptive sentimentality. But his unprecedented capacity to mould retail behaviour around the world is almost certainly lost for ever. We still buy the products, but that is because retail choices tend to outlast the advertising strategies that created them.

The power of advertising is often remarked upon, but we think of it in terms of other people and not ourselves. But sit back and think of the products you purchase and even the beliefs you hold. Think long enough and, if you are as malleable as me, you will begin to see rational decisions as the product of subliminal impulses, unseen and unfelt. Marx called it false consciousness, which is a neat label. Perhaps behind the gruff beard, he, too, understood the power of advertising.

I am not suggesting anything sinister or conspiratorial. Advertising, as far as it goes, is open and transparent – we know what big companies are doing, and how they are doing it. But that, perhaps, is the scariest thing of all. Knowing about it doesn't make you wise to it. Indeed, I rather suspect that those who most fervently believe in their own independence of thought are those who are most hopelessly trapped in the invisible forces that animate our behaviour.

At some level, we are all powerless in the face of the Tiger Effect.

Jake LaMotta
11 September 2007

He is standing at the doorway of his apartment on the corner of Fifty-Seventh Street and First Avenue and exuding the menace that has shadowed him since he forged his demonic reputation on the streets of The Bronx in pre-war New York.

Jake LaMotta: self-confessed rapist to read his 1970 autobiography, wife-beater, misogynist and former middleweight champion of the world; the first boxer to lick the great Sugar Ray Robinson; the man lauded as having the most indestructible chin in the history of the ring; the sociopath immortalised by Martin Scorsese in his seminal 1980 biopic *Raging Bull*. 'What's the emoygency,' he growls as I quicken my pace to shake his hand.

He beckons me through the door of his studio apartment. Tiny but comfortable, it is on the seventeenth floor of a portered block in a slick part of midtown Manhattan. Sir Harry Evans, former Editor of *The Times*, and Tina Brown, the author and columnist, live across the street, and around the corner is the home of the late Katharine Hepburn.

LaMotta, eighty-six, is wearing nothing more than a pair of colourful Bermuda shorts, which seem to exaggerate his distinctive top-heavy anatomy: large head on a short body. His torso is lean and healthy. 'Take a seat,' he says, gesturing to a chair in a mirrored corner of the room. His weathered face is a complex study in irritability, complacency and charm.

It is the autumn of 1938. Franklin D. Roosevelt is President, *Snow White and the Seven Dwarfs* is on general release, the Munich Pact has just been signed and the Great Depression is eating away at the fabric of American society. The seventeen-year-old LaMotta is living with his family in a rat-infested tenement building in an immigrant Bronx slum and, despite his youth, has already forged a reputation as a violent small-time hoodlum.

The youngster has spent the day figuring out how to mug Harry Gordon, a local bookie, who always carries a few bucks in his pocket after doing the rounds in the neighbourhood. Gordon tends to take the same route home and, as the clock ticks past midnight, LaMotta is poised in a dark corner with a length of lead piping wrapped in a newspaper.

Gordon appears, walking slowly, and LaMotta creeps up behind. He whacks his quarry around the back of the head with the lead pipe; Gordon staggers but stays on his feet. LaMotta is so enraged that his victim has not lost consciousness that he loses control, bludgeoning Gordon again and again across the skull until he crashes to the ground. LaMotta then reaches inside his coat pocket, removes his wallet and vanishes.

The story in one of the next day's newspapers is depicted as follows: Harry Gordon, forty-five, with a record of bookmaking arrests, was found beaten to death in an alley off Brook Avenue in the Bronx at four o'clock this morning.

'Harry Gordon played on my mind for a while,' LaMotta says. 'For more than ten years I thought I had killed the fella. It kind of messed me up a bit. I felt that I had done something I hadn't paid for. I was in stir as a youngster at Coxsackie [a notorious reform school in New York] but for something else [the attempted burglary of a jewellery store]. I guess it felt like a safe place to be whilst the cops were looking for the murderer.

'It was only in 1949 that I found out what really happened. I was celebrating after beating Marcel Cerdan for the championship and this man with scars on his forehead comes over. It was Harry. "You remember me?" he says. It was like a ghost had turned up. Turns out Harry was so bashed up when he got to the hospital that the newspaperman thought he was a goner. We didn't know any better because he moved out of town as soon as he was released from hospital. He'd decided The Bronx was too rough.'

How did Harry react when he found out that it was you who half-killed him that night? 'He never found out,' LaMotta says. 'I didn't damn well tell him and by the time my book came out he was dead.'

LaMotta's phantasmagoric life contains some of the darkest episodes in twentieth-century sport. He turned to boxing as a teenager as the only quick-buck alternative to the Mob, but soon found himself at odds with the local hoods. He raged at everyone and everything: at his close friends because he feared they were shafting him; at his various wives because he was paranoid that they were cheating on him; at the Mob because they wanted to control him; and at himself because of his terrible knowledge of the crimes he had committed.

He has been angry for as long as he can remember: a man trapped in a labyrinth of intolerable emotion. 'When I was eight I was already getting mad at people,' he says. 'I would clock them for talking to each other because I thought they might be talking about me. Sometimes I would get so crazy at nothing that I didn't give a damn what happened, whether I killed them or they killed me. There could have been an explosion across the street but I wouldn't have heard it.'

LaMotta's homicidal unpredictability was such that even the Mob feared to go heavy on him when he declined their over-tures in his early days as a prize fighter. This was a time when boxing was less a legitimate sport and more an extension of the criminal underworld, with many fighters forced to hand over 50 per cent of their purses to the shadowy figures that haunted the gyms of the big cities.

It was only after seven years as a leading contender without a sniff of a title shot that LaMotta finally fell into line, throwing a bout with Billy Fox in one of the myriad gambling scams master-minded by the New York Mob. LaMotta was too proud to drop to the canvas, but the contest was waved over as he stood on the ropes taking dozens of unanswered punches. Within two years he was given a shot at Marcel Cerdan for the middleweight championship of the world.

'They blew the Fox fight out of all proportion,' LaMotta says. 'I testified to the Senate committee [which had launched an investigation into corruption in boxing in 1960] but people went crazy saying that nobody should ever throw a fight. I was only talking so that people would know what it was really like in boxing. That kind of stuff happened all the time and if I hadn't done it I would never have got a shot at the title.'

Even after achieving his dream of becoming champion, LaMotta remained as volatile as ever. His jealousy and paranoia were causing ructions with family and friends. On one occasion he heard a malicious rumour that Vicky, his second wife, and Pete, his best friend, had been seeing a lot of each other. He drove home in a blind rage, battered Vicky in their living room and then drove around to Pete's workplace and beat him to a pulp. He and Pete did not talk for more than a decade.

I ask whether he feels any sense of guilt for having beaten Vicky and his other wives. 'If you had a girl and she was beautiful and other people were trying to invite her out and seduce her, wouldn't you get angry?' he says.

'That's the thing. I saw these obvious jerks and schmucks coming on with their lines and it bothered me. I never really and truly hit my wives. If I had hit them properly they would be dead. You know how it is: you slap around a broad just a little bit and everything is blown out of proportion.'

As the conversation progresses it is increasingly clear that LaMotta has not come to terms with his past. One had expected to meet an old man who had taken the time to empathise with those who suffered at his hands; someone who had sought and found atonement. Instead, LaMotta is a man in denial; an ageing thug seeking to escape from his crimes despite cashing in on them, not only through his 1970 autobiography but in a recent deal that could lead to the cinematic release of *Raging Bull II*.

When I ask him about his rape of a young woman in New York, which is harrowingly described in his book, LaMotta reverts to type, attempting first to deny and then to evade responsibility.

'Rape?' he says. 'I never really raped anybody.' 'But what about the woman you describe in your autobiography?' I ask. LaMotta pauses for a long moment. 'Well, I suppose I gave her a little push or something,' he says. 'You know what it's like to give a little extra pressure. It often happens when women get their first sex, they pretend that they didn't want it to happen. It's a game to them.'

Meeting LaMotta in the flesh is to realise that even Scorsese's commendably unsentimental depiction fails to get to the heart of the matter. *Raging Bull* portrays the violence and pathos of LaMotta's life, but fails to capture his essential narcissism. His violence was not merely the product of his inner rage, but of his sociopathic indifference to the suffering of anyone but himself.

On one occasion, after necking a few drinks, he punched his first wife so hard that he thought he had killed her. His first reaction on coming out of his alcohol-induced slumber was not one of remorse but of how the murder might affect his boxing career: 'Beautiful. Absolutely beautiful. A minimum of three years.' But Joey, his brother, has a plan: 'Throw her in the river.' It turned out she was alive but unconscious.

After defeating Cerdan in 1949, LaMotta defended his title twice before being dethroned by Sugar Ray Robinson on Valentine's Day in 1951. He continued to fight for three years but was at the end of his rope, finally retiring to open a night-club in Florida. In 1957 he was imprisoned for six months for acting as a pimp to a fourteen-year-old, despite claiming that he did not know the girl in question. For the past half-century he has made a living from personal appearances, book signings, acting and stand-up comedy.

He is now engaged to Denise Baker, a fifty-six-year-old divorcee. 'Ain't she beautiful,' he says, pointing to a photo on the wall. 'She is younger than my daughter. You know how I get such beautiful women? I bulls*** them. I tell them what they want to hear. It's easy if you flatter them; they don't even care when they realise you are talking s***. Look at her face on this photo. Amazing face, don't ya think? She's gonna be my seventh wife; lucky number seven. I get lucky once in a while.'

Lance Armstrong
19 January 2013

We have heard many long and lingering laments about Lance Armstrong. About how we have been betrayed by the messianic figure who turned out to be Satan in Lycra. About how our dreams have been snatched away by the machinations of a congenital cheat. The truth, I think, is rather different. Rarely has a story given so much pleasure to quite so many.

The pursing of lips, the mumblings of how 'he let the children down', the moralising about the nastiness of a man who seemed whiter than white but who betrayed us like a second-rate chiseller: this is as good as it gets. The bottomless pit of pleasure can perhaps be measured by the length and tone of the comments at the bottom of any article on the Texan sportsman. The outrage, the sense of betrayal, the breathlessness at his vertiginous fall: it is almost orgasmic.

This is about more than *Schadenfreude*. For decades we have witnessed the cyclical nature of the tabloid media and regarded it as a peculiarly British ritual.

It begins with the building up of a hero: lionising his virtues, airbrushing his flaws, creating a messianic caricature that we can love without inhibition. And then, with the inevitability of a lion kill, we witness the relish with which he is decapitated, his erstwhile heroism wielded as the perfect tool for the evisceration.

But this was never really about the tabloids or Britishness; it goes far deeper. We see it in Greek mythology and Shakespearean tragedy. We see it, too, in the treatment of football managers. They are built up, revered, imbued with all sorts of mysterious powers to influence results. And then, when results taper off, even for a few weeks, they are sacrificed. There is no economic or sporting rationality to this, but then the sacking of managers was never about logic.

Lance Armstrong

In *The Golden Bough*, the anthropologist Sir James George Frazer wrote about the phenomenon of the temporary king. This is someone with all-encompassing rule and a flawless character: able to control the rain, wind and crops. But his real function is not to rule but to die. When the crops fail he is sacrificed, paving the way for a new king. And thus the ritual of hope and cleansing can start afresh.

The narrative that surrounds Armstrong (and other modern messiahs) follows this atavistic pattern. His elevation to moral bastion never had any basis in reality. We closed our eyes to his faults independently of his drug-taking. We pretended that his temper, megalomania and vindictiveness didn't exist. When the evidence became overwhelming, we excused his flaws as part of the repertoire of any driven winner. After all, the temporary king can only serve his function as a lamb: faultless and without sin. And then we pounced.

The Armstrong story represents, above all, our love of moral caricature. When he was winning his seven Tours de France, Armstrong was the quintessential cartoon character: vivid, angelic, and with rousing music playing behind the scenes. Today, after his fall from grace, he remains a cartoon character: shadowy, Machiavellian, black wings sprouting from his muscular back, and with Mussorgsky's *Night on Bald Mountain* playing in the background. When his life story is dramatised, only Disney will be able to do it full justice.

The lack of nuance can also be seen in the way in which his shrinking coterie of hardcore fans, clinging to their temporary king, debate the issue with his detractors. For the former, Armstrong was part of a wider culture of cheating, merely following the pack. For the latter, he was a free moral agent who betrayed his fans and conscience. Anything else, they say, is an attempt to forgive the unforgivable.

As so often, the truth is halfway in-between. Armstrong did not invent doping in cycling: it existed for decades before he arrived in the sport and was endemic when he did so. According to one former teammate, 90 per cent of the peloton were on drugs, including the Briton David Millar. The sheer scale of doping reflects the power of a culture to corrupt those who may have wanted to do the right thing. There but for the grace of God . . .

But it is also true that not everyone succumbed to temptation. Christophe Bassons, the French rider, stood against the pack and proved that, even in the most insistent of cultures, we all exercise moral choice. And it has to be said that Armstrong did not merely exercise moral choice in taking drugs, but also in bullying, intimidating and defaming his accusers. When he was at the top of his game, his worst qualities came to the fore.

Lance Armstrong is not the first and will not be the last to run the gauntlet of our primal need for a temporary king. We projected our own hopes and anxieties on to the Texan, just as we have with so many others down the years. Perhaps Armstrong has more human flaws than most. But the Satanic parody we are left with today is as partial and one-dimensional as the saintly figure we once revered.

Michael Schumacher

1 January 2014

There is something rather odd about so many people referring to Michael Schumacher's crash as ironic. The idea seems to be that it is somehow paradoxical that the world's most famous motor-racing driver, who spent a lifetime in a dangerous sport, has been injured on the slopes of a ski resort.

Yet where is the irony? Skiing is dangerous. Two people died at the weekend while skiing in the same region as Schumacher.

High-profile fatalities include Alfonso, Duke of Anjou and Cádiz, Michael Kennedy, the son of Senator Robert Kennedy, and Natasha Richardson, the actress. It might have been ironic if the world's greatest racing driver had injured himself getting out of the shower or opening the fridge, but to injure himself while bombing down snow at an estimated 60 m.p.h.?

Schumacher loves skiing precisely because it is hazardous. Danger makes him tick. After his Formula One career, he took up motorcycling and competed in a few races under the pseudonym 'Marcel Niederhausen'. At a practice session in Cartagena, Spain, in February 2009, his bike crashed and Schumacher fractured bones in his head and neck, preventing him from deputising for Felipe Massa in F1 five months later.

He took up skydiving, taking leaps over the canyons of Colorado. He tried bungee jumping. Partly under the influence of Corinna, his wife, he gave horse racing a go. He returned to Formula One in 2010 and had three more years behind the wheel of a 250 m.p.h. racing car. Dancing with danger is more than a thrill; for Schumacher, it is something closer to a *raison d'être*.

Skiing is not some tranquil escape from this compulsion, it is part and parcel of it. He has a chalet at the resort from where he was airlifted to a hospital's brain injury unit on Sunday. He regularly went off-piste and tested the limits of his skill and daring. He was aware of the risks. Indeed, he skied because of the risks.

In a beautifully crafted piece yesterday, Kevin Garside, the journalist, described an encounter with Schumacher during his first retirement, post-Ferrari. It was at the private Ascari circuit in Andalusia, southern Spain, where Schumacher gestured Garside into a Maserati for a spin. 'Before we set off he asked the engineer to check the tyres,' Garside wrote. '"They are shot, down to the thread. We need to change them."

"OK," Schumi said, "One more lap."

'And off we went, sparks showering the asphalt as what was left of the tyres dug into the black stuff through the first corner . . . As we closed out the lap and the pit entry beckoned, I finally let go of the door handle and relaxed. I should have known. There is no such thing as one more lap for Schumacher. Round we went a second time before he said, "OK, we slow down now. The rears have gone, too." '

Schumacher is not the only racing driver to have had an infatuation with danger, as Kevin Eason, the motor-racing correspondent of *The Times*, has pointed out. Robert Kubica was about to break into the big time in F1 when he took up rally driving during the closed season. A crash in an event in Italy in 2011 almost sliced off his forearm. Mike Hawthorn, the 1958 world champion, died six months after retirement, on the A3 Guildford bypass. He was thought to be speeding in his Jaguar saloon.

Accidents, for certain people, are no deterrent. Patrick Depailler broke both his legs hang-gliding in 1979 before his return to F1. He was killed the next year in an accident during testing in a car with adapted brakes.

Didier Pironi took up offshore powerboat racing after he had broken both legs in an accident in practice for the 1982 German Grand Prix. He was killed in an accident off the Isle of Wight in 1987.

Schumacher also had his fair share of injuries, even before his motorcycling crash: at Silverstone in 1999, he ploughed into a barrier shortly after the start of the race when his brakes failed. He broke bones in his right shin, the tibia and fibula. The injury forced him out of half a dozen races and ended his title challenge. Five years earlier, Ayrton Senna crashed and died as he rounded the Tamburello corner on lap seven in San Marino while fending off a youthful Schumacher.

Many people will find this litany of incidents incomprehensible. Why take such dangers when there is so much to live for? The question misses the point. For such people, life is (at least in

part) about danger. Nobody expressed this truth more eloquently than Schumacher himself. 'Despite the accidents, I'm not afraid,' he said in a television interview. 'It may well be true that some things have changed in my life, yes. What won't change is the way I live, I'm not about to consciously deny myself the things that bring me joy.'

This does not mean that drivers take risks for the sake of it. Schumacher, like many of his colleagues, expressed deep gratitude to the likes of Max Mosley, who transformed the safety of motor racing. The point, however, is that with many high-octane activities, risk cannot be eliminated altogether.

Formula One at 10 m.p.h. would have held no attractions for Schumacher, or anyone else. The danger may have been mitigated by helmets, high-efficiency barriers and medical staff, but it is nevertheless an indispensable aspect of the sport's meaning.

George Mallory, the great adventurer and mountaineer, spoke for many thrill-seekers when he answered those who questioned his desire to climb Everest, with all its attendant dangers. 'What do we get from this adventure? What we get is sheer joy,' he wrote in *Climbing Everest*. 'And joy is, after all, the end of life. We do not live to eat and make money. We eat and make money to be able to live. That is what life means and what life is for.'

Some may scoff at these sentiments, but they go deep. It is curious just how often those who choose to live close to death have an overpowering zest for life. It is almost as if by confronting mortality, by coming face to face with the void that awaits us all, they find meaning in the here and now.

As Jonathan Waterman, the peerless mountaineering writer, put it: 'By bringing myself over the edge and back, I discovered a passion to live my days fully, a conviction that will sustain me like sweet water on the periodically barren plain of our short lives.'

Schumacher pushes himself to limits that any mountaineer would recognise. He was a fine driver, perhaps the greatest to have drawn breath. His will to win is implacable, his meticulousness unmatched. He crossed moral boundaries from time to time, and he could be a nightmare to work with, but he pursued greatness, just as he pursued danger.

And this brings us to the deepest question of all: can we really describe what happened on the slopes of Meribel as a tragedy? We all dearly hope that Schumacher lives, and if he does not, we will feel profound sympathy for his wife and his children. For them, the pain will linger. Whatever happens (and reports yesterday were rather more positive), they will surely take comfort from the thought that the irrepressible German has lived his life doing the things that give him meaning. And how many of us can say that?

Cristiano Ronaldo
15 January 2014

It was not the most beautiful goal of that unforgettable season. Perhaps it was not the most important, either. But there was something mesmerising about the way Cristiano Ronaldo leapt vertically to connect with the inswinging cross from Wes Brown, defying gravity as he hung in the Moscow air, a picture-perfect header from a man who had, even by that stage of his career, changed the way many of us think about football.

As the ball sped into the net, there was a delightful picture of Ronaldo coming back down to earth, his body still slightly contorted by the centrifugal force of his movement, but perfectly under control.

As he wheeled away, his face etched with emotion, we knew two things: the Portuguese had given Manchester United a vital lead in the 2008 Champions League final against Chelsea, and he had racked up an astonishing forty-two goals in all competitions for the season. We knew one other thing, too: he wanted more.

The 2007–08 season was the one in which the youngster signed by United in 2003 for £12.24 million – a risky purchase was the verdict of many commentators – made the transition from a very good player to a footballing immortal. He scored with blockbuster free kicks, solo dribbles and, in the case of that insouciant flick against Aston Villa, a back-heel. He also contributed to the wider tapestry of the team. Sir Alex Ferguson said that he 'raised the quality of everyone'.

But there is something deeply aesthetic about Ronaldo that goes beyond the stats and goals. It is about the almost perfect symmetry between his two feet. It is about the sense that on every dimension of skill – dribbling, passing, shooting, or charging forward to make a courageous header, like the thunderbolt from near the penalty spot against Roma in the Champions League quarter-finals of 2008 – he is in the top rank.

It is about his supreme balance and athleticism. You could almost say that, in footballing terms, Ronaldo is complete. Everything is in perfect proportion. He is football's *Vitruvian Man*.

And, like that seminal work by Leonardo da Vinci, it has taken an inordinate amount of sweat and sacrifice to turn Ronaldo into the masterpiece he has become. His odyssey in football started on the streets of Madeira at the age of two. His council house was too small for the family of six, but his father, a gardener, and his mother, a cook who took a sabbatical in France to clean houses, couldn't afford more. He played all day, slept with a football and dreamt of making it into the top leagues.

Life was tough. His brother was, for a time, a drug addict; his father was an alcoholic. When he was signed by Sporting Lisbon at the age of twelve and left home for the first time, he was heartbroken. He was teased, this young boy with a strange regional accent, and spent hours each evening on the phone to his beloved mother. She had to beg him to continue, to stick at it, not to throw it all away.

At fifteen, it was discovered that he had an abnormally slow resting heart-rate and he endured laser surgery to repair the damaged area of his heart. He kept working, striving through his teenage years, building the skill that would soon be recognised by scouts from around the world, including Carlos Queiroz, the Portuguese who was at the time assistant manager for United.

He was signed by the club in the summer of 2003 after a friendly game in which his performance blew Ferguson away. 'He is one of the most exciting young players I've ever seen,' the Scot said.

His application on the training pitches at Carrington astonished his new team-mates. 'You don't become a great player like Cristiano without a serious work ethic,' Gary Neville would later say. 'Take free kicks. He didn't have a dead-ball technique when he first came to United, but he developed that incredible dipping shot off the laces of his boot, toes pointing downwards, through hours and hours of hard work and perseverance on the training ground. Ronaldo was a machine.'

Greatness was not assured even then, however. The death of his father from liver failure on the eve of an international match in 2005 played havoc with his mind. Six weeks later, a tabloid ran a front-page story that he had been arrested for rape after meeting a girl at the Sanderson Hotel in London. The allegation provoked headlines around the world. Less coverage was devoted to a later newspaper story claiming that the girl was a prostitute who specialised in ensnaring the rich and famous. No charges were ever brought.

After the sending-off of Wayne Rooney at the 2006 World Cup finals, Ronaldo faced a fresh onslaught. His face was turned into a dartboard by the *Sun*, which described him as a 'nancy boy'. 'We've made Ronaldo's wink the bull's-eye', the story said. Ferguson had to travel to the Algarve to convince Ronaldo to return to England. He was booed and jeered for the entire season, but he proved his mettle once again: he scored twenty-three goals and won the PFA Player of the Year award. In the way he dealt with adversity, it was reminiscent of David Beckham eight years previously.

One of my favourite Ferguson quotes was uttered just over a year later, after United had won the Premier League and Champions League in 2008. Ronaldo had been nominated for the Ballon d'Or and Ferguson found himself musing upon a player whose relationship with the British public remained complex. There was a suspicion, even then, that he was a preener, a player who went to ground too easily, a showboater who lacked the substance of the truly great players.

Ferguson scoffed at this distorted caricature. 'Courage in football, as in life, manifests itself in different ways,' he said. 'But the courage to move forward, no matter how many times he is going to be kicked, identifies Ronaldo. Some believe the greatest courage is the courage to win the ball. The other kind of courage – and it's a moral courage – is the courage to keep a ball. That's what Ronaldo has. All the great players had it.'

Ronaldo won the combined FIFA World Player of the Year and Ballon d'Or for the first time on Monday evening. I have never cared much for these awards, with their horse-trading and hidden deals, but have no doubt that he deserved his victory.

His performances for Real Madrid have taken his skill to a level that has, at times, defied the imagination. It makes a mockery of any residual ambivalence about his claims to greatness. When he is in full flight, galloping down the wing with that distinctive gait, terrorising defenders, he is one of the supreme sights in sport.

Some will say he is not a perfect human being, but then who is? Some will mock his concern with his appearance and occasional bouts of petulance. What we can say for certain is that, in his chosen profession, he has reached the top through merit and astonishing application. From the dusty streets of Madeira to the pinnacle of the most popular cultural institution on the planet, he has done it the hard way. Cristiano Ronaldo dos Santos Aveiro deserves every plaudit he gets.

Andre Agassi
28 February 2015

Andre Agassi has spent most of his life trying to come to terms with his childhood. He started playing tennis in his cot, a mobile of balls hung above his head, a ping-pong bat taped to his hand, his dad standing above encouraging little Andre to hit, hit, hit.

When he was old enough to walk, he played in the yard against the so-called Dragon, a mechanical device custom-made by his father to spit tennis balls from a steep angle at more than 100 m.p.h. in the Las Vegas haze. Agassi estimates that he hit one million balls per year throughout his childhood, his dad screaming every time he missed.

At the age of thirteen, he was packed off to boarding school to play yet more tennis at the Bollettieri academy in Florida. 'It was more like a prison than a tennis academy,' he says. 'It was on an old tomato farm and the courts stretched one after the other into the distance. We only went to school for four hours a day. The rest of the time we played tennis.'

To meet Agassi in the flesh is to feel the contradictions in one of the most revelatory of modern sporting lives. He hated tennis, but loved it, too. He begrudged his upbringing, but acknowledges that it laid the foundations for everything he has achieved in life. He resented his dad, but has gradually come to recognise that for all the pain, mistakes and shouting matches, this complex man, still railing against the world at the age of eighty-four, acted out of love.

'He is an extraordinary and complex man,' Agassi says. 'I have spent a lifetime trying to understand him. His mum was a Russian Armenian who moved to Tehran after the Armenian genocide in 1915. Dad grew up in Tehran as a Christian and he had some pretty horrible experiences. They were very poor. I think that taught him to fight. He took up boxing, won two golden gloves and competed in two Olympic Games for Iran.

'When he came to America, he had one ambition: "I will spend my life trying to create an environment where my kids can have the one thing I never had, money." He conditioned us to leave our heritage behind. His attitude was: "We are Americans. We are going to live the American dream." He didn't want us to learn [Persian]. We changed our name from Aghassian to Agassi. He didn't want anyone to think we were Muslim.'

The parental urge for betterment, for leaving a former world behind, will strike a chord with many second-generation immigrants. So will the vision of a tortured dad, who felt that everyone was against him, seeking to ensure that his children had every opportunity to succeed. But the sheer intensity of what Agassi endured will seem extreme, even to immigrant eyes. He was pushed, cajoled, urged and goaded, every spare hour of every day.

'The irony is that I had it pretty easy,' Agassi says. 'It was my three older siblings who really felt the heat of my father's ambition. I was the baby. Thank god he had the sense to save me from himself. That is why he sent me away at thirteen to the tennis academy. Our relationship was on the brink of self-destruction. He just couldn't stop himself pushing, pushing, pushing.'

The experience has shaped Agassi's attitude profoundly to his own children from his marriage to Steffi Graf: Jaden, thirteen, and Jaz, eleven. 'I didn't want to make the same mistakes,' he says. 'Even when the children were very young, I didn't define their ambitions for them. I try to let them decide what they are passionate about. But once they define it, I hold them to a standard of commitment. Their dreams become my dreams and I won't allow them to stop caring just because they have had a disappointment or two.

'I am not saying it is easy to get the balance right. My daughter used to ride horses and she flew off a couple of years ago, and the horse stomped around a foot from her head. And it changed her on a dime. She didn't want to get back on her horse. And that was kind of an interesting one for me. I don't know if I handled it right. I didn't push her to carry on, but that was because I didn't want to see her on the back of a 1,200lb animal.

'My son had a tough experience, too. He is very into baseball and he was hit by the ball and broke his palate last year. I would have understood if that had affected him. But he went out the next day and on the very first pitch, he hit it to deep right. That took character. I celebrated that. That is what I try to do with my kids: to give them context. I don't tell them what to do, but I encourage them to keep going at the things they love, even when the going gets tough.'

Perhaps it is the experience of mentoring his children that has triggered a reinterpretation of his upbringing. In recent years he has come not merely to respect, but to admire his father, a man so vigilant to insults, so proud, so driven by an inner turmoil that he never fully resolved, that he would step out of his car and offer to fight anyone who cut him up on the Vegas strip.

'It is only recently that I have realised how difficult life has been for him,' he says.

Andre Agassi

'Even my tennis career was tough on him. He watched me play live on average once a year. I never knew when that time would be. It might be in Palm Springs. It might be in LA. But he never missed a single match on TV, wherever I was playing in the world. He would record it and watch it fifty times. He lived and died with it. Watching me lose, watching me suffer. He was suffering, too.

'What I can say for certain is that my dad was motivated for all the right reasons. He was not acting out of betterment for himself; he was acting out of love for me. Whether he was right or wrong, whether he made good or bad judgement calls, I know he just wanted his boy to live the American Dream. All that work, all that pressure, all that angst: he was pushing me to have the success that was denied to him. And that realisation goes a long way.'

Today, they are reconciled. They have a relationship that works, at least in a way that they can both live with. Agassi would love to shower his father with gifts, but he has to be conscious of his dad's pride. 'To say this man has life-force is an understatement,' he says. 'He worked until he was eighty. He just kept going. He only accepts gifts from me today if he is convinced they aren't costing me much. He wouldn't accept a thing if he felt it was a sacrifice for me.'

Today, Agassi lives in a small community a few miles from the intensity of the Vegas strip and divides his time between his family and his charitable foundation. The school that bears his name – he donated a reported $35 million (about £23 million) to create it – has segued into a new business venture with a social conscience, funding Charter schools across the United States. He is busy, but has found a balance, both in his professional life and the personal relationships that matter most.

Perhaps the deepest irony about the fragile rapport he has found with his father is that it was most imperilled by the book that lifted the lid on their relationship. When Agassi brought out his tell-all autobiography in 2010, he was terrified that his father would take offence. 'I called him up before publication and said, "Dad, you haven't read the book. You haven't even let me talk to you about the book. Can I at least walk you through how I have portrayed you, so you are clear about why I did it?"

'He just said: "I am eighty years old. Why would I give a s*** about what people think about me? I know what I did and why I did it. And I would do the same all over again." I sort of smiled because that was my dad all over: strong, proud, never prepared to admit a weakness.

'But then he suddenly said: "Actually, there is one thing I would do different."

'I had to pull over to the side of the road. I couldn't believe he was going to admit a mistake. "What would you have done different, Dad?" I asked. He said: "I wouldn't let you play tennis. You would be playing baseball or golf if I had my time over. You would have made a lot more money."'

Brian Clough

28 December 2011

By chance, I visited the grave of Brian Clough yesterday. It is situated in the grounds of one of the most beautiful small churches in England, St Alkmund's near Derby, a chapel that dates back to the first millennium and is only half a mile or so from the home of my in-laws. Clough's final resting place is a few yards in front of the entrance, with a small and dignified headstone.

The grave is cherished by close family – yesterday there was a semi-circular wreath of white flowers on it – but it is striking that Clough is remembered in so many other ways in these parts. The road linking Derby and Nottingham, the cities whose clubs

Brian Clough

Clough led to triumph, is called Brian Clough Way. In Nottingham city centre is a bronze statue, paid for by donations. Another statue stands outside Pride Park.

Clough touched the area, and the wider world, in the way that many sporting icons do, and not just football managers. Sports people are, in many ways, the cultural heroes of the early twenty-first century. We idolise them, we mythologise their virtues, we buy replica shirts with their name on the back. We read their biographies, pore over their interviews and, when they die, the greatest among them, we mourn.

And there is something rather uplifting in all this. In his final years, when the battle with alcohol and illness began to take its toll, Clough was still deeply loved. Principally by his wife and family, of course, but also, in a different way, by the legions of admirers he amassed as he and Peter Taylor, his assistant, redefined the art of the possible in football management.

Almost until his death, youngsters would visit his house in Quarndon to pay homage and Clough would share his reminiscences of the glory days. I like to think that he was as cantankerous and lacking in sentimentality even as the door was closing on his remarkable life. Certainly, he must have found meaning in the pleasure he brought to so many. As was once said of Shankly: 'He made the people happy.'

But, in many ways, Clough was one of the lucky ones. Like Muhammad Ali, he was one of those sporting icons who remained a hero after the Midas touch had deserted him. The glory clung to him, perhaps because of his unique charisma, even when his reputation became tainted by allegations of financial misdealing. Indeed, it is possible that Clough, partly because of the books and films that have been made about his life, will become even more cherished as the years pass.

Unlike Ali, Joe Louis did not die surrounded by love and compassion, but by poverty and ignominy. He lost his money to the taxman, went to gambling haunts, and towards the end of his life was admitted to an asylum, afflicted by advanced paranoia. Sonny Liston died alone in a dingy home in Las Vegas. Police could only estimate the time of death from the advanced state of decomposition.

These are extreme cases, but they convey a chastening truth. Idolisation rarely outlasts success. When the legs go, the acclamation goes, and the hero is left like Coriolanus, crying into the heavens.

I often wonder what Shakespeare would have made of the ironies of modern stardom, and the complex relationship between the masses and those upon whom they bestow their acclaim. As Billie Jean King said: 'Fame is the most confusing thing in the world, and not just for the famous.'

There is a saying in investment banking, perhaps the least sentimental of professions, that, whatever you achieve, however much money you amass, however popular you become, you eventually leave 'in a coffin'. This is not literal, of course, merely a metaphor for the industry's defining assumption: as soon as you lose the ability to make money, you are kicked out of the door, escorted by security guards, with your personal possessions in a small box.

Sport, in many ways, is just as brutal. There is no room for emotion, only the remorseless examination of competition. When a player is too old, he disappears, and we move on to the next hero.

We are a promiscuous public. When I interviewed Jake LaMotta, one of the most storied of sporting champions, he felt betrayed. 'They loved me, but only for as long as I was winning,' he said. 'When I started losing, they hated me.'

LaMotta's premise was flawed, of course. He was not really loved. Yes, his skill was loved, the way he handled himself in the ring was loved, the drama he created was loved. He was acclaimed, fêted, richly rewarded, and he had his pick of the women who surrounded the fight game. But this was not love. It was stardom. And stardom is fleeting, transient and brutally conditional. We love only for as long as the gladiator amuses us.

I sometimes wonder if the metaphors we apply to our sporting heroes should come with a health warning.

In banking, as with most jobs in life, the assumptions are well understood. Everybody recognises that they are employed only for as long as they are of use. In sport, the vernacular is different. We talk of love, of idolisation. We speak of heroism. Is it any wonder that so many former champions feel a sense of confusion when the love flickers and dies?

Every now and again, a story will appear of a former sporting great who has fallen on hard times, and it always makes for powerful and disconcerting reading. We almost feel morally affronted that once-legendary figures are now eking out fringe existences, short of money, shorn of majesty, largely forgotten. But we also cannot figure out at whom to direct our outrage.

The reason is simple: it is not any person or group who has let these heroes down; it is the ambiguity of stardom. Clubs do not owe their former players a living any more than those who cheered their names from the terraces. They, and we, are left in a state of moral confusion because we have never fully defined the rules of fame, the subclauses of mass adulation. We use the metaphor of love, without realising that true love is unconditional.

The gravestone of Clough has a powerful inscription. It talks of how he was loved by the masses, but how he was most dearly loved by Barbara, his wife, and his family. It is powerful, because it contains an important truth. Even for a man such as Clough, who continues to be revered years after his death, the most meaningful love came from his family, those who really knew him. Stardom is only ever secondary.

Unquestionably The Greatest

6 June 2016

Norman Mailer, perhaps his most eloquent chronicler, once described Muhammad Ali as 'beautiful'. 'There is always a shock in seeing him again,' Mailer wrote in his seminal book *The Fight*. 'Not live as in television but standing before you, looking his best. Then the World's Greatest Athlete is in danger of being our most beautiful man . . . Women draw an audible breath. Men look down . . . If Ali never opened his mouth to quiver the jellies of public opinion, he would still inspire love and hate. For he is the Prince of Heaven – so says the silence around his body when he is luminous.'

Ali was, indeed, beautiful. In the way he moved, the way he talked, and in the high-voltage charisma that seemed to flow whenever he stood near a TV camera, he redefined the nature of twentieth-century celebrity. He could box, too. When he took on Cleveland Williams in 1966 at the height of his powers, he altered the way many observers thought about sport. He danced and glided, connecting with 100 punches and taking just three. As one pundit put it: 'This is the closest sport has come to perfection. For seven or so minutes, Ali turned boxing into ballet.'

But Ali was not always beautiful. He could be ugly, vindictive and, at times, hypocritical. Indeed, the only way to fully understand how a 'mere' sportsman rose to become one of the most influential figures of the last century, you have to engage with both the light and the darkness. Over recent decades, particularly since his descent caused by Parkinson's disease, the image of Ali has been carefully sanitised. He was positioned by his commercial handlers as saintly, unifying, pacifistic and unthreatening. But the real Ali, the man who shocked, outraged, fascinated and ultimately endeared the world, was a polarising and controversial figure. In his words and deeds, there was always a whiff of Semtex. Now, more than ever, it is time to rediscover the real Ali.

His arrival on the world stage can be pinned to a particular date: 25 February 1964. Ali had already won Olympic gold in the light-heavyweight event in Rome, but it was his challenge for the so-called richest prize in sport that transformed him into a cultural icon. It would not be entirely true to say that nobody gave this unorthodox pugilist, who carried his hands low, a hope. Three of the forty-plus journalists at ringside picked Cassius Clay, as he was then called, to defeat Sonny Liston, the defending heavyweight champion. It was not the first time that pundits would underestimate the courage and skill of the man who was about to turn their world upside down.

Of all Ali's title bouts, this remains the most electric. He edged the contest until the fourth, when an illegal substance from Liston's glove found its way into his eyes. Partially blinded, Ali kept Liston at bay by holding his arms out horizontally but, as his vision began to clear, he started to dominate. Liston seemed to age as Ali danced around him, and he failed to answer the bell for the seventh round (some observers claim he was ordered to throw the contest by the Mob). It was a breathtaking performance. As Ferdie Pacheco, his long-time doctor put it: 'Beethoven wrote some of his greatest symphonies when he was deaf. Why couldn't Cassius Clay fight when he was blind?'

It wasn't until the next day, however, that the story shifted to the front pages. Ali informed a press conference that he had converted to the Nation of Islam, an extremist, anti-white religious group. He also said that he had dropped his 'slave name' (Cassius Clay was, in fact, the name of a nineteenth-century abolitionist). Soon afterwards, he became Muhammad Ali. Mainstream America, accustomed to compliant black athletes in the mould of Joe Louis, the former heavyweight champion, was outraged. The Nation had a surrealist theology, preaching that blacks were the first humans and that whites had been created in a botched experiment conducted by a rogue scientist. They also believed that blacks would be rescued from a looming apocalypse by a wheel-shaped spaceship.

But it was their political vision that caused the deepest anxiety. They argued for a separation between the races, campaigning aggressively (and with a stated belief in the use of force) for a homeland for blacks within the borders of the United States. That put them in direct opposition to the integrationist agenda of Martin Luther King and, curiously enough, on the same page as white supremacist groups, who also believed in racial segregation. Soon after his conversion, Ali himself addressed a meeting of the Ku Klux Klan, saying: 'Blue birds with blue birds, red birds with red birds, pigeons with pigeons, eagles with eagles! God didn't make no mistake!'

How could Ali have fraternised with an organisation that had lynched and murdered across the former Confederacy? How could he associate with people whose declared aim was to create a state of terror among black people south of the Mason-Dixon line? To his detractors, then and now, Ali was a racist, pure and simple. He believed that whites were congenitally evil, just as the Klan believed that blacks were congenitally subhuman. In multiple interviews, Ali proclaimed his ideology. 'We cannot live in harmony because we are different,' he said. 'Whites have a bad nature, they cannot be trusted . . . We need to have our own land, our own government, our own way of doing things.' Mark Kram, in his book *Ghosts of Manila*, wrote: 'Seldom has a public figure of such superficial depth been more wrongly perceived – by the right and the left. Today, he would be looked upon as a contaminant, a chronic user of hate language.'

But the context of Ali's views should not be overlooked. He grew up in Louisville, Kentucky, a city called the 'gateway to the south'. The indignities of Jim Crow were part of everyday experience. When asked to write a school project on slavery, he was so shocked when confronted by the full horrors of the Middle Passage that he openly wept.

His radicalisation was complete when, in 1955, he read about the murder of Emmett Till, a boy of the same age as Ali, who had been lynched for wolf-whistling at a white shop assistant in Mississippi. Till's body had been mutilated and an eye gouged from its socket. The two men charged with murder were acquitted by an all-white jury in sixty-seven minutes. 'If we hadn't stopped to drink pop, it wouldn't have taken so long,' one juror said.

From this perspective, Ali's demonisation of whites can at least be understood, if not condoned. The Black Muslims may have had a similar ideology to the Klan on paper, but the historical context could not have been more different. The Klan wished to sustain a reign of hatred against blacks in the South. The anti-white racism of the Nation of Islam was more a cry for help, the vigilante response of an impotent and pitiful minority.

Either way, there is no doubt that Ali's position as heavy-weight champion handed the Nation a political significance out of all proportion to their small base. For a brief period, the fear of a rising black underclass – disciplined, well organised, and intent on insurrection – struck fear into Middle America. And it was at this moment that Luther King played his trump card. Concerned that the Civil Rights Bill was bogged down in Congress, he realised that the extremist rhetoric of the new heavyweight champion might be used to secure concessions. In one of his biggest political gambles, he painted a chilling vision of what might happen if reforms were delayed further, pushing more young blacks into the arms of the extremists.

In a watershed article in the *Chicago Defender*, Jackie Robinson, the first black player to cross the colour line in Major League Baseball, made the case. 'I don't think Negroes en masse will embrace Black Muslimism any more than they have communism. Young and old, Negroes by the tens of thousands went into the streets of America and proved their willingness to suffer, to fight, and even die for their freedom. These people want more democracy – not less. They want to be integrated into the mainstream of American life, not invited to live in some small cubicle of this land in splendid isolation. If Negroes ever turn to the Black Muslim movement, in any numbers, it will not be because of Cassius Clay or even Malcolm X. It will be because white America has refused to recognise the responsible leadership of the Negro people and to grant us the same rights that any other citizen enjoys.'

President Johnson got the point, strengthening the act against the wishes of his party. The 1964 Bill went further than anyone had believed possible only months earlier and, along with the Voting Rights Act in 1965, banned employment discrimination and obliterated the disenfranchisement of blacks throughout the South. It is perhaps the deepest irony of Ali's life that, in allying himself with a creed fanatically opposed to integration, he smoothed the passage of the most seminal integrationist legislation in American history. Jim Crow had finally expired.

America was a-changing, and, soon, Ali was changing, too. By 1967, he had defended the title nine times (including a rematch with Liston), almost without breaking sweat. And yet, even as the nation was starting to warm to a man they had previously vilified, he took a stance that would divide it again. His refusal to accept the draft for Vietnam was another calculated act of hostility against the establishment. 'I ain't got no quarrel with them Viet Cong,' Ali said. The words would ultimately become a rallying cry for critics of the war, but at the time it still commanded support and his stance was regarded as an act of betrayal. The boxing authorities stripped him of his title, and he spent three and a half years in the wilderness.

By the time he returned, however, the world had shifted. Opinion had swung against the war, and Ali was on the verge of being embraced by mainstream America for the first time. His courage convinced many of his severest critics that he was a man of principle whose stances pierced the surface assumptions of American society. He even won his case against the United States government, avoiding jail and garnering an apology.

In 1974, as he travelled to Zaire to take on George Foreman for the heavyweight title (he had been defeated by Joe Frazier in his first attempt to regain the championship in 1971), he had become a hero to millions at home and abroad. It was a stunning turnaround, reflecting not only Ali's personality, but a growing consensus, even in the South, that the dismantling of Jim Crow had changed the nation for the better. The cultural meaning of Ali was morphing, too. This was a period of mass entertainment driven by television satellites and the first attempts at global marketing. Ali's bouts in Kinshasa, Kuala Lumpur, Manila, San Juan, Munich, New York and Nassau became an international roadshow, creating what we would today call a global brand. He was, by now, the most famous person on the planet, able to charm and delight audiences with effortless charisma. For the US, still traumatised by Watergate and Vietnam, these mega-bouts offered much-needed escapism. The pre-bout vaudeville and hype became essential to the drumbeat of the Seventies.

To many, the 1974 clash with Foreman remains Ali's definitive bout. However, he was way past his best. Three and a half years out of the ring had created a very different boxer: one who had slowed dramatically. Ali called his tactics against Foreman 'rope-a-dope', taking mighty shots on his body and arms that would have previously hit thin air. He won with a stoppage in the eighth round, but urinated blood for weeks afterwards. After the savage, fourteen-round epic with Frazier in the Philippines, the fabled Thrilla in Manila in 1975, he looked as if he had been in a traffic accident. But America loved him for it. This was an authentic champion, rather than the defensive artist who had dominated the Sixties. He took punishment. He bled. For some people, this represented heroism.

In 1978, Ali faced Leon Spinks in an attempt to win the title for an unprecedented third time before a record TV audience. Howard Cosell, the legendary announcer, used the closing moments to provide one of the most cherished pieces of sports commentary, citing Bob Dylan. 'May your hands always be busy, may your feet always be swift. May you have a strong foundation, when the winds of changes shift. May your heart always be joyful, and may your song always be sung. May you stay for ever young.' Ali won, but his decline was evident. Within months of his retirement in 1981, the signs of Parkinson's were already manifest. The descent into illness had begun.

For most of the years following, Ali lived a curious half-life, both in the spotlight and beyond it. He renounced the Nation and converted to moderate form of Sunni Islam. Gradually, however, the melodious voice was silenced. An 80 per cent share in his name, image and likeness were sold for $50 million to CKX, an entertainment conglomerate, which started the process of airbrushing his image.

He was positioned, doubtless for commercial reasons, as a Gandhi-like caricature who preached peace and tolerance. The real Ali, the man whose explosive stances subtly altered American history, was drowned in a deluge of misleading sentimentality. In the eyes of a new generation, Ali was a teddy bear: safe, unthreatening, and devoid of the contradictions that symbolised the deep schisms in postwar American consciousness.

Soon after retirement, he married Lonnie, his fourth wife, and apologised for the womanising that had characterised his youth, stating 'the man who views the world at fifty the same as he did at twenty has wasted thirty years of his life.' In his final years, he spent much of his time watching videos of old fights and interviews. 'He does have advanced Parkinson's disease, so he is challenged,' Lonnie said recently. 'The thing he loves most is watching himself on YouTube. He becomes so intense. It's as if he hasn't ever seen it before. He watches the [Michael]

Parkinson interviews. I remember in Michigan one time, he was watching himself, and said: "I was crazy, wasn't I?" I said: "Yes!"'

Only a historian lacking imagination could fail to place Ali among the most influential cultural figures of the last century. He was a sportsman with a conscience, a man whose desire to right the injustices in American society led him down many roads, both dark and light. In his life, we glimpse not only the moral complexity of the most transformative epoch in modern American history, but also the story of a boy from a small town who, against all odds, 'shook up the world'. He was imperfect and flawed, courageous and so very beautiful.

He was, unquestionably, the greatest.

Index

Index

Index

Ashton, Chris, 56, 58
Augusta National golf course,
    Georgia, USA, 53–5
authority, 15
    see also delegation

Baker, Denise, 245
Bale, Gareth, 30, 137
Ballesteros, Seve, 54–5
Ballon d'Or (award), 121, 123
Banks, Gordon, 104
Bannister, Moyra, Lady, 233–6
Bannister, Sir Roger, 103, 209,
    232–6
Barakzai, Diana, 185
Barbarians (rugby club), 89, 91
Barcelona Football Club, xii, 89,
    95, 105, 112–13, 119, 122,
    135–6
Barcelona Olympics (1992), 21
Barclay, Patrick, 112
Barnes, John, 188
Barnes, Simon
    on Sampras' state of mind,
        47
    The Meaning of Sport, xiv
Barnett, Marilyn, 212–13
Barrett, Frank J., 90
baseball
    Billy Beane and, 28
    in Cuba, 159–61
    reserve clause, 173–4
    statistics, 28–9
Bassons, Christophe, 129–30,
    248
Bastien, David, 90

Bayern Munich: in 1999
    European Cup final against
    Manchester United, 73
BBC Sports Personality of the
    Year, 20
Beane, Billy, 28–32
Beardsley, Peter, 123
Beckham, David
    goal-scoring, 105
    honoured, 176
    learns from mistakes, 45
    natural ability, 11
    out of favour with Capello,
        58
    style and influence, 176–8,
        255
    team play, 120–1, 123
Bell, Alexander Graham, 26
Benayoun, Yossi, 171
Bengtsson, Stellan, 74
Benítez, Rafael, 71–2
Bennett, Phil, 91
Billie Jean King National Tennis
    Center, New York, 211
Black Muslims, 267–8
Blair, Tony, 169, 175, 177–8
Blitzkrieg, 69
Bolt, Usain, 12
Botham, Ian, 76
Bowman, Bob, 232
boxing
    fatality, 180–1
    see also Ali, Muhammad;
        LaMotta, Jake
Bradman, Don, 127
Brailsford, Sir Dave, 16, 33–41

Index

Brazil
    football team, 13, 26, 112,
        123–4
    heavy defeat by Germany in
        2014 World Cup, 69–71
Brearley, Mike, 77
Brentford Football Club, 138–41
Brown, Rita Mae, 224, 227
Brown, Tina, 241
Brown, Wes, 252
Buford, Bill, 197–8
Butt, Nicky, 120

Cameron, David, 18
Camus, Albert, 171
Capello, Fabio, 58
capitalism: and competition,
        124–5
Capriati, Jennifer, 62–3
Capuano, Chris, 175
Carneiro, Eva, 199
Casartelli, Fabio, 146
Castle, Andrew, 226
Castro, Fidel, 151, 158, 160–2,
        195
Cato Journal, 198
Caulkin, George, 144
Cerdan, Marcel, 242–3, 245
César, Júlio, 71
Chambers, Dwain, 129
champions: making of, 3
Chapman, Herbert, 126
Charters, Peter, 19
cheating
    in ancient Olympics, 203–4
    in sport, 128–31

chess: and visual awareness, 67
Chichester, Sir Francis, 233
China
    Cultural Revolution, 154–8
    table tennis, 153–7, 194–5
Christie, Linford, 21
Čilić, Marin, 24, 27
Clancy, Gil, 179
Clarke, Michael, 127
Clarkson, Jeremy, 187, 190
Clinton, Hillary, 169
Clough, Barbara, 263
Clough, Brian, 260–3
coaches: and delegation, 15
Coe, Sebastian, 116
Cole, Andy, 189
Coleman, Chris, 50, 52–3
collective zone, the, 88–91
Collins, Brian, 189
comebacks, 72–4
Comolli, Damien, 30–1
competition (rivalry), 24–7,
        124–5
Conger, Jay, 15
Connors, Jimmy, 217–21
Connors, Patti, 220
conscious mind, 61–2
Conway, Sally, 108
Cook, Alastair, 76
Cooper, Henry, 6
Coote, Ken, 140
CORE (Commitment, Ownership,
        Responsibility, Excellence),
        16
Coroebus of Elis, xi
Cosell, Howard, 270

Index

Index

Index

Index

Index

Index

Index

Index

Index